LIVING LANGUAGE®
SPANISH
BEYOND THE BASICS

LIVING LANGUAGE®
SPANISH

BEYOND THE BASICS

Written by
ENRIQUE MONTES

Edited by
SUZANNE MCQUADE

Based on the original by
ROBERT E. HAMMAR STRAND, PH.D.,
HUNTER COLLEGE

LIVING LANGUAGE®

Published in the United States by Living Language, A Random House Company

www.livinglanguage.com

Editor: Suzanne McQuade
Production Editor: John Whitman
Production Manager: Heather Lanigan
Interior Design: Sophie Ye Chin

ISBN 1-4000-2161-8

PRINTED IN THE UNITED STATES OF AMERICA

10 9 8 7 6 5 4 3 2 1

ACKNOWLEDGMENTS

Thanks to the Living Language staff: Tom Russell, Sanam Zubli, Christopher Warnasch, Zviezdana Verzich, Suzanne McQuade, Suzanne Podhurst, Sophie Chin, Denise De Gennaro, Linda Schmidt, Alison Skrabek, John Whitman, Helen Kilcullen, and Heather Lanigan. Special thanks to Mary Lee.

CONTENTS

INTRODUCTION

Living Language® *Spanish: Beyond the Basics* is a perfect follow-up to any beginner-level Spanish course. It focuses on the specific needs of the intermediate student: vocabulary expansion, review of basic grammar, introduction of more challenging grammatical constructions, and natural conversational and idiomatic speech. If you've recently completed a beginner-level course in Spanish, or if you're looking for a way to reactivate the Spanish that you may have studied years ago, *Spanish: Beyond the Basics* is a great course for you.

The complete program includes this course book, four hours of recordings, and a reference dictionary. The recordings include the dialogues and other material from the course book; they're an essential tool for perfecting pronunciation and intonation as well as building listening comprehension. The book may also be used on its own if you're confident of your pronunciation.

COURSE MATERIALS

There are twenty lessons in *Spanish: Beyond the Basics*. Each lesson begins with a dialogue that focuses on a particular setting designed to highlight certain vocabulary or grammatical constructions. These settings will also give you a good idea of various cultural issues and put the language you're learning into a realistic context. In addition to the dialogues, each of the twenty lessons also contains language notes, grammar and usage explanations and examples, and several exercises. There is also a reference section at the end of the book containing a grammar summary, a section on letter writing, and e-mail and Internet resources.

DIALOGUE: The dialogue in each lesson features standard, idiomatic Spanish and presents a realistic situation that demonstrates natural language use in a real context. The idiomatic English translation is provided below each line of dialogue.

NOTES: The notes refer to specific words, expressions, or cultural items used in the dialogue that are worthy of further comment. A note may clarify a translation, expand on a grammatical construction, or provide a cultural context. The notes are numbered to refer back to particular lines of dialogue for easy reference.

GRAMMAR AND USAGE: This section focuses on a few key grammatical or structural points. There is a clear and simple explanation first, followed by examples to further illustrate the point. Many of the grammar points are included as a review of key basic structures, but the overall scope of this course also includes more challenging and higher level grammar.

EXERCISES: The final section of each lesson gives you an opportunity to practice the material covered in that lesson. There are several different types of exercises, including fill-in-the-blanks, multiple choice, translation exercises, and more.

GRAMMAR SUMMARY: The Grammar Summary contains a concise and comprehensive summary of Spanish grammar. This section is an invaluable tool for use either with the course or on its own for independent reference.

LETTER WRITING: This section includes examples of business, formal, and personal letters. There are also forms of salutations and closings, as well as sample envelopes.

E-MAIL AND INTERNET RESOURCES: This section includes sample e-mail correspondence with vocabulary and expressions related to the internet. There is also a list of Internet resources of interest to the student of Spanish.

THE RECORDINGS

The recordings include the complete dialogues from all twenty lessons in the course book, as well as a number of example sentences taken from the grammar and usage sections. Each dialogue is first read at conversational speed without interruption, and then a second time with pauses inserted, allowing you to repeat after the native speakers. By listening to and imitating the native speakers, you'll improve your pronunciation and build your listening comprehension while you reinforce the new vocabulary and structures that you've learned in the book.

HOW TO USE THIS COURSE

Take as much time as you need to work through each lesson. Do not be afraid to look over material that you've already covered if you don't feel confident enough to move ahead. The course is organized so that you can move through it at a pace that is exactly right for you.

Start each lesson by reading through it once to get a sense of what it includes. Don't try to memorize the vocabulary from the dialogue or master the grammar items, and don't attempt to do any of the exercises. Simply familiarize yourself with the lesson in a general sense.

Then start again by reading through the dialogue a first time to get a general sense of it. Then look over the notes to help clarify points that may be confusing. Next, read the dialogue more carefully, focusing on each line and its translation. If you come across new or unfamiliar vocabulary, write it down in a notebook or somewhere else you can return to for practice. Re-read the dialogue until you're comfortable with it.

After you've carefully read the dialogue a few times, turn on the recordings and listen as you read along. The dialogue is first read at normal conversational speed, and then again with pauses inserted for you to repeat. Follow along in your book as you listen, and then again as you repeat, in order to activate two senses—sight and hearing. After you've listened while reading along, close your book and try to follow without any written material. See how much of each sentence and phrase you can successfully repeat. Again, feel free to repeat these steps as many times as you'd like.

After you've finished reading and listening to the dialogue, turn to the Grammar and Usage section. Read each point carefully until it makes sense to you, and take a close look at the example sentences to see how they relate to the point at hand. If you're using a notebook, it's a good idea to take notes on the grammar and try to restate each point in your own words. Try to come up with other examples if you can. After you've completed each point in a similar way, turn on your recordings and listen through the section in the same way as you did for the dialogue. Listening and repeating will serve as an excellent review.

The exercises at the end of each lesson will help you review the material and check your overall progress. If you're unsure of a particular exercise, go back and cover the grammar again. If you're not comfortable moving ahead, make sure you take the time you need.

Turn to the Grammar Summary while you're working through the course to remind yourself of a grammar point you may have forgotten, or to provide yourself with another way of explaining a point you're working on. Also, take a look at the Internet Resources for suggestions of how you can use the internet as a reference tool or as a way to enhance your studies.

Now, you're ready to begin.

LESSON 1

UNA CITA EN UN CAFÉ
MEETING AT A CAFE

A. DIALOGUE

0. *Carlos y Juana acaban de llegar a Madrid de México y deciden llamar a su amigo Miguel para reunirse esa tarde.*
Carlos and Juana have just arrived in Madrid from Mexico and decided to call their friend Miguel and arrange a meeting for the afternoon.

1. Miguel: **¿Diga?**
Hello.

2. Carlos: **Soy Carlos Andrade, de México.**
This is Carlos Andrade, from Mexico.

3. Miguel: **¡Qué gusto! ¿Dónde te encuentras?**
What a pleasure! Where are you?

4. Carlos: **Estoy en el Hotel Plaza. Acabamos de llegar mi esposa y yo.**
At the Hotel Plaza. We have just arrived, my wife and I.

5. Miguel: **¡Tengo ganas de veros lo más pronto posible! ¿Podemos vernos esta tarde? ¿Qué tal a las dos?**
I'd like to see you as soon as possible! Can we get together this afternoon? How about at two o'clock?

6. Carlos: **Claro que sí. ¿Dónde podemos encontrarnos?**
Of course. Where can we meet?

7. Miguel: **En el Café Gijón. Toma un taxi y ve a la Castellana cerca de la plaza Colón.**
At the Café Gijón. Take a taxi and go to the Castellana near Colón Square.

8. Carlos: **Muy bien. ¿Pero será posible encontrar una mesa a esa hora?**
All right. But will it be possible to get a table at that time?

9. Miguel: **Sin duda, hombre. Hasta luego, entonces.**
No doubt about it. (Of course.) See you soon, then.

10. Carlos: **Muy bien. Adiós.**
Sounds good. Bye.

Se encuentran en el café. They meet at the café.

11. Miguel: **Bueno, Carlos, por fin estás aquí. ¡Bienvenido a Madrid!**
Well, Carlos, it's so good to see you. Welcome to Madrid!

12. Carlos: **Gracias, Miguel. Juana y yo estamos muy contentos de estar en Madrid finalmente.**
Thank you, Miguel. Juana and I are very happy to finally be in Madrid.

13. Juana: **Es una ciudad muy bonita. Quiero visitar tantos lugares . . .**
It's a beautiful city. I want to visit so many places . . .

14. Carlos: **Ya tenemos un programa bastante cargado.**
We already have a rather busy schedule.

15. Miguel: **Ya veo. ¿Preferís sentaros adentro o afuera, al aire libre?**

I see. Do you prefer to sit in here or outside in the fresh air?

16. Juana: **¡Al aire libre, claro!**
In the fresh air, of course!

17. Miguel: **¡Ah! Allí hay una mesa libre.**
Ah! There's an empty table.

18. Camarera: **¿Qué quieren tomar?**
What would you like?

19. Juana: **Una limonada para los dos, por favor. ¡Hace tanto calor!**
A lemonade for the two of us, please. It's so hot!

20. Carlos: **Y para mí una cerveza.**
And for me, a beer.

21. Camerera: **En seguida.**
Right away.

22. Juana: **¡Qué manera más agradable de empezar la estancia en Madrid! ¡Ah! Aquí está la camarera con las bebidas. ¡Salud!**
What a pleasant way to begin our stay in Madrid! Ah! Here's the waitress with our drinks. Cheers!

23. Miguel: **¡Salud! ¡Y que lo paséis bien en Madrid!**
Cheers! And I hope you have a good time in Madrid!

24. Carlos: **Se está muy bien aquí. Tengo ganas de quedarme aquí todo el día.**
It's really nice here. I feel like staying here all day.

25. Miguel: **Uno puede quedarse en el café toda la tarde, si quiere.**
You can stay at the café all afternoon, if you want.

26. Carlos: **¿Y jamás hacen marcharse a los clientes?**
Don't they ever ask the customers to leave?

27. Miguel: **¡No, nunca! Y, si queréis, podéis leer el periódico, escribir cartas, charlar con los amigos, o simplemente observar a la gente que pasa.**
No, never! And, if you want, you can read the newspaper, write letters, chat with friends, or simply look at the people passing by.

28. Carlos: **En el mundo de los negocios, uno pierde fácilmente el arte de relajarse.**
In the business world, one easily loses the art of relaxing.

29. Miguel: **Es cierto. Espero que hayáis tenido un buen viaje.**
That's true. I hope you had a good trip.

30. Juana: **Sí, el vuelo estuvo bien.**
Yes, the flight was fine.

31. Miguel: **Bueno, si no tenéis planes para mañana, tal vez podríamos pasear un poco.**
Well, if you don't have any plans for tomorrow, perhaps we could do a little sightseeing.

32. Carlos: **¡Me parece bien! Estoy seguro de que nos servirás de buen guía. Gracias.**
What a good idea! I'm sure you'll be a good guide. Thank you.

33. Miguel: **Camarera, la cuenta, por favor. Pago la cuenta, y nos marchamos. . . No, no, Carlos. Yo te invito, hombre, que es para celebrar tu llegada a Madrid.**
Waitress, the check, please. I'm going to pay the bill, and we'll go . . . No, no, Carlos. It's my treat, to celebrate your arrival in Madrid.

B. NOTES

1. *Diga:* In Spain, *Diga* or *Dígame* (imperative of *decir*) is the equivalent of the English "hello" when answering the telephone. There is considerable variety in other Spanish-speaking countries: *Bueno* in Mexico, *A ver* in Colombia, *Oigo* or *¿Qué hay?* in Cuba, *Hola* in Argentina, and *Aló* in most other countries.

3. *¡Qué gusto!:* Note the use of *qué* before nouns to express "What a . . ." in exclamations.

4. *acabamos de llegar:* Note the use of *acabar de* plus the infinitive to express "to have just."

5. *vernos:* Note the use of the reflexive pronoun to indicate mutual action: "to see each other" or "to meet one another." Compare *encontrarnos,* used later.

7. *Café Gijón* is a popular rendezvous for writers, directors, and actors on the long and beautiful, tree-lined boulevard *Paseo de Recoletos,* near the lovely fountain and statue of *Cibeles* in front of Madrid's main post office, *el Correo.*

8. *Muy bien:* All right, OK. Used to express agreement.

10. *Adiós:* Good-bye. *Adiós* is used in Mexico, while *Hasta luego* is more common in Spain.

15. *sentaros:* sit down, from the verb *sentarse.* Note the use of the reflexive pronoun, attached here to the infinitive.

18. *tomar:* to take; used in the sense of "to eat" or "to drink."

19. *¡Hace tanto calor!:* The verb *hacer* is generally used with expressions concerning weather conditions.

Compare *hace frío* (it's cold); *hace fresco* (it's cool); *hace buen tiempo* (the weather is fine); *hace viento* (it's windy).

21. *En seguida:* Right away. Equivalents: *inmediatamente, ahora mismo.*

22. *¡Salud!:* Cheers!, literally, "health." In toasting one another, Spanish-speaking people generally exchange this single word.

23. *Y que lo paséis bien:* In expressing a wish or desire, the verb "to hope" (*esperar*) is frequently omitted and the statement begins with the introductory *que,* followed by a verb in the subjunctive. Equivalent to the English "(May you) have a good time." Compare *¡Que vivan mil años!* ([May they] live a thousand years!) and *¡Que siga usted bien!* ([May you] continue in good health!)

24. *Se está:* Note the use of the reflexive here for the impersonal "one feels."
    tengo ganas de; me gustaría: I feel like, I'd like to.
    todo el día: all day. Note the use of the article in such expressions as *todo el año* (all year), *toda la tarde* (all afternoon), *toda la semana* (all week), *todo el verano* (all summer), etc.

26. *hacen marcharse a:* literally, "make go away." Note the use of the personal *a* before *los clientes.*

29. *hayáis tenido:* Note the use of the subjunctive after the verb of emotion, "to hope."

31. *pasear:* to stroll, to walk around, to go sightseeing. This verb can also be used with *pasear en coche* (to

drive around in a car), *pasear a caballo* (to ride around on horseback).

32. *¡Me parece bien!:* What a good idea! That sounds good!

C. GRAMMAR AND USAGE

1. Notice that the expression *acabar de* translates as "to have just done something." The verb *acabar* is conjugated regularly, and then followed by *de* + infinitive.

Acabo de llegar.
I have just arrived.

Juan acaba de llamar.
Juan has just called.

2. The expression *tener ganas de* means "to feel like," and is also followed by an infinitive. See the Summary of Spanish Grammar for the full conjugation of *tener*.

Tengo ganas de comer helado.
I feel like eating ice cream.

María tiene ganas de salir.
María feels like going out.

Ellos tendrán ganas de acostarse.
They will feel like going to bed.

3. The verb *poder* means "can" or "to be able" and is followed directly by an infinitive, without *de*.

Puedo hacer el trabajo.
I can do the work.

Juan puede estudiar la lección mañana.
Juan can study the lesson tomorrow.

Podemos pasar las vacaciones allí.
We can spend our vacation there.

Ellos pueden ver a María la semana que viene.
They can see María next week.

Note in the last example above that *a* is used after the verb *ver* and before nouns or pronouns referring to people.

He visto a papá.
I have seen Dad.

Object pronouns can be attached to the verb that follows *poder*, or they may also precede *poder*.

Él podía hacerlo. / Él lo podía hacer.
He was able to do it.

Ellos podrán comerlo. / Ellos lo podrán comer.
They will be able to eat it.

Ella puede mandarlo. / Ella lo puede mandar.
She can send it.

Poder generally implies physical ability to do something. When knowledge or learned skills are implied, *saber* is generally used. Compare:

Puedo leerlo. ("I can read it" in the sense of having the ability to read it; i.e., in spite of the darkness, fog, bad script, etc.)

Sé leerlo. ("I can read it" in the sense of "knowing how to," as a language, a code, etc.)

4. In English, adjectives are often followed by certain prepositions and the -ing form of a verb or its infinitive (ex: interested in reading, happy to go, afraid of flying) Similarly, Spanish adjectives are followed by a preposition plus the infinitive:

Estoy contento de saberlo.
I'm happy to know it.

Estaba desesperado por irse.
He was desperate to leave.

Estarán interesados en pasear con nosotros.
They will be interested in walking with us.

EXERCISES

A. Substitute each of the words or expressions in parentheses for the underlined word or expression in the model sentence. Write each new sentence and say it aloud.

1. *Juan acaba de <u>comer</u>.* (estudiar, entrar, salir, acostarse, lavarse)

2. *Los hombres acaban de <u>llegar</u>.* (verlo, escucharlo, hablar, telefonear)

3. *Tengo ganas de ir <u>al cine</u>.* (al concierto, a la biblioteca, al museo, al parque, al restaurante)

4. *Tienen ganas de <u>bailar</u>.* (cantar, leer, mirar la televisión, escuchar la radio, ir al cine)

5. *Puedo <u>hacerlo</u>.* (comer, beber, comprar, estudiar, ganar, aprender)

6. *<u>Los niños</u> están contentos de estar aquí.* (Los padres, Los hombres, Juan y José, Los profesores, María y Rafael)

B. Convert these sentences to the plural, making appropriate verb changes. Write the complete sentence and translate.

1. *Acabo de llegar.*

2. *El niño tiene ganas de comer.*

3. *Usted puede hacerlo.*

4. *La muchacha está contenta de verlos.*

5. *Lo puedo hacer ahora.*

C. Translate the following sentences into Spanish, then say them aloud.

1. He has just come in.

2. She has just eaten.

3. We feel like going to the movies.

4. I feel like dancing.

5. I can do it now.

6. We can see her tomorrow.

7. They'll be able to go there.

8. I am happy to see you.

9. We are surprised to hear it.

10. They are pleased to know it.

D. From among the three choices given, choose the best equivalent of the English term (in parentheses) for each sentence, and translate.

1. (Who) ¿_____ habla?
    (a) *Qué*
    (b) *Cuál*
    (c) *Quién*

2. (What a) ¡_____ gusto!
    (a) *Qué*
    (b) *Cuál*
    (c) *Cuál un*

3. (way) ¡Qué _____ más agradable de empezar el día!
    (a) *vía*
    (b) *manera*
    (c) *camino*

4. (had) *Espero que hayáis* _____ *buen viaje.*
   (a) *habido*
   (b) *tenido*
   (c) *comido*

5. (at) *Vimos a Miguel* _____ *el Café Gijón.*
   (a) *al*
   (b) *en*
   (c) *entre*

6. (all) *Estuvimos allí* _____ *el día.*
   (a) *todos*
   (b) *toda*
   (c) *todo*

7. (There are) _____ *muchos monumentos en Madrid.*
   (a) *Están*
   (b) *Allí son*
   (c) *Hay*

8. (sit down) *¿Quiere usted* _____ *aquí?*
   (a) *sentarte*
   (b) *sentarse*
   (c) *sentar*

9. (so much) *El señor tiene* _____ *dinero.*
   (a) *tan*
   (b) *tantas*
   (c) *tanto*

10. (arrived) *Acabamos de* _____.
    (a) *llegado*
    (b) *llegar*
    (c) *llegamos*

Answer Key

B.
1. *Acabamos de llegar.*
   We have just arrived.

2. *Los niños tienen ganas de comer.*
   The children want to eat.

3. *Ustedes pueden hacerlo.*
   You can do it.

4. *Las muchachas están contentas de verlos.*
   The girls are happy to see them.

5. *Lo podemos hacer ahora.*
   We can do it now.

C.
1. *Él acaba de entrar.*

2. *Ella acaba de comer.*

3. *Tenemos ganas de ir al cine.*

4. *Tengo ganas de bailar.*

5. *Puedo hacerlo ahora.*

6. *Podemos verla mañana.*

7. *Ellos podrán ir allí.*

8. *Estoy contento de verle (verte).*

9. *Estamos sorprendidos de oírlo.*

10. *Están contentos de saberlo.*

D.
1. *¿Quién habla?*
   Who's speaking?

2. *¡Qué gusto!*
   What a pleasure!

3. *¡Qué manera más agradable de empezar el día!*
   What a pleasant way to begin the day!

4. *Espero que hayáis tenido buen viaje.*
   I hope that you have had a good trip.

5. *Vimos a Miguel en el Café Gijón.*
   We saw Miguel at the Café Gijón.

6. *Estuvimos allí todo el día.*
   We were there all day.

7. *Hay muchos monumentos en Madrid.*
   There are many monuments in Madrid.

8. *¿Quiere usted sentarse aquí?*
   Do you want to sit down here?

9. *El señor tiene tanto dinero.*
   The man has so much money.

10. *Acabamos de llegar.*
    We have just arrived.

LESSON 2

LAS NOTICIAS
THE NEWS

A. DIALOGUE

0. *Pedro y Alberto están mirando la televisión cuando
   empiezan a conversar sobre un nuevo canal de noticias de veinticuatro horas.*
   Pedro and Alberto are watching television when
   they start discussing a new twenty-four hour TV
   news channel.

1. Pedro: *(Mirando la televisión)* **No conozco bien
   este nuevo canal de televisión. ¿Has tenido la
   oportunidad de verlo?**
   (Watching television) I really don't know this new TV
   channel. Have you had the opportunity to watch it?

2. Alberto: **No, no he tenido suficiente tiempo para
   mirar la televisión últimamente; he estado muy
   ocupado, pero parece ser muy similar a los otros
   canales de noticias. Hay otros canales que trans-
   miten noticias las veinticuatro horas del día. Si
   tienes conexión por satélite puedes ver varios
   canales de noticias de varios países.**
   No, I haven't had enough time to watch TV lately;
   I've been very busy, but it seems similar to other
   news channels. There are other channels that offer
   news twenty-four hours a day. If you have satellite
   connection you can get various news channels from
   various countries.

3. Pedro: **¿Y también hay canales que ofrecen noticias en otros idiomas? ¿Hay un canal en francés**

u holandés? Hablo bastante bien el francés y estoy aprendiendo holandés actualmente.

Are there news channels in other languages as well? Is there a news channel in French or Dutch? I speak French rather well and I'm currently learning Dutch.

4. Alberto: **Sí, puedes recibir canales en francés, inglés, alemán, italiano y, por supuesto, español. No sabía que estabas estudiando holandés. Yo no sé hablar ningún otro idioma.**

Yes, you can receive channels in French, English, German, Italian, and, of course, Spanish. I didn't know that you were learning Dutch. I don't speak any other languages.

5. Pedro: **Yo creo que es muy buena idea escuchar las noticias en otro idioma. Así puedes practicar mientras te informas de lo que está ocurriendo en el mundo.**

I think it's a great idea to listen to the news in other languages. That way you can practice while you learn what's happening around the world.

6. Alberto: **Sí. ¿Qué tipo de noticias te suele interesar?**

Yes. What type of news are you normally interested in?

7. Pedro: **A mí me gusta leer todo tipo de noticias. Me gusta saber de todo un poco: economía, deportes, cultura, espectáculos y política internacional.**

I like to read all types of news. I like to know a bit of everything: the economy, sports, the arts, entertainment and world politics.

8. Alberto: **¡A mí me encanta leer la sección de ciencia y tecnología! Me gusta mucho todo lo rela-**

cionado con los acontecimientos científicos, desde
la salud hasta la meteorología.
I really like to read the science and technology section! I like everything related to scientific events,
from health to weather.

9. Pedro: **Mira, ahora están dando el pronóstico del
tiempo para este fin de semana. Parece que va a
hacer muy buen tiempo. Verdaderamente nos
hace falta: ha estado lloviendo mucho todos los
fines de semana y en el verano me gusta mucho
irme a la playa.**
Look, now they're giving the weather forecast for
this weekend. It seems like it will be good weather.
We really need it: it has been raining every weekend,
and in the summer I like to go to the beach.

10. Alberto: **Pues, de acuerdo al informe, el domingo
va a ser mejor día que el sábado. ¿En cuál de los
dos días pensabas ir a la playa?**
According to the forecast, Sunday will be a better
day than Saturday. On which of the two days were
you thinking of going?

11. Pedro: **Pensaba ir el domingo, aunque parece que
va a estar a tope.**
I was thinking of going on Sunday; although it
might be very crowded.

12. Alberto: **Mira, están dando el informe financiero.**
Look, they're giving the financial report.

13. Pedro: **Por lo que veo la bolsa no parece mejorar
nada. Llevamos varios meses sin ver mucha
mejoría.**
It seems like the stock market isn't getting any better. We've spent several months without seeing
much improvement.

14. Alberto: **Pero no te debes preocupar tanto. Como sabes, es normal que los mercados financieros pasen largos períodos estancados. A lo largo de los años la bolsa ha pasado por los mismos ciclos.**
But you shouldn't worry so much. As you know, it's normal for financial markets to remain stagnant for long periods. Throughout the years the stock market has gone through the same cycles.

15. Pedro: **Por lo que veo eres un optimista.**
I can see that you're an optimist.

16. Alberto: **Sí, aunque a veces las noticias que ponen en la televisión me hacen sentir más pesimista.**
Yes, although sometimes the news they show on TV makes me feel more pessimistic.

17. Pedro: **Yo sé que hay muchas cosas en las noticias que nos pueden preocupar. Pero también debes saber que la prensa a veces se enfoca mucho en noticias negativas.**
I know there are many things on the news that can make us worried. But you should also know that the media sometimes focuses on negative news.

18. Alberto: **Es cierto. Es una pena que cuando dan reportajes de noticias sensacionalistas adquieren más popularidad y venden más ejemplares.**
It's true. It's a shame that when they report sensational news they gain more popularity and sell more issues.

19. Pedro: **Y a veces dejan de informar noticias constructivas e interesantes.**
And sometimes they stop giving constructive and interesting news.

20. Alberto: **De todas formas, me gusta saber qué está pasando en el mundo.**
In any case, I like to know what's happening in the world.

21. Pedro: **La solución perfecta sería obtener las noticias de más de una fuente noticiera.**
The perfect solution would be to get the news from more than one news source.

22. Alberto: **Lo mejor es tener la costumbre de comprarse un periódico serio, suscribirse a una revista semanal buena y escoger un buen noticiero por televisión. Así se puede tener una impresión más completa de los acontecimientos mundiales.**
The best way is to get in the habit of buying a serious newspaper, subscribing to a good weekly magazine and choosing a good TV news program. That way you can get a more complete impression of what's happening in the world.

23. Pedro: **Me tengo que ir, Alberto.**
I have to go, Alberto.

24. Alberto: **¿Adónde vas?**
Where are you going?

25. Pedro: **Me voy a comprar un buen periódico. . . ¡Quiero asegurarme de que va hacer buen tiempo para ir a la playa este fin de semana!**
I'm going to buy a good newspaper . . . I want to make sure that there will be good beach weather this weekend!

B. NOTES

1. *no conozco:* I don't know. From *conocer,* "to be familiar with."

2. *las veinticuatro horas del día:* Notice the articles used in this expression; compare with the English "twenty-four hours a day."

3. *francés u holandés:* Note that *o* (or) changes to *u* before a word beginning with *o* (or with *ho* since *h* is silent in Spanish).

   actualmente: currently. Not to be confused with "actually," which can be expressed in a few ways: *de hecho, en realidad, realmente.*

6. *te (suele) interesar:* Note that "to be interested in" in Spanish is the verb *interesar* plus the direct object pronoun placed before the verb. *Me interesan los periódicos extranjeros.* Foreign newspapers interest me.

   Me encanta: I really like it very much. In English, we would usually say "I love." It literally means "It enchants me." Notice that the infinitive form of the verb follows: *Me encanta leer* (I love to read), *me encanta comer* (I love to eat), etc.

9. *nos hace falta:* From *hacer falta,* "to be lacking (to someone)." Compare *Me hace falta un libro:* I need a book. *Nos hace falta más dinero:* We need more money.

11. *a tope:* flat out, jam-packed. It literally means "to the limit" or "to the end." *La sala estaba a tope.* The hall was jam-packed.

15. *Por lo que veo:* I can see that. Literally, "from what I see."

18. *es una pena:* it's a shame. It literally means "it's a sorrow."

19. *constructivas e interesantes:* constructive and interesting. Notice that *y* and *e* both mean "and." You use

e when the second word begins with the letter *i*. Compare: *José y Raúl son amigos. José e Ignacio son amigos también.*

22. *tener la costumbre de:* to be in the habit of, to be used to. This expression is followed by the infinitive of the verb.

C. GRAMMAR AND USAGE

1. Notice that the verbs *conocer* and *saber* both mean "to know" in different connotations. *Conocer* means "to be acquainted with something or someone" or "to meet a person." The verb *saber* means "to know in terms of having information, knowledge or skill."

conocer

Conozco a los señores Hernández.
    I know Mr. and Mrs. Hernández.

No conocemos el norte de España.
    We do not know (are not familiar with) the north of Spain.

Ellos conocen bien el sistema.
    They know the system well.

Conocí a María en Francia.
    I met María in France (i.e., we met for the first time, became acquainted).

saber

Sé que los señores Hernández están aquí.
    I know that Mr. and Mrs. Hernandez are here.

Todos sabemos la verdad.
    We all know the truth.

Ella lo sabrá mañana.
> She will know it (i.e., some fact) tomorrow.

Él sabe cocinar.
> He knows how to cook.

2. The Spanish word *hay* means "there is" and "there are." The same word is used for both the singular and the plural.

Hay muchos libros sobre la mesa.
> There are many books on the table.

Habrá un desfile mañana.
> There will be a parade tomorrow.

Había mucha gente allí.
> There were many people there.

3. The following are very useful and common question words in Spanish: *¿Qué?*: What? *¿Cuál?*: Which? *¿Quién(es)?*: Who?

¿Qué sabe usted de la familia?
> What do you know about the family?

¿Cuál de los niños es amigo tuyo?
> Which of the children is a friend of yours?

¿Quién es aquel niño?
> Who is that child?

4. *Hacer falta* means "to need" or "to lack." Notice that the phrases begin with the object pronoun followed by *hacer falta* and the subject.

Me hace falta más dinero.
> I need more money.

Te hacen falta tres euros.
> You need three euros.

Le hará falta (a él) mucha experiencia.
He will need a lot of experience.

EXERCISES

A. Substitute each of the words or expressions in parenthe-
    ses for the underlined word or expression in the model
    sentence. Write each new sentence and say it aloud.

1. *Acaba de conocer a María.* (a tu hermano, a los
    señores La Torre, a la señora de Aguirre, a la
    señorita Domenech, a los amigos de mi padre)

2. *Ellos conocen a Juan.* (María y yo conocemos, Yo
    conozco, Pepe conoce, Francisco y Miguel conocen,
    Todo el mundo conoce)

3. *Ellos deben saber el número.* (la dirección, la ver-
    dad, el precio, la fecha, el nombre, la palabra)

4. *Hay muchas personas en el hotel.* (una peluquería,
    varios salones, un comedor, algunas reuniones, un
    conserje)

5. *Me hace(n) falta un libro.* (unos discos, más infor-
    mación, un corte de pelo, más tiempo, los nombres)

6. *¿Quién(es) es (son) aquel muchacho?* (tu amigo,
    María Velarde, estos señores, el profesor, los alum-
    nos)

B. Convert these sentences to the plural, making appropri-
    ate verb changes. Write out the complete sentence and
    translate.

1. *Él sabe bailar.*

2. *Usted conocerá a los señores Pérez.*

3. *Hay una clase por la tarde.*

4. *Me hace falta un euro.*

5. *¿Quién es el médico?*

C. Translate the following sentences into Spanish, then say them aloud.

1. Do you know the number?

2. They know how to dance.

3. There were many parades.

4. Which of these books do you want?

5. Who are those men on the corner?

6. What do you need?

7. Do they know the address?

8. Who knows María?

9. They need many classes.

10. We need more time.

D. From among the three choices given, choose the best equivalent of the English term (in parentheses) for each sentence, and translate.

1. (know) *Estoy seguro de que ellos* _____ *a María.*
   (a) *sepan*
   (b) *conocer*
   (c) *conocen*

2. (knew) *Me dijeron que ellos* _____ *el título del libro.*
   (a) *sabían*
   (b) *conocerán*
   (c) *conozco*

3. (need) *Me hace* _____ *un libro nuevo.*
   (a) *necesito*
   (b) *falta*
   (c) *faltas*

4. (good) *Hay una revista muy* _____ *que sale el lunes.*
   (a) *bueno*
   (b) *buenas*
   (c) *buena*

5. (which one) *No me dijo* _____ *de estas novelas es mejor.*
   (a) *qué*
   (b) *quién*
   (c) *cuál*

6. (there are) *En este lado* _____ *muchos periódicos extranjeros.*
   (a) *hay*
   (b) *estarán*
   (c) *habían*

7. (German) *Esta revista* _____ *es interesante.*
   (a) *alemanes*
   (b) *alemana*
   (c) *alemán*

8. (should be) *Este librito* _____ *lo que quieren ustedes.*
   (a) *debe ser*
   (b) *tiene que estar*
   (c) *son*

9. (feel like) *Ellos* _____ *de ir a la fiesta.*
   (a) *sienten como*
   (b) *tienen ganas*
   (c) *quieren*

10. (you) *Este libro* _____ *da a usted muchos informes.*
    (a) *le*
    (b) *os*
    (c) *les*

Answer Key

B. 1. *Ellos saben bailar.*
   They know how to dance.

   2. *Ustedes conocerán a los señores Pérez.*
   You will meet Mr. and Mrs. Pérez.

   3. *Hay unas clases por la tarde.*
   There are some classes in the afternoon.

   4. *Me hacen falta unos euros.*
   I need some euros.

   5. *¿Quiénes son los médicos?*
   Who are the doctors?

C. 1. *¿Sabe(s) usted (tú) el número?*

   2. *Ellos saben bailar.*

   3. *Había muchos desfiles.*

   4. *¿Cuál de estos libros quiere(s) usted (tú)?*

   5. *¿Quiénes son esos hombres en la esquina?*

   6. *¿Qué necesita(s) usted (tú)? ¿Qué le (te) hace falta a usted (ti)?*

   7. *¿Saben la dirección?*

   8. *¿Quién conoce a María?*

   9. *Les hacen falta muchas clases. Necesitan muchas clases.*

   10. *Nos hace falta más tiempo. Necesitamos más tiempo.*

D. 1. *Estoy seguro de que ellos conocen a María.*
   I'm sure they know María.

   2. *Me dijeron que ellos sabían el título del libro.*
   They told me that they knew the title of the book.

3. *Me hace falta un libro nuevo.*
   I need a new book.

4. *Hay una revista muy buena que sale el lunes.*
   There is a very good magazine that comes out on Monday.

5. *No me dijo cuál de estas novelas es mejor.*
   He didn't tell me which one of these novels is better.

6. *En este lado hay muchos periódicos extranjeros.*
   On this side there are many foreign newspapers.

7. *Esta revista alemana es interesante.*
   This German magazine is interesting.

8. *Este librito debe ser lo que quieren ustedes.*
   This little book should be what you want.

9. *Ellos tienen ganas de ir a la fiesta.*
   They feel like going to the party.

10. *Este libro le da a usted muchos informes.*
    This book gives you a great deal of information.

LESSON 3

AL TELÉFONO
ON THE TELEPHONE

A. DIALOGUE

0. *Roberto se ha ido de compras para comprarle a su amigo Rafa un regalo de cumpleaños y decide llamar a Laura.*
   Roberto is shopping for a gift for Rafa's birthday and decides to call Laura.

1. Roberto: (*en Madrid hablando por un teléfono móvil*) **¡Buenas tardes, Laura! ¿Cómo estás?**
   (*In Madrid speaking on a cell phone*) Good afternoon, Laura! How are you?

2. Laura: **Muy bien, gracias. Aquí con mucho trabajo; tengo un examen final mañana.**
   Very well, thanks. I have a lot of work here; I have a final exam tomorrow.

3. Roberto: **¿Puedes hablar ahora?**
   Can you talk now?

4. Laura: **Sí, claro. Me hacía mucha falta tomarme un descanso. Llevo horas leyendo; me ha dado dolor de cabeza de tanto leer.**
   Yes, of course. I really needed to take a break. I've been reading for hours. I got a headache from reading so much.

5. Roberto: **Laura, ¿puedes hablar más alto, por favor? No te oigo muy bien.**
   Laura, can you speak a little louder, please? I can't hear you very well.

6. Laura: **Sí, ya me he dado cuenta; me has estado gritando todo este tiempo.**
Yes, I've noticed; you've been screaming at me all this time.

7. Roberto: **Disculpa, Laura. Es que estoy en un sitio donde hace mucho ruido. Estoy justo enfrente de la parada de autobuses en la Puerta del Sol.**
Sorry, Laura. I'm at a place that's very noisy. I'm right in front of the bus station in Puerta del Sol.

8. Laura: **¿Y qué vas a hacer hoy?**
So what are you going to do today?

9. Roberto: **Pues, decidí irme de compras hoy. El cumpleaños de Rafa es el domingo y quería comprarle algo. Voy a escoger algo que le guste.**
I decided to go shopping today. Rafa's birthday is Sunday and I wanted to get him something. I'm going to choose something that he likes.

10. Laura: **¿Por qué no planificamos una fiesta sorpresa?**
Why don't we plan a surprise party?

11. Roberto: **Pero Laura, me habías dicho que estabas muy ocupada, que tenías mucho que estudiar.**
But Laura, you said that you were very busy, that you had a lot of studying to do.

12. Laura: **Sí, pero el examen es mañana; después estaré libre. Además, tú puedes comenzar con los preparativos.**
Yes, but the test is tomorrow; after that, I'll be free. Besides, you can get started with the planning.

13. Roberto: **Bueno, me parece estupendo. ¿Qué quieres que haga?**
OK, it sounds great. What do you want me to do?

14. Laura: **Antes que nada, llama a Juan y a Luis. Pregúntales si están disponibles el sábado por la noche.**

   First of all, call Juan and Luis. Ask them if they are available Saturday night.

15. Roberto: **Ellos no tienen planes; ya les hablé esta mañana.**

   They have no plans. I already spoke to them this morning.

16. Laura: **Roberto, ¿puedes irte a una calle más tranquila? Apenas te oigo.**

   Roberto, could you go to a quieter street? I can barely hear you.

17. Roberto: **Vale, estoy caminando a un área más tranquila. ¿Qué más quieres que haga?**

   OK, I'm walking to a quieter street. What else do you want me to do?

18. Laura: **También dale una llamada a Rosita. Ella tiene muchísimas amistades. Luego, pasa por casa de Paula y Gloria. Ellas tienen más amigos aun que Rosita.**

   Call Rosita first. She has a lot of friends. Then stop by Paula and Gloria's house. They have even more friends than Rosita.

19. Roberto: **Espera, Laura. ¿Dónde va a ser esta fiesta?**

   Wait a second, Laura. Where is this party going to be?

20. Laura: **Tranquilo. . . en mi casa. Pregúntale a Juan si puede traer algo de comida y a Luis si puede traer algo de bebida. Ve al supermercado esta noche. Compra cualquier cosa que haga falta.**

Relax . . . at my house. Ask Juan if he can bring
some food and Luis if he can bring some drinks. Go
to the supermarket tonight. Buy anything that we
may need.

21. Roberto: **Perfecto, pero no tengo dinero.**
    Perfect, but I have no money.

22. Laura: **No te preocupes, entre todos vamos a
    pagar. Usa tu tarjeta de crédito. No van a ser más
    de cien euros.**
    Don't worry, we will all pay. Use your credit card. It
    won't be more than one hundred euros.

23. Roberto: **¿Y qué hago con toda la comida?**
    And what should I do with all the food?

24. Laura: **Trae todo a mi casa mañana por la tarde.
    Yo vuelvo de la universidad a las tres de la tarde.**
    Bring everything to my house tomorrow afternoon.
    I get back from the university at 3 p.m.

25. Roberto: **No tengo el número de teléfono de
    Rosita. ¿Sabes su número?**
    I don't have Rosita's phone number. Do you know
    the number?

26. Laura: **Sí, es el noventa y uno, tres, treinta y ocho,
    veinte y cinco, quince.**
    Yes, it's ninety-one, three, thirty-eight, twenty-five,
    fifteen.

27. Roberto: **Pues la voy a llamar ahora.**
    I am going to call her now.

28. Laura: **Roberto, no llames desde la Puerta del Sol
    donde hace tanto ruido.**
    Roberto, don't call from Puerta del Sol where it's so
    noisy.

29. Roberto: **No, tranquila, Laura. No me gustaría que todos se presentaran a tu casa el martes por la noche.**
I won't, Laura. I wouldn't want everyone showing up at your house on Tuesday night.

30. Laura: **Muy bien. Ahora vuelvo a mis estudios. . .**
Very good. Now I'm going to get back to my books . . .

31. Roberto: **Buena suerte. . . ¡Te llamo mañana!**
Good luck . . . I'll call you tomorrow!

B. NOTES

4. *dolor de cabeza:* headache; literally, "pain of the head." There is also *dolor de estómago* (stomach ache), *dolor de muelas* (tooth ache) and *dolor de espalda* (back ache).

7. *Disculpa:* excuse me or sorry. Other similar expressions are *perdona, dispensa* or *lo siento.*
Puerta del Sol: The geographical center of Spain. The square marks Kilometer Zero, where all of Spain's major highways begin. *Puerta del Sol* is also where Spaniards congregate every year to celebrate the New Year. With each of the twelve chimes, revelers eat one grape to represent good luck and prosperity for the year ahead.

9. Notice that in Spanish the names of days of the week and months of the year are not capitalized unless they appear at the beginning of a sentence.

13 & 17. Notice there are a number of ways to signal agreement: *Bueno, vale* (used mostly in Spain), *está bien.* All these are equivalents to the English "Okay," "Alright," "That's fine."

20. *cualquier cosa*: anything. *Cualquier* can be used with other nouns: *cualquier momento* (any moment); *cualquier nivel* (any level).

30. *volver a mis estudios*: The verb *volver* means "to go back." This phrase literally means "to go back to my studies."

C. GRAMMAR AND USAGE

1. The expression *ir a* + infinitive indicates the immediate future. It is the equivalent of the English "going to."

ir   a   Infinitive Complement

Voy a estudiar la lección.
   I'm going to study the lesson.

Vamos a ir a la tienda.
   We're going to go to the store.

Van a hacer una llamada.
   They're going to make a phone call.

2. The expression *más que* or *más de* means "more than." Notice that *más de* is used with numbers. Also notice that the negative *no . . . más que/de* usually means "only."

más que

Juan tiene más libros que María.
   Juan has more books than María.

Yo estudio más que Juan.
   I study more than Juan.

Ellos viajan más que nadie.
   They travel more than anyone.

No tengo más que cien euros.
   I have only (I have no more than) a hundred euros.

más de (used with numbers)

Él vendió más de cien libros.
　　He sold more than a hundred books.

Ellos compraron más de cuatro casas.
　　They bought more than four houses.

Ustedes tienen más de tres horas.
　　You have more than three hours.

3. When selecting commands or request forms, keep in mind that in Spanish you have to pay attention to the degree of familiarity (polite or familiar) and to the number (singular or plural).

POLITE FORMS

Notice that the polite command forms are the third person singular (for *usted*) and the third person plural (for *ustedes*) of the present subjunctive.

Ponga usted el libro allí.
　　Put the book there.

Vengan ustedes mañana.
　　Come tomorrow.

Vaya usted a verlo.
　　Go see it.

No fumen ustedes.
　　Don't smoke.

Entre usted.
　　Come in. (Enter.)

No coman ustedes tanto.
　　Don't eat so much.

FAMILIAR SINGULAR

The familiar singular affirmative command (*tú*) is usually the same as the third person singular of the present indicative. However, keep in mind that there are some irregular forms: *ten, pon, ven, ve, sal*. The negative form uses the second person singular of the present subjunctive.

Mira. No mires.
> Look. Don't look.

Escucha. No escuches.
> Listen. Don't listen.

Come el helado. No comas el helado.
> Eat the ice cream. Don't eat the ice cream.

Ven aquí en seguida. No vengas aquí.
> Come here at once. Don't come here.

Ponte el sombrero. No te pongas el sombrero.
> Put on your hat. Don't put on your hat.

Vete. No te vayas.
> Go away. Don't go away.

Notice also that the object pronouns (reflexive, indirect, and direct) are attached to both polite and familiar affirmative verb commands:

Dámelo (tú). Démelo (usted).	Give it to me.
Póntelo (tú). Póngaselo (usted).	Put it on.
Tráemelo (tú). Tráigamelo (usted).	Bring it to me.

but not to negative commands:

No me lo des (tú).	Don't give it to me.
No me lo dé (usted).	
No te lo pongas (tú).	Don't put it on.
No se lo ponga (usted).	

No me lo traigas (tú).   Don't bring it to me.
No me lo traiga (usted).

FAMILIAR PLURAL (*VOSOTROS*)

The affirmative familiar plural command is formed by changing the final *r* of the infinitive to *d*. The negative is the second person plural form of the present subjunctive. Note the position of the pronouns. *Vosotros* forms, including these commands, are only used in Spain. In Latin America, there is no difference between the familiar plural and polite plural; both are designated by *ustedes*.

Hablad más alto. No habléis más alto.
  Speak louder. Don't speak louder.

Escuchad. No escuchéis.
  Listen. Don't listen.

Venid. No vengáis.
  Come. Don't come.

Compradlo. No lo compréis.
  Buy it. Don't buy it.

Traédmelo. No me lo traigáis.
  Bring it to me. Don't bring it to me.

Dádnoslo. No nos lo deis.
  Give it to us. Don't give it to us.

4. The expression *querer* + infinitive means "I want."

Quiero llamarle ahora.
  I want to call him now.

No queremos ir al cine.
  We don't want to go to the movies.

Querían hablar con Pablo.
  They wanted to speak with Pablo.

EXERCISES

A. Substitute each of the words or expressions in the parentheses for the underlined word or expression in the model sentence. Write each new sentence and say it aloud.

1. *Van a comprar <u>la casa</u>.* (los libros, el disco, un coche, dos entradas, el sombrero)

2. *Voy a <u>estudiar</u> mañana.* (escribir, comprarlo, salir, llamar, descansar)

3. *Tengo más de tres <u>clases</u>.* (libros, problemas, billetes, programas, euros)

4. *Juan y María viajan más que <u>yo</u>.* (el profesor, nadie, la Sra. Andrade, ella, nosotros)

5. *No escuches <u>la radio</u>.* (el programa, la música, las noticias, la broma, el cuento)

6. *Ellos quieren <u>cantar</u>.* (bailar, comer, comprarlo, irse, verlo)

B. Change these commands to the negative. Write the complete sentence and translate.

Example: *Dámelo.*   *No me lo des.*   Don't give it to me.

1. *Dígamelo.*

2. *Vete.*

3. *Póngaselo.*

4. *Quítatelo.*

5. *Cómpramelo.*

C. Translate the following sentences into Spanish, then say them aloud.

1. I work more than Juan.

2. They will travel more than three hours today.

3. We have more than ten pages to read *(que leer)*.

4. They are going to buy a new car.

5. He is going to rest tomorrow.

6. We were going to sell the house.

7. Do you want to see the doctor?

8. He wants to give me the book.

9. Don't send it to him.

10. They don't want to leave.

D. From among the three choices given, choose the best equivalent of the English term (in parentheses) for each sentence, and translate.

1. (the telephone book) *Usted encontrará* _____ *allí.*
   (a) *la guía telefónica*
   (b) *el libro de teléfonos*
   (c) *la telefónica*

2. (than) *Tenemos más dinero* _____ *ellos.*
   (a) *de*
   (b) *que*
   (c) *el que*

3. (send to him) *Quieren* _____ *el libro.*
   (a) *mandarnos*
   (b) *mandarse*
   (c) *mandarle*

4. (go inside) *Tenía que* _____ *la cabina.*
   (a) *ir a*
   (b) *entrar por*
   (c) *entrar en*

5. (Tell him) _____ *que estoy en Madrid.*
   - (a) *Dale*
   - (b) *Dígale*
   - (c) *Dícele*

6. (make) *Puedo* _____ *una llamada de larga distancia a Madrid.*
   - (a) *dar*
   - (b) *poner*
   - (c) *hacer*

7. (know) ¿_____ *usted el número?*
   - (a) *Sé*
   - (b) *Sabe*
   - (c) *Conozco*

8. Don't tell (it to) him.
   - (a) *No dígaselo.*
   - (b) *No le lo diga.*
   - (c) *No se lo diga.*

9. (send it to us) _____ *usted mañana.*
   - (a) *Mándelonos*
   - (b) *Mándenoslo*
   - (c) *Mándenoslos*

10. (to send them) *Ellos quieren* _____ *en seguida.*
    - (a) *mandarle*
    - (b) *mandarlos*
    - (c) *mandarlo*

Answer Key

B. 1. *No me lo diga.*
       Don't tell (it to) me.

    2. *No te vayas.*
       Don't go away.

    3. *No se lo ponga.*
       Don't put it on.

    4. *No te lo quites.*
       Don't take it off.

    5. *No me lo compres.*
       Don't buy it for me.

C. 1. *Trabajo más que Juan.*

    2. *Viajarán más de tres horas hoy.*

    3. *Tenemos más de diez páginas que leer.*

    4. *Van a comprar un coche nuevo.*

    5. *Va a descansar mañana.*

    6. *Íbamos a vender la casa.*

    7. *¿Quiere (usted) ver al médico? ¿Quieres (tú) ver al médico?*

    8. *Quiere darme el libro.*

    9. *No se lo mande (a él). No se lo mandes (a él).*

   10. *(Ellos) no quieren marcharse.*

D. 1. *Usted encontrará la guía telefónica allí.*
       You will find the telephone book there.

    2. *Tenemos más dinero que ellos.*
       We have more money than they do.

3. *Quieren mandarle el libro.*
   They want to send him the book.

4. *Tenía que entrar en la cabina.*
   He had to go inside the cabin.

5. *Dígale que estoy en Madrid.*
   Tell him that I am in Madrid.

6. *Puedo hacer una llamada de larga distancia a Madrid.*
   I can make a long-distance call to Madrid.

7. *¿Sabe usted el número?*
   Do you know the number?

8. *No se lo diga.*
   Don't tell (it to) him.

9. *Mándenoslo usted mañana.*
   Send it to us tomorrow.

10. *Ellos quieren mandarlos en seguida.*
    They want to send them at once.

LESSON 4

TRANSPORTES URBANOS
CITY TRANSPORTATION

A. DIALOGUE

El metro. The subway.

0. *Julieta y Leandro son turistas de Argentina. Han estado andando por Madrid durante mucho tiempo descubriendo la ciudad. De repente se dan cuenta de que están muy lejos del hotel y no saben si tomar un taxi de regreso.*

   Julieta and Leandro are tourists from Argentina. They have been walking around Madrid for a long time getting to know the city. They suddenly realize that they are too far from the hotel and don't know whether to go back by taxi.

1. Leandro: **¿Cómo es que terminamos tan lejos del hotel? Tenemos bastante camino para regresar. Tal vez deberíamos pedir un taxi.**

   How did we end up so far from the hotel? We have a long way to get back. Maybe we should take a taxi.

2. Julieta: **¿Te has vuelto loco? Un taxi nos costará un ojo de la cara.**

   Have you gone crazy? A taxi will cost us an arm and a leg.

3. Leandro: **¿Desde cuándo piensas en ahorrar?**

   Since when did you start thinking of saving?

4. Julieta: **Es que prefiero gastar el dinero en otras cosas.**

It's just that I prefer to spend the money on other things.

5. Leandro: **Bueno, creo que podemos tomar el metro y luego el autobús por el resto del camino. Necesitaremos un taxi para el último trecho. Podremos llegar al hotel por poco dinero.**
Well, I think we can take the subway and then the bus the rest of the way. We'll just need a taxi for the last stretch. We'll be able to get to the hotel for very little money.

6. Julieta: **Muy bien. Compremos los boletos para el metro. Espero que no sea difícil.**
Alright. Let's get our tickets for the subway. I hope it's not too difficult.

7. Leandro: **¿Cómo hacemos para ir a Correos?**
How do we get to Correos (the Central Post Office)?

8. Empleada: **Es muy fácil. Es la cuarta parada en esta misma línea.**
It's very easy. It's the fourth stop on this very line.

9. Leandro: **¿Lo ves, Julieta? Es facilísimo. Y tan rápido. Estaremos allí en pocos minutos.**
You see, Julieta? It's very easy. And so fast. We'll be there in a few minutes.

10. Julieta: **Sí, ya veo. . . pero hay tanta gente y con el calor que hace. . .**
Yes, I see . . . but there are so many people, and with this heat . . .

11. Leandro: **Bueno. Piensa en el dinero que estamos ahorrando. Y podemos bajarnos dentro de poco.**
Well, think of the money we're saving. And we can get off in a little while.

12. Julieta: **Gracias a Dios. Espero que los autobuses no vayan tan llenos de gente.**
Thank God. I hope the buses aren't so crowded.

El autobús. The bus.

13. Julieta: *(En la parada de autobús)* **¡Mira la cantidad de gente que hay!**
(At the bus stop) Look at all the people!

14. Leandro: **Sí, desgraciadamente es la hora en que salen todos del trabajo. Tendremos que hacer cola.**
Yes, unfortunately it's the hour when everyone gets off work. We'll have to stand in line.

15. Juliana: **¿Qué hacemos si no podemos subir?**
What do we do if we can't get on?

16. Leandro: **Hay muchos que van por Recoletos. Necesitamos un número veintidós.**
There are many that go up Recoletos. We need a number twenty-two (bus).

17. Julieta: **Ya viene uno. ¡Y está casi vacío! A ver si podemos subir.**
Here comes one. And it's almost empty! Let's see if we can get on.

18. Leandro: **¿Estás contenta? Vamos sentados, cómodos, con una vista magnífica.**
Are you happy? We are seated, comfortable, and we have a magnificent view.

19. Julieta: **Desde luego es muchísimo más cómodo que el metro, y Recoletos es preciosa... los árboles, la sombra. Me gusta ver a los niños jugando por aquí.**

Of course, it's much more comfortable than the subway, and Recoletos is beautiful . . . the trees, the shade. I like to see the children playing along here.

20. Leandro: **Estamos casi en la parada de Colón. Vamos a bajar allí.**
We're almost at the Colón stop. Let's get off there.

21. Julieta: **¡Ah! ¡Qué día más hermoso! Podremos sentarnos allí en la terraza, a la sombra, y tomar un refresco.**
Ah! What a beautiful day! We could sit down at the sidewalk café, in the shade, and have something to drink.

22. Leandro: **Claro, no estamos muy lejos del hotel ahora. Luego podemos tomar un taxi al hotel, echar una siesta. . .**
Sure, we're not far from the hotel now. Then we can take a taxi to the hotel, take a nap . . .

23. Julieta: **¡Esa sí es una idea magnífica! Estoy un poco cansada.** *(Se bajan del autobús y van hacia el café.)*
Now that is a wonderful idea! I'm a little tired.
(They get off the bus and go to the sidewalk café.)

24. Leandro: **¡Camarera! Tráiganos un café helado y una limonada, por favor.**
Waitress! Bring us an iced coffee and a lemonade, please.

25. Camarera: **En seguida.**
Right away.

26. Julieta: **¡Ah, qué delicia! ¿No es cierto que Madrid es agradable, Leandro?**
Ah, how delightful! Isn't Madrid pleasant, Leandro?

27. Leandro: **¡Ya lo creo!**
    It certainly is!

El taxi. The taxi.

28. Leandro: **¡Taxi! ¡Taxi!**
    Taxi! Taxi!

29. Julieta: **Ese está ocupado. Es mejor que vayamos al otro lado de la calle. Allí está la parada de taxis.**
    That one is taken. Let's go to the other side of the street. The taxi stand is there.

30. Leandro: *(En el taxi)* **¿Cuánto cuesta ir al Hotel Emperatriz?**
    (In the taxi) How much is it to the Hotel Emperatriz?

31. Taxista: **Aproximadamente unos seis euros, pero depende del taxímetro.**
    Approximately six euros, but it depends on the taxi meter.

32. Leandro: **Muy bien. Tomemos el taxi de regreso.**
    Very well. Let's take the taxi back.

33. Julieta: **Perfecto. Ya me empezaban a doler los pies.**
    Perfect. My feet were beginning to hurt.

34. Leandro: **¡Ya, ya! Cuando lleguemos al hotel, podremos descansar un rato, porque luego tenemos que arreglarnos para salir a cenar. . . y tal vez ir a una discoteca a bailar.**
    OK, OK. When we get to the hotel, we'll rest awhile, because then we have to get ready to go out to dinner . . . and perhaps go to a nightclub and dance.

B. NOTES

0. *El metro*: abbreviated form of *El metropolitano*, the name of the Madrid subway system.

2. *¿Te has vuelto loco?*: *volverse loco* = to go crazy.
   un ojo de la cara: a fortune, comparable to "an arm and a leg" (literally, "an eye from your face").

3. *¿Desde cuándo?*: literally, "since when." Notice *pensar en*.

7. *Correos*: The Central Post Office. The central post office in Madrid is sometimes affectionately called *Nuestra Señora de Correos* ("Our Lady of the Mail") because of its Gothic, churchlike architecture.

11. *podemos bajarnos*: we can get off. *Subir* and *bajar* are used to express the idea of "getting on" and "getting off" any vehicle.

12. *Espero que los autobuses no vayan*: Note the use of the subjunctive after *esperar*, "to hope."

17. *ya*: approximately, it means "already" or "now." Often used to preface an expression of pleasant surprise, the sense is difficult to translate, as in *¡Ya lo creo!* (I really *do* believe it!). Can be equivalent to positive agreement: "You bet!" or "indeed."

21. Note the use of *sentarse* (to sit down); not to be confused with *sentirse* (to feel).

26. *¡Ah, qué delicia!*: Often *qué* is used to express surprise. In English, we often express this with "how": How delightful!, How interesting! *¡Qué interesante!*

34. *discoteca*: nightclub. Other equivalents are *cabaret*, *club nocturno* (often just *club*), *sala de fiestas* (less

used), the French word *boîte,* or the English "night-club."

C. GRAMMAR AND USAGE

1. The preposition *por* means "in exchange for," "in place of," or "per."

    Él me dio diez dólares por el libro.
    He gave me ten dollars for the book.

    Ellos ganan tres mil pesos por hora.
    They make (earn) three thousand pesos an hour.

    Carlos vendió el coche por muy poco dinero.
    Carlos sold the car for very little money.

2. The preposition *para* means "to," "in order to," or "for" (purpose or use). Notice the examples below:

    Él me dio un libro para leer.
    He gave me a book to read.

    Trabajan mucho para ganarse la vida.
    They work hard in order to make (earn) a living.

    El regalo es para nuestro vecino.
    The gift is for our neighbor.

    Entraron aquí para buscar a Juan.
    They came in here to look for Juan.

3. The expression *tener que* means "to have to." The verb *tener* is conjugated and then followed by *que* and an infinitive.

    Tenemos que ir temprano.
    We have to go early.

    Ellos tendrán que comprar el libro.
    They'll have to buy the book.

Tengo que quedarme aquí.
  I have to stay here.

4. To express the fact that an action is in progress, you must use the verb *estar* followed by the present participle. Notice that the verb *estar* is conjugated.

Estoy esper<u>ando</u> el autobús.
  I am waiting for the bus.

Estaban durm<u>iendo</u> cuando sonó el timbre.
  They were sleeping when the bell rang.

Estamos aprend<u>iendo</u> mucho.
  We are learning a lot.

EXERCISES

A. Substitute each of the words or expressions in the parentheses for the underlined word or expression in the model sentence. Write each new sentence and say it aloud.

  1. *Juan lo compró por <u>seis euros</u>.* (poco dinero, diez dólares, más de cien pesos, un precio muy bajo, mucho menos dinero)

  2. *Juan lo compró para <u>dárselo</u> a su padre.* (regalar, enviar, despachar, mandar, enseñar)

  3. *Tendremos que <u>estudiar</u> mucho.* (aprender, trabajar, escribir, practicar, andar)

  4. *Estarán <u>comiendo</u> cuando lleguemos.* (bailando, estudiando, leyendo, durmiendo, hablando)

  5. *Juan estaba leyendo <u>el periódico</u> cuando entré.* (el libro, la lección, una revista, la comedia, el primer acto)

6. *María y Juana* tienen que hacer el trabajo. (Los chicos, José y su hermano, Ellas, Todos, Los alumnos)

B. Change the subject of these sentences to the plural. Write the complete sentence and translate it.

1. *Él tiene que verlo mañana.*

2. *Yo tendré que levantarme temprano.*

3. *Ella está lavando los platos.*

4. *Tú tienes que leer la novela.*

5. *Usted me dio veinte dólares por el libro.*

C. Translate the following sentences into Spanish, then say them aloud.

1. Juan bought the car for his wife.

2. They paid two thousand pesos for the tickets.

3. We have to leave at once.

4. They are writing letters now.

5. How much do you want for the suit?

6. You have to go through the park in order to get to the museum.

7. They gave him five hundred euros in order to pay for the trip.

8. They were listening to the radio when I arrived.

9. In order to see well, you have to be in the front row.

10. Miguel has to buy a new book.

D. From among the three choices given, choose the best equivalent of the English term (in parentheses) for each sentence, and translate.

1. (to) *Juàn cree que tenemos _____ ir al banco.*
   - (a) *a*
   - (b) *que*
   - (c) _____

2. (for) *Paco pagó _____ la entrada.*
   - (a) ___
   - (b) *por*
   - (c) *para*

3. (per) *Alcanza cuarenta kilómetros _____ hora.*
   - (a) *para*
   - (b) *por*
   - (c) *el*

4. (walking) *Los vimos _____ por la calle.*
   - (a) *andando*
   - (b) *andados*
   - (c) *andandos*

5. (sitting) *Nosotros estábamos _____ en la terraza.*
   - (a) *sentado*
   - (b) *sentando*
   - (c) *sentados*

6. (reading) *Juan está _____ el periódico.*
   - (a) *lee*
   - (b) *leyendo*
   - (c) *leído*

7. (for) *Esta propina es _____ el camarero.*
   - (a) *de*
   - (b) *para*
   - (c) *a*

8. (She has to) *_____ comprar el traje.*
   - (a) *Ella hay que*
   - (b) *Ella tiene que*
   - (c) *Ella ha que*

9. (they want) *No sé lo que* _____.
   (a) *quieren*
   (b) *querer*
   (c) *queremos*

10. (we) *Ellos van a los mismos sitios que* _____.
    (a) *nosotros*
    (b) *ir*
    (c) *van*

Answer Key

B. 1. *Ellos tienen que verlo mañana.*
       They have to see it (or him) tomorrow.

    2. *Nosotros tendremos que levantarnos temprano.*
       We will have to get up early.

    3. *Ellas están lavando los platos.*
       They are washing the dishes.

    4. *Vosotros tenéis que leer las novelas.*
       You have to read the novels.

    5. *Ustedes me dieron veinte dólares por el libro.*
       You gave me twenty dollars for the book.

C. 1. *Juan compró el coche para su esposa.*

    2. *Pagaron dos mil pesos por los billetes.*

    3. *Tenemos que marcharnos en seguida.*

    4. *Están escribiendo cartas ahora.*

    5. *¿Cuánto quiere(s) usted (tú) por el traje?*

    6. *Tiene(s) que pasar por el parque para llegar al
       museo.*

    7. *Le dieron quinientos euros para pagar el viaje.*

    8. *Estaban escuchando la radio cuando llegué.*

    9. *Para ver bien, tiene(s) que estar en la primera fila.*

   10. *Miguel tiene que comprar un libro nuevo.*

D. 1. *Juan cree que tenemos que ir al banco.*
       Juan thinks that we have to go to the bank.

    2. *Paco pagó la entrada.*
       Paco paid for the ticket.

3. *Alcanza cuarenta kilómetros por hora.*
   It goes forty kilometers per hour.

4. *Los vimos andando por la calle.*
   We saw them walking along the street.

5. *Nosotros estábamos sentados en la terraza.*
   We were sitting (seated) on the terrace.

6. *Juan está leyendo el periódico.*
   Juan is reading the newspaper.

7. *Esta propina es para el camarero.*
   This tip is for the waiter.

8. *Ella tiene que comprar el traje.*
   She has to buy the suit.

9. *No sé lo que quieren.*
   I don't know what they want.

10. *Ellos van a los mismos sitios que nosotros.*
    They are going to the same places we are. Or,
    They go to the same places as we do.

LESSON 5

VAMOS A DAR UN PASEO
LET'S TAKE A WALK

A. DIALOGUE

0. *Cecilia y Enrique se están hospedando en un hotel en Barcelona. Ellos deciden dar un paseo por la ciudad.*

   Cecilia and Enrique are staying at a hotel in Barcelona. They decide to go for a walk.

Antes del paseo. Before the walk.

1. Cecilia: **¡Vamos a dar un paseo! ¿Qué te parece? Los dos solos. Podríamos ir por La Rambla hasta el Monumento a Colón. ¿No tienes ganas de verlo? Yo, sí.**

   Let's take a walk! What do you think? Just the two of us. We could walk down Rambla to the Columbus Monument. Don't you feel like seeing it? I do.

2. Enrique: **¿Dar un paseo los dos? No sabría dónde ir. Hace tanto tiempo que no salgo solo en Barcelona.**

   Take a walk, the two of us? I wouldn't know where to go. It's such a long time since I've been out in Barcelona by myself.

3. Cecilia: **Podemos preguntar a la mujer en la recepción. Ella nos dirá donde debemos ir. Y si nos perdemos, podemos volver aquí en taxi.**

   We can ask the woman at the reception desk. She will tell us where we should go. And if we get lost we can get back by taxi.

4. Enrique: **Bueno, ¡vámonos! Pero... como es un día tan espléndido, vamos a visitar la Rambla y la parte antigua de la ciudad.**
OK, let's go! But . . . since it's such a beautiful day, let's visit the Rambla and the old part of the city.

En la recepción. At the reception desk.

5. Enrique: **Dígame, señora, ¿cómo se puede ir a la Rambla?**
Tell me, ma'am, how does one get to the Rambla?

6. Empleado: **Pues, ustedes pueden tomar aquí en la esquina el autobús número...**
Well, here on the corner you can get bus number . . .

7. Enrique: **No, perdone. Yo quería decir a pie.**
No, I'm sorry. I meant on foot.

8. Empleada: **¡Ah! Bueno, pues, es bastante lejos para ir andando. Pero si ustedes quieren... miren este plano de la ciudad. Nosotros estamos aquí, y ¿ven la Rambla allí?**
Oh! Well, then, it's pretty far to go walking. But if you want to . . . look at this map of the city. We are here, and . . . do you see the Rambla there?

9. Cecilia: **Sí que es lejos. Pero tenemos muchas ganas de andar. Nos gusta mucho.**
It is a long way. But we really feel like walking. We enjoy it very much.

10. Empleada: **Bueno... Ustedes tendrán que seguir la Avenida Diagonal hasta llegar al Paseo de Gracia. ¿Se acuerdan? Es la calle donde están los edificios modernistas. Allí hay que doblar a la derecha y bajar por el Paseo de Gracia. Sigan hasta la Plaza de Cataluña...**

Well, you'll have to walk down Avenida Diagonal to
Paseo de Gracia. You remember? It's the street with
the Art Nouveau buildings. There, you must turn
right and go down Paseo de Gracia. Keep going until
Plaza Cataluña. . .

11. Cecilia: **Ah, sí, la Plaza de Cataluña. Me acuerdo
de haber visto muchas fotos de ella.**
Oh, yes, the Plaza Cataluña. I remember having seen
many pictures of it.

12. Empleada: **Sí, señora. Bueno, como iba diciendo
. . . Doblen a la derecha allí y bajen por La Rambla. ¿La ven ustedes?** *(indicando el plano)* **Al
pasar el Teatro del Liceo, doblen a la izquierda
otra vez y verán los arcos de la Plaza Mayor.**
Yes, ma'am. Well, as I was saying . . . Turn right
there and go down Rambla. Do you see it? *(pointing
to the map)* When you pass the Lyceum Theater, turn
to the left again and you will see the arches of the
Plaza Mayor.

13. Enrique: **Gracias, señora. Parece muy claro y bastante fácil.**
Thank you, ma'am. It seems very clear and quite easy.

14. Empleada: **De nada, señores. Que lo pasen bien.**
You're welcome. I hope you enjoy it.

15. Cecilia: **¿Ves? Ya te lo había dicho . . . Es
facilísimo.**
You see? I told you . . . it's very easy.

16. Enrique: **Pero será una caminata de media hora,
por lo menos. ¿No te parece demasiado?**
But it will probably be a half hour walk, at least.
Don't you think it's too much?

17. Cecilia: **Claro que no, cariño. Ya verás. ¡Qué gusto!**
   Of course not, darling. You'll see. What a pleasure!

Un cuarto de hora más tarde... Fifteen minutes later . . .

18. Enrique: **Nos falta muy poco para llegar al Paseo de Gracia.**
   We have just a little way to go to Paseo de Gracia.

19. Cecilia: **Sí, ya lo veo. Es donde hay que doblar a la derecha, ¿verdad?**
   Yes, I can see it. That's where we have to turn right, isn't it?

20. Enrique: **Eso es. Y si te parece, podemos sentarnos un rato en aquella terraza tan agradable y descansar un poco antes de seguir.**
   That's right. And if you want, we can sit down for a while at that nice sidewalk café and rest a bit before going on.

21. Cecilia: **Sí, pero me parece que eres tú el que quiere descansar.**
   Yes, but it seems to me that you're the one who wants to rest.

22. Enrique: *(Después del descanso)* **Creo que nos hemos equivocado. ¿Será éste el Paseo de Gracia? ¿Tienes la guía de la ciudad?**
   (After resting) I think we've made a mistake. Can this be Paseo de Gracia? Do you have the map of the city?

23. Cecilia: **¡Ay! La dejé sobre la mesa en aquella terraza. No vale la pena volver a buscarla ahora. Pregúntale a esa señora si vamos bien.**
   Oh! I left it on the table at the café. It's not worth the trouble to go back to look for it now. Ask that woman if we're on the right track.

24. Enrique: **Perdone, señora. ¿Vamos bien para llegar a la Plaza de Cataluña?**
    Pardon me, ma'am. Are we going the right way to get to the Plaza Cataluña?

25. Una señora: **¿A la Plaza de Cataluña? No, no. Éste es el Paseo de San Juan. Ustedes tienen que volver atrás hasta el punto donde se separan el Paseo de Gracia y la Avenida Diagonal. ¿Ven aquel edificio grande? Pues, es allí donde tienen que doblar a la izquierda.**
    To the Plaza Cataluña? No, no. This is the Paseo San Juan. You have to go back to the point where the Paseo de Gracia and Avenida Diagonal separate. Do you see that big building? Well, that's where you have to turn left.

26. Enrique: **Muchísimas gracias, señora. Vamos, Cecilia, o no llegamos nunca.**
    Thank you very much, ma'am. Come on, Cecilia, or we'll never get there.

27. Cecilia: **No me importa tanto. El paseo es agradable de todas maneras y estamos viendo cosas muy interesantes. Las tiendas por aquí son muy elegantes.**
    It doesn't matter much to me. The walk is pleasant anyway, and we're seeing interesting things. The shops along here are very elegant.

De vuelta en el hotel. Back at the hotel.

28. Empleada: **Buenas tardes, señores. ¿Les ha gustado el paseo?**
    Good afternoon. Did you like the stroll?

29. Enrique: **No llegamos hasta la Rambla. Nos equivocamos de camino varias veces y perdimos tanto**

tiempo en los escaparates del Paseo de Gracia que se hizo demasiado tarde para eso.
We didn't even get to the Rambla. We lost our way several times and wasted so much time with the shop windows of the Paseo de Gracia that it got to be too late for that.

30. Cecilia: **Pero mañana iremos de compras y por la tarde continuaremos el paseo.**
But, tomorrow we'll go shopping, and in the afternoon we'll go continue our stroll.

B. NOTES

0. Barcelona is a city on the Mediterranean coast of Spain. It is in the region of Catalonia. Catalonia has two official languages: Spanish and Catalan.

1. *dar un paseo*: to take a walk.
The Rambla is a boulevard that connnects the Plaza Catalonia to the Columbus Monument by the waterfront. The Rambla is known for its pedestrian traffic and for its many street performers and artists.

10. *los edificios modernistas*: Art Nouveau buildings. Make sure not to confuse *modernista* with *moderno* or "modern."

30. *ir de compras*: to go shopping.

C. GRAMMAR AND USAGE

1. The construction *hacer* + time expression + *que* is used to indicate that an action has been taking place for some time in the past and is still happening in the present. Notice that both *hacer* and the following verb are used in the present tense. Pay attention to the examples below:

Hace una semana que estoy aquí.
I've been here for a week.

Hace dos horas que esperamos.
We have been waiting for two hours.

Hace un año que Carlos estudia español.
Carlos has been studying Spanish for a year.

Note:

- *Hace* (without *que*) may go at the end of the sentence, as in *Estoy aquí hace una semana.*

- The present tense is used in this construction to indicate that an action has been, and still is, taking place.

2. Notice the contraction *al* in the sentences below. When personal *a* is followed by the singular masculine definite article (*el*), they contract to become *al*.

Vamos a preguntarle al hombre.
Let's ask the man.

Tengo que ver al dentista.
I have to see the dentist.

Ellos llamaron al médico.
They called the doctor.

When the personal *a* is followed by other definite articles (*la, las, los*), there is no contraction.

Hay que preguntarles a los hombres.
You *(impersonal)* must ask the men.

Tengo que ver a la costurera.
I have to see the dressmaker.

Veo a María.
I see María.

3. The impersonal pronoun *se* is used to express an action that doesn't have a specific subject.

¿Se puede fumar?
  Is smoking permitted? (May one smoke?)

Se puede ir de prisa en esta carretera.
  One can go fast (speed up) on this road. You *(impersonal)* can go fast on this road.

Se come bien aquí.
  One eats well here. (The food is good here.)

4. The phrase *acordarse de* means "to remember."

Me acuerdo muy bien de ella.
  I remember her very well.

¿Se acuerda usted del accidente?
  Do you remember the accident?

Nos acordamos frecuentemente de aquel viaje.
  We frequently remember that trip.

EXERCISES

A. Substitute each of the words or expressions in parentheses for the underlined word or expression in the model sentence. Write each new sentence and say it aloud.

  1. *Hace una semana que vivo en Buenos Aires.* (un año, dos meses, mucho tiempo, varias semanas, muy poco [tiempo])

  2. *Hace tres horas que Juan trabaja.* (viaja, estudia, duerme, escribe, lee)

  3. *Usted tiene que llamar al médico.* (al dentista, al sereno, al oficial, al camarero, al recepcionista)

  4. *Se come bien en Barcelona.* (duerme, bebe, está, habla, canta)

   5. *Nos acordamos mucho de México.* (del viaje, de San Juan, de Teresa, de ustedes, del médico)

   6. *No me acuerdo de nada.* (ella, María, Juan y Francisco, ellos, él)

B. Change these sentences to the negative. Write the complete sentence and translate.

   1. *Usted se acuerda de María.*

   2. *Hace una semana que Juan está aquí.*

   3. *Teresa tiene que llamar al médico.*

   4. *Se come bien en este restaurante.*

   5. *Ellos se acuerdan del viaje.*

C. Translate the following sentences into Spanish; then, say them aloud.

   1. They've been here for a month.

   2. You have to call the doctor.

   3. I remember you very well.

   4. I have been sleeping for two hours.

   5. It is believed that there are ghosts here.

   6. I don't see María.

   7. We can sit down to rest awhile.

   8. We feel like walking.

   9. You have to turn right.

   10. Let's visit the museum.

D. From among the three choices given, choose the best equivalent of the English term (in parentheses) for each sentence, and translate.

1. (I have been) _____ aquí hace dos años.
   (a) Estuve
   (b) He estado
   (c) Estoy

2. (for three months) Ellos viven en Madrid
   _____.
   (a) en tres meses
   (b) hace tres meses
   (c) de tres meses

3. (have you been) ¿Cuánto tiempo hace que
   _____ aquí?
   (a) ha estado usted
   (b) está usted
   (c) usted estuve

4. (is spoken) Aquí _____ ruso.
   (a) hablamos
   (b) se habla
   (c) está hablando

5. (You [impersonal] can find) _____ muchos
   anuncios en el periódico.
   (a) Se encuentran
   (b) Se encuentra
   (c) Encontrar

6. (remember) Creo que ellos _____ la fecha.
   (a) se acuerda
   (b) se acuerdan de
   (c) acordarse

7. (you [impersonal] can meet) Esta es una fiesta en la
   que _____ a mucha gente simpática.
   (a) se conoce
   (b) se conocen
   (c) se encuentran

8. (my friend) ¿Conoce usted _____?
   (a) *amigo mío*
   (b) *a mi amigo*
   (c) *mi amigo*

9. (they have been) *Hace tres años que* _____ *en Nueva York.*
   (a) *son*
   (b) *están*
   (c) *habían estado*

10. (for an hour) *Hace* _____ *que espero.*
    (a) *por una hora*
    (b) *una hora*
    (c) *un hora*

Answer Key

B. 1. *Usted no se acuerda de María.*
    You don't remember María.

    2. *Hace una semana que Juan no está aquí.*
    Juan hasn't been here for a week.

    3. *Teresa no tiene que llamar al médico.*
    Teresa doesn't have to call the doctor.

    4. *No se come bien en este restaurante.*
    The food isn't good in this restaurant. Or, one
    doesn't eat well in this restaurant.

    5. *Ellos no se acuerdan del viaje.*
    They don't remember the trip.

C. 1. *Hace un mes que están aquí.*

    2. *Tiene(s) que llamar al médico.*

    3. *Me acuerdo muy bien de usted (ti).*

    4. *Hace dos horas que duermo.*

    5. *Se cree que hay fantasmas aquí.*

    6. *No veo a María.*

    7. *Podemos sentarnos a descansar un rato.*

    8. *Tenemos ganas de andar.*

    9. *Tiene(s) que doblar a la derecha.*

    10. *Vamos a visitar el museo.*

D. 1. *Estoy aquí hace dos años.*
    I have been here for two years.

    2. *Ellos viven en Madrid hace tres meses.*
    They have been living in Madrid for three months.

3. *¿Cuánto tiempo hace que está usted aquí?*
   How long have you been here?

4. *Aquí se habla ruso.*
   Russian is spoken here.

5. *Se encuentran muchos anuncios en el periódico.*
   One finds many ads in the newspaper. Or, You can find many ads in the newspaper.

6. *Creo que ellos se acuerdan de la fecha.*
   I think that they remember the date.

7. *Esta es una fiesta en la que se conoce a mucha gente simpática.*
   This is a party where one meets (or, you can meet) many nice people.

8. *¿Conoce usted a mi amigo?*
   Do you know my friend?

9. *Hace tres años que están en Nueva York.*
   They have been in New York for three years.

10. *Hace una hora que espero.*
    I have been waiting for an hour.

LESSON 6

DE COMPRAS
SHOPPING

A. DIALOGUE

0. *Ernesto ha decidido pasarse la tarde haciendo unas
   compras en Plaza Las Américas, el centro comercial
   más grande del Caribe, ubicado en San Juan,
   Puerto Rico.*
   Ernesto has decided to spend the afternoon shopping
   in Plaza Las Americas, the largest shopping mall in
   the Caribbean, located in San Juan, Puerto Rico.

En la sección de camisas. In the shirt department.

1. Dependienta: **¿Puedo servirle en algo, señor?**
   Can I help you with something, sir?

2. Ernesto: **Sí, por favor. Me gustaría una camisa
   informal pero elegante a la vez.**
   Yes, please. I'd like a casual shirt that looks elegant
   at the same time.

3. Dependienta: **Las tenemos de todos los estilos y
   colores. Aquí tiene usted unas muy bonitas de
   manga corta.**
   We have all styles and colors. Here are some nice
   ones with short sleeves.

4. Ernesto: **Sí, son muy bonitas. ¿Las tiene de manga
   larga?**
   Yes, they're very nice. Do you have them with long
   sleeves?

5. Dependienta: **No están aquí, pero tal vez las tenemos en el interior. Un momento, por favor.**

They're not here, but maybe we have them in the back room. Just a minute, please.

6. Ernesto: **Gracias.**
Thanks.

7. Dependienta: **Aquí la tiene usted. Es la última.**
Here you are. It's the last one.

8. Ernesto: **¡Qué suerte! ¡Cuánto cuesta?**
How lucky! How much is it?

9. Dependienta: **Son cincuenta y cinco dólares, señor.**
That'll be fifty-five dollars, sir.

10. Ernesto: **Está bien. ¿Me la puede envolver?**
That's fine. Will you wrap it, please?

11. Dependienta: **Con mucho gusto. Aquí la tiene usted. Muchas gracias.**
With pleasure. Here you are. Thank you very much.

12. Ernesto: **¿Tienen ustedes chaquetas deportivas?**
Do you have sports jackets?

13. Dependienta: **Sí, muchas. Creo que ésta le va muy bien con la camisa que lleva. ¿Qué talla usa?**
Yes, many. I think this one goes very well with the shirt you are getting. What size do you wear?

14. Ernesto: **Depende, pero por lo general cualquier tamaño mediano me queda bien.**
It depends, but usually any medium size fits me well.

15. Dependienta: **A mí me gusta muchísimo. Se la puede probar allí.**
I like it a lot. You can try it on in there.

16. Ernesto: **Yo la encuentro un poco ancha de espalda y mangas, y demasiado larga.**
I find it a little wide in the shoulders and sleeves, and too long.

17. Dependienta: **Desde luego, lo es. Probemos con una talla más pequeña entonces. ¡Ah! Ésta le va de maravilla. ¿Qué le parece?**
Of course, it is. Let's try a smaller size, then. Ah! It fits you marvelously. What do you think?

18. Ernesto: **Me gusta muchísimo. Me la llevo también. ¿Aceptan cheques de viajero?**
I like it very much. I'll take it as well. Do you take traveller's cheques?

19. Dependienta: **Si tiene identificación no hay problemas. Por favor, fírmelos.**
If you have I.D. there is no problem. Please sign them.

20. Ernesto: **Muchas gracias, señora. ¿Me puede decir dónde están las corbatas?**
Thanks a lot, ma'am. Could you tell me where the ties are located?

21. Dependienta: **En el segundo piso. Gracias y que disfrute su visita.**
On the second floor. Thanks and enjoy your visit.

En la sección de corbatas. In the men's tie section.

22. Dependienta: **¿Necesita ayuda, señor?**
May I help you, sir?

23. Ernesto: **Sí, estoy buscando una corbata de seda para esta camisa.**
Yes, I'm looking for a silk tie for this shirt.

24. Dependienta: **Este tipo de corbata es de última moda, y una verdadera ganga a cincuenta dólares.**
    This type of tie is the latest style, and a real bargain at fifty dollars.

25. Ernesto: **¡Ah! Es demasiado. ¿No tendría usted otra menos cara?**
    Oh, that's too much. Don't you have another, less expensive one?

26. Dependienta: **Hay esta otra a treinta dólares. Vea que no es tan ancha.**
    There's this one at thirty dollars. Notice that it's not as wide.

27. Ernesto: **¿Aceptan tarjetas de crédito?**
    Do you accept credit cards?

28. Dependienta: **Aceptamos las tarjetas de crédito principales. Venga por aquí. Le acompaño a la caja.**
    We accept all major credit cards. Come this way. I'll accompany you to the cashier.

29. Ernesto: **¿Dónde está la sección de teléfonos celulares?**
    Where is the cell phone department?

30. Dependienta: **Para eso tendrá que ir al quinto piso.**
    For that you will have to go to the fifth floor.

En el mostrador de teléfonos celulares. At the cell phone counter.

31. Dependiente: **¿Le puedo ayudar, señor?**
    May I help you, sir?

32. Ernesto: **Sí. Busco un teléfono celular nuevo.**
    Yes, I'm looking for a new cell phone.

33. Dependiente: **Tenemos una selección muy grande. ¿Ve usted algún modelo que le guste?**
    We have a very large selection. Do you see any model that you like?

34. Ernesto: **Sí, pero quiero uno que tenga cámara.**
    Yes, but I want one that has a camera.

35. Dependiente: **Todos éstos tienen cámara. ¿Le importa el tamaño?**
    All of these have cameras. Do you mind the size?

36. Ernesto: **Me interesa que sean compactos.**
    I want them to be compact.

37. Dependiente: **Sí, pero son un poco más caros.**
    Yes, but they're a little more expensive.

38. Ernesto: **No importa. Me gusta poder llevarlos en el bolsillo. ¿Cuánto cuesta éste?**
    It doesn't matter. I like to be able to carry them in my pocket. How much is this one?

39. Dependiente: **Son ciento cincuenta dólares.**
    It's a hundred and fifty dollars.

40. Ernesto: **Está bien.**
    That's fine.

B. NOTES

0. Puerto Rico is the easternmost of the Greater Antilles. Even though Spanish is by far its dominant language of communication, Spanish and English are both official languages. Since Puerto Rico became a

territory of the United States in 1898 as a result of the Spanish-American war, language has become an important educational and cultural issue. During the first three decades, the U.S. government insisted upon English-only instruction in schools. In 1930, Spanish became the official language for the classroom. In 1991, Spanish was declared the official language of Puerto Rico by the pro-commonwealth government, but the decision was overturned in 1993 by Pedro J. Rossello, a pro-statehood governor. Spanish and English currently share equal status on the island.

2. *a la vez*: at the same time. Literally, "at the time."

9. The Commonwealth of Puerto Rico has very strong ties to the United States economy. After the Spanish American War in 1898, Puerto Rico went from being a Spanish colony to being a U.S. territory. The official currency in Puerto Rico is the U.S. dollar.

13. *talla, tamaño*: size, used for articles of clothing. *Talla* is generally used for suits and dresses (cf. *talle*: waist measurement). *Tamaño* refers to the largeness or smallness of any article, whether clothing or otherwise.

29. *teléfonos celulares*: cell phones. They are also referred to as *(teléfonos) móviles* in some other Spanish speaking countries.

C. GRAMMAR AND USAGE

1. The indirect and direct object pronouns may be attached to the infinitive of the verb. Notice that you attach the indirect object pronoun first, followed by the direct object pronoun.

Infinitive + Indirect/Direct Object pronoun

Juan quiere dárselo (a él).
   Juan wants to give it to him.

María va a mandármelo.
   Maria is going to send it to me.

Ellos tienen que pagárnoslo.
   They have to pay us for it.

Indirect and direct object pronouns may also be placed separately before the main verb. Notice that the indirect object pronoun comes before the direct object pronoun.

Juan se lo quiere dar.
   Juan wants to give it to him.

María me lo va a mandar.
   María is going to send it to me.

Ellos nos lo tienen que pagar.
   They have to pay us for it.

• Notice that indirect *le* and *les* change to *se* before the third person (*lo, la*, etc.) direct object pronouns.

Juan se lo quiere dar a él.
   Juan wants to give it to him.

2. The expression *Aquí* + (third person) direct object pronoun + *tener* has the English equivalent of "Here it is" or "Here they are."

¿El libro? Aquí lo tiene usted.
   The book? Here it is.

¿Los libros? Aquí los tiene usted.
   The books? Here they are.

¿La novela? Aquí la tienes.
   The novel? Here it is.

¿Las novelas? Aquí las tiene usted.
 The novels? Here they are.

3. When expressing likes and dislikes, use the verb *gustar* in the following construction:

Indirect object + *gusta(n)* + subject

Me gusta el vestido.
 I like the dress.

Me gustan los vestidos.
 I like the dresses.

Nos gusta el hotel.
 We like the hotel.

Nos gustan los hoteles.
 We like the hotels.

EXERCISES

A. Substitute each of the words or expressions in parentheses for the underlined word or expression in the model sentence. Write each new sentence and say it aloud.

1. *Mi padre quiere <u>dárselo</u> a él.* (regalar, mandar, vender, pedir, preguntar)

2. *Ellos me lo <u>quieren</u> comprar.* (pueden, van a, desean, tienen que, podrán)

3. *Me gusta <u>comer</u>.* (bailar, cantar, beber, dormir, trabajar)

4. *<u>Nos</u> gustan los viajes.* (Te, Me, Le, Os, Les)

5. *A él le gustan <u>los vestidos</u>.* (los trajes, los libros, las películas, los barcos, los coches)

6. *Aquí lo <u>tiene usted</u>.* (tienes, tienen, tenéis, tenemos, tengo)

B. Change the nouns to pronouns. Write the complete sentence and translate.

    1. *María va a comprar el libro para Juan.*

    2. *Ellos quieren mandarle la carta al señor Hernández*

    3. *Nosotros podemos regalarle los vestidos a tu madre.*

    4. *Tú prefieres pedirle el dinero a su padre.*

    5. *Tenéis que enviarle las flores a mis padres.*

C. Translate the following sentences into Spanish, then say them aloud.

    1. They want to give it (the gift) to me.

    2. You will have to ask him for it (the letter).

    3. We want to send it (the package) to them.

    4. He will have to try it (the tie) on.

    5. We like to travel in Spain.

    6. Here they (the books) are.

    7. You (familiar singular) like ice cream.

    8. I'm going to look for it (the hat) for you.

    9. Do you want to carry the package?

    10. We can send it (the jacket) to you, if you prefer.

D. From among the three choices given, choose the best equivalent of the English term (in parentheses) for each sentence, and translate.

    1. (they are) *Aquí* _____ *usted.*
       (a) *lo tiene*
       (b) *los tiene*
       (c) *la tiene*

2. (them to me) *Quiere dár* _____ *ahora.*
   (a) *-losme*
   (b) *-melos*
   (c) *ellos me*

3. (Give it [*el libro*] to me.) _____
   (a) *Dámelo.*
   (b) *Me lo das.*
   (c) *Dámela.*

4. (We have them [*corbatas*]) _____ *de todas clases.*
   (a) *Tenémoslas*
   (b) *Las tenemos*
   (c) *Ellos tenemos*

5. (it [*el pasaporte*]) *Aquí* _____ *tiene usted.*
   (a) *los*
   (b) *lo*
   (c) *el*

6. (for you) *Voy a buscar* _____ *el paquete.*
   (a) *-le*
   (b) *-se*
   (c) *-los*

7. (silk dress) *Quiero comprarme un* _____.
   (a) *vestido seda*
   (b) *seda vestido*
   (c) *vestido de seda*

8. (it is) *¿Es demasiado caro? Creo que sí* _____.
   (a) *está*
   (b) *lo es*
   (c) *el es*

9. (Here it is—Here you are.) _____
   (a) *Aquí lo tiene usted.*
   (b) *Aquí lo está.*
   (c) *Aquí estamos.*

10. (send them [*las cartas*] to me) *¿Quiere usted* _____?
    (a) *mandárlasme*
    (b) *me las mandar*
    (c) *mandármelas*

Answer Key

B. 1. *Ella va a comprárselo (a él).*
She is going to buy it for him.

2. *Ellos quieren mandársela (a él).*
They want to send it to him.

3. *Nosotros podemos regalárselos (a ella).*
We can give them to her.

4. *Tú prefieres pedírselo (a él).*
You prefer to ask him for it.

5. *Tenéis que enviárselas (a ellos).*
You have to send them to them.

C. 1. *Quieren dármelo (a mí).*

2. *Usted tendrá que pedírsela (a él). Or, Tendrás de pedírsela.*

3. *Queremos mandárselo a ellos.*

4. *Tendrá que probársela.*

5. *Nos gusta viajar por España.*

6. *Aquí los tiene(s). Aquí están.*

7. *Te gusta el helado.*

8. *Voy a buscárselo. Or, Voy a buscártelo* (informal).

9. *¿Quiere(s) usted (tú) llevar el paquete?*

10. *Podemos mandársela, si quiere. Or, Podemos mandártela, si quieres* (informal).

D. 1. *Aquí los tiene usted.*
Here they are.

2. *Quiere dármelos ahora.*
He/She wants to give them to me now.

3. *Dámelo.*
   Give it to me.

4. *Las tenemos de todas clases.*
   We have them in all styles.

5. *Aquí lo tiene usted.*
   Here it is.

6. *Voy a buscarle el paquete.*
   I am going to look for the package for you.

7. *Quiero comprar un vestido de seda.*
   I want to buy a silk dress.

8. *¿Es demasiado caro? Creo que sí lo es.*
   Is it too expensive? I think it is.

9. *Aquí lo tiene usted.*
   Here it is. (Here you are.)

10. *¿Quiere usted mandármelas?*
    Do you want to send them to me?

LESSON 7

NUEVOS AMIGOS
NEW FRIENDS

A. DIALOGUE

0. *Juan y Noel están esperando a Carolina y a su amiga en un bar en Bogotá. Juan y Noel no conocen a la amiga de Carolina.*
   Juan and Noel are waiting for Carolina and her friend at a bar in Bogota. Juan and Noel have not met Carolina's friend.

1. Juan: **¿A qué hora te dijo Carolina que vendría?**
   What time did Carolina say that she was coming?

2. Noel: **Me dijo que a las nueve. Seguramente está por llegar.**
   She said nine o'clock. I'm sure she is about to get here.

3. Juan: **Seguro que estarán en el bar de la otra calle. Carolina es a veces muy despistada.**
   They must be in the bar on the other street. Carolina is sometimes so absent-minded.

4. Noel: **Nosotros hablamos por la tarde y le dije que nos encontráramos en este bar. Fui muy claro.**
   We spoke this afternoon and I told her to meet us in this bar. I was very clear.

5. Juan: **Pero ya son las nueve y media. Deberías llamarla.**
   But it's already nine thirty. You should call her.

6. Noel: **Tienes razón. Pero dejé mi móvil en el coche. Voy a buscarlo, vuelvo en seguida.**
You're right. But I left my cell phone in the car. I'm going to get it, I'll be right back.

7. Juan: **No tardas mucho, ¿verdad?**
You won't take long, will you?

8. Noel: **No, vuelvo en cinco minutos.**
No, I'll be back in five minutes.

Al rato, Noel entra al bar y se encuentra a Carolina y a su amiga hablando con Juan.
Moments later, Noel enters the bar and finds Carolina and her friend talking to Juan.

9. Noel: **¡Por fin has llegado! Fui a buscar el móvil. Estaba a punto de llamarte.**
You finally arrived! I went to get my cell phone. I was about to call you.

10. Carolina: **Sí, es que había mucho tráfico. Nos tomó mucho tiempo llegar y conseguir aparcarnos.**
Yes, there was a lot of traffic. It took us very long to get here and find parking.

11. Noel: **Disculpa, no me has presentado a tu amiga.**
Excuse me, you haven't introduced me to your friend.

12. Carolina: **¡Ay, perdona! Claudia, te presento a Noel. Noel, Claudia.**
Oh, I'm sorry! Claudia, let me introduce you to Noel. Noel, Claudia.

13. Claudia: **Mucho gusto. Es un placer conocerte.**
Nice to meet you. It's a pleasure meeting you.

14. Noel: **El placer es mío.**
    The pleasure is mine.

15. Carolina: **Claudia es una buena amiga de la universidad. Es brasileña y está estudiando español en Bogotá.**
    Claudia is a good friend from college. She is Brazilian and is studying Spanish in Bogota.

16. Juan: **Pero habla el español perfectamente, es increíble. Parece que es de aquí.**
    But she speaks Spanish perfectly, it's incredible. She seems to be from here.

17. Claudia: **Muchas gracias pero están exagerando. Me cuesta mucho trabajo todavía.**
    Thanks a lot, but you are exaggerating. It is still very difficult for me.

18. Noel: **¿Y qué te parece la ciudad? ¿Habías visitado Colombia anteriormente?**
    And what do you think of the city? Had you visited Colombia before?

19. Claudia: **Pues no, es mi primera vez, pero en Río de Janeiro tengo muchas amistades que hablan español. Mi mejor amiga es colombiana. Y sí, me gusta mucho la ciudad.**
    No, it's my first time, but in Rio de Janeiro I have a lot of friends who speak Spanish. My best friend is Colombian. And yes, I like the city very much.

20. Noel: **Por eso lo hablas tan bien. Apenas te noto el acento portugués.**
    That's why you speak it so well, I can barely notice a Portuguese accent.

21. Carolina: **A Claudia le gusta mucho el teatro. Le había dicho que eras actor.**
Claudia loves theater. I had told her that you are an actor.

22. Noel: **Pues en este momento estamos ensayando una obra. Estrenamos en dos semanas. No sé si te gustaría ir. . .**
Well, right now we're rehearsing for a play. We're opening in two weeks. I don't know if you'd like to go . . .

23. Claudia: **¡Me encantaría! ¿Cuántos boletos puedes conseguir?**
I would love to! How many tickets can you get?

24. Noel: **Los que tú quieras.**
As many as you would like.

25. Claudia: **¿Podríamos ir los tres? Carolina, Juan y yo. . .**
Could the three of us go? Carolina, Juan, and I . . .

26. Noel: **Me parece una idea estupenda.**
It seems like a great idea.

27. Claudia: **¿Y cómo nos contactamos?**
And how do we get in touch?

28. Noel: **Pues te dejo mi teléfono y mi correo electrónico.**
Well, I'll give you my phone number and e-mail address.

29. Claudia: **¡Perfecto! Al volver a casa te voy a mandar un correo para que te acuerdes.**
Perfect! When I get home I'll send you an e-mail to remind you.

30. Carolina: **¿Y qué hacen mañana?**
And what are you doing tomorrow?

31. Claudia: **Yo no tengo ningún plan, ¿y tú, Noel?**
I don't have any plans, and you, Noel?

32. Noel: **Ninguno, voy a estar por el área de la universidad.**
None, I'm going to be around the university.

33. Juan: *(a Carolina)* **Estos dos se han caído muy bien.**
These two are getting along very well.

B. NOTES

3. *despistado*: clueless. The word *pista* means "clue." *Los detectives siguen esa pista.* The detectives are following that clue. Another word that means "absent-minded" is *distraído* (distracted).

7. *¿verdad?*: The word verdad literally means "truth." When used after a question it is used as a question tag. It may mean "Right?", "Will you?", "Don't you?", "Are you?", etc. . . . *Te gusta la pizza, ¿verdad?* You like pizza, don't you?

9. *a punto de*: about to. This construction is always followed by *de* and the infinitive.

15. Notice that in Spanish adjectives of nationality are not capitalized unless they appear at the beginning of a sentence. The same is true of days of the week and months of the year.

17. *Me cuesta trabajo*: It literally means "It costs me a lot of work."

20. *Apenas te noto*: I can barely notice. *Apenas* (barely), *te* (you), *noto* (I notice) . . . "I barely notice in you . . . (the Portuguese accent)."

31 & 32. Notice the usage of *ningún* and *ninguno* in these two sentences. *Ninguno* is used on its own, whereas *ningún* is used when followed by a noun. *Ninguna* can be used alone or followed by a noun.

33. *caerse bien:* to get along. From the verb *caer* (to fall). It literally means "to fall well on each other."

C. GRAMMAR AND USAGE

1. You may use the future tense to express probability. Notice the examples below:

¿Quién será?
   Who can it be?

Ellos habrán ido al cine.
   They must have gone (they probably went) to the movies.

Estarán aquí en alguna parte.
   They must be (they probably are) here somewhere.

2. The expression *tener razón* means "to be right."

Usted tiene razón.
   You're right.

Ellos siempre creen tener razón.
   They always think they are right.

Tenemos razón, como siempre.
   We are right, as usual.

3. The present tense may be used to imply future meaning. The same construction is often used in English. Notice the usage and compare the following sentences:

¿Se lo corto del mismo modo?
   Shall I cut it in the same way?

¿Qué haces esta tarde?
   What are you doing (will you do) this afternoon?

Vuelvo en seguida.
   I'll come back right away.

4. The Spanish construction *al* + infinitive means "on," "upon," or "when (doing something)."

Usted lo puede hacer al pagar la cuenta.
   You can do it when you pay (on paying) the bill.

Al volver a casa, te llamo.
   Upon returning home (when I return home), I'll call you.

Me saludó al entrar.
   He greeted me on entering (when he entered).

EXERCISES

A. Substitute each of the words or expressions in the parentheses for the underlined word or expression in the model sentence. Write each new sentence and say it aloud.

   1. *¿Dónde estará el libro?* (el lápiz, la novela, Miguel, el profesor, el lápiz de labios)

   2. *¿Qué le habrá pasado a Teresa?* (al señor Andrade, a Miguel, al libro, a mi amigo, al profesor)

   3. *Los libros estarán en alguna parte.* (Los señores, Juan y José, María y Juana, Ellas, Los jóvenes)

4. *¿Se lo hago mañana?* (digo, pregunto, pido, mando, pago)

5. *Los chicos siempre tienen razón.* (Las chicas, Los profesores, Juan y Francisco, Mis padres, Las hermanas)

6. *Puedes hacerlo al entrar.* (salir, pagar, acostarte, llegar, despertarte)

B. Change these sentences to the present tense. Write the complete sentence and translate.

1. *Te lo diré al volver.*

2. *Juan me lo dará.*

3. *Usted tendrá razón.*

4. *Vendré por la mañana.*

5. *Ellos podrán dártelo.*

C. Translate the following sentences into Spanish, then say them aloud.

1. Where can the tickets be? (future of probability)

2. They must have gone home.

3. When he came in, he greeted us.

4. You can pay it when you leave.

5. I think he's right.

6. I'll give it (the book) to you tomorrow.

7. How handsome you are!

8. You need a haircut.

9. I was going to look for you.

10. Do you like the color?

D. From among the three choices given, choose the best equivalent of the English term (in parentheses) for each sentence, and translate.

1. (It will be) _____ *difícil.*
   (a) *Será*
   (b) *Es*
   (c) *Sería*

2. (when you leave) *Usted puede dármelo* _____.
   (a) *cuando salir*
   (b) *al salir*
   (c) *en salir*

3. (you are right) *Creo que siempre* _____.
   (a) *está derecho*
   (b) *tienes razón*
   (c) *es razón*

4. (can it be) *¿Quién* _____?
   (a) *lo puede ser*
   (b) *será*
   (c) *sea*

5. (next door) *La señora está aquí* _____ *en la peluquería.*
   (a) *próxima puerta*
   (b) *lado*
   (c) *al lado*

6. (I'm going) *Creo que* _____ *mañana.*
   (a) *va*
   (b) *voy*
   (c) *estoy yendo*

7. (before) *Claro que usted empezó* _____ *yo.*
   (a) *antes que*
   (b) *antes de*
   (c) *delante*

8. (to be right) *Le gusta* _____ *siempre.*
    (a) *ser derecho*
    (b) *tener razón*
    (c) *estar razón*

9. (upon arriving) *Nos saludamos* _____ *al hotel.*
    (a) *al llegar*
    (b) *en llegando*
    (c) *sobre llegar*

10. (else) *¿Hay algo* _____ *?*
    (a) *otro*
    (b) *demás*
    (c) *más*

Answer Key

B. 1. *Te lo digo al volver.*
      I'll tell it to you when I return.

    2. *Juan me lo da.*
      Juan gives it to me.

    3. *Usted tiene razón.*
      You are right.

    4. *Vengo por la mañana.*
      I am coming in the morning.

    5. *Ellos pueden dártelo.*
      They can give it to you.

C. 1. *¿Dónde estarán los billetes?*

    2. *Habrán ido a casa.*

    3. *Al entrar, él nos saludó. Él nos saludó al entrar.*

    4. *Usted puede pagarlo al salir.*

    5. *Creo que él tiene razón.*

    6. *Se lo doy a usted mañana.* Or, *Te lo doy mañana.*

    7. *¡Qué guapo estás!*

    8. *Le (Te) hace falta un corte de pelo.*

    9. *Iba a buscarte.*

    10. *¿Le (Te) gusta el color?*

D. 1. *Será difícil.*
      It must be difficult. (It will be difficult.)

    2. *Usted puede dármelo al salir.*
      You can give it to me when you leave.

    3. *Creo que siempre tienes razón.*
      I think you are always right.

4. *¿Quién será?*
   Who can it be?

5. *La señora está aquí al lado en la peluquería.*
   The lady is right next door in the beauty shop.

6. *Creo que voy mañana.*
   I think that I'm going tomorrow.

7. *Claro que usted empezó antes que yo.*
   Of course you began before I did.

8. *Le gusta tener razón siempre.*
   You always like to be right. Or, He always likes to be right.

9. *Nos saludamos al llegar al hotel.*
   We said hello upon arriving at the hotel.

10. *¿Hay algo más?*
    Is there anything else?

LESSON 8

EN EL CINE
AT THE MOVIES

A. DIALOGUE

0. *Natalia, Agustín y Mercedes son tres chicos de Santo Domingo, República Dominicana, que han decidido ir a ver el estreno de la última película de Almodóvar.*
Natalia, Agustin, and Mercedes are three guys (*see notes*) from Santo Domingo, Dominican Republic, who have decided to see the premiere of the latest Almodóvar film.

Caminando por la calle en camino al cine. Walking down the street on the way to the movies.

1. Agustín: **Espero que podamos conseguir entradas para la tanda de las ocho.**
I hope we can get tickets for the eight o'clock showing.

2. Natalia: **Yo también. La película se estrena este fin de semana y solamente la exhiben en este cine. Ojalá que todavía queden boletos.**
Me too. This film opens this weekend and they only show it in this theater. I hope they still have tickets.

3. Mercedes: **¡Mira la fila que hay! Por lo que veo no vamos a tener suerte.**
Look at the line! It seems like we won't have any luck.

4. Natalia: **Vamos a ver. Yo nunca encuentro entradas para las películas que quiero ver los sábados por la noche.**
We'll see. I never find tickets for the movies I want to see on Saturday nights.

En la taquilla. At the ticket window.

5. Agustín: **¿Tiene usted entradas para la función de las ocho?**
   Do you have tickets for the eight o'clock showing?

6. Empleado: **¿Para qué película?**
   For which film?

7. Agustín: **Para la de Almodóvar, por favor. . .**
   For the Almodóvar film, please . . .

8. Empleado: **No, ya no quedan para la de Almodóvar. La próxima tanda es la de las diez. Para ésa sí tengo entradas disponibles.**
   No, there are no tickets left for the Almodóvar film. The next showing is at ten. I do have tickets available for that showing.

9. Agustín: **¿Qué les parece? Podemos tomarnos algo y volver más tarde para la función de las diez.**
   What do you think? We could get something to drink and come back later for the ten o'clock showing.

10. Natalia: **Yo no estoy cansada. No me importa ir más tarde.**
    I'm not tired. I don't mind going later.

11. Mercedes: **Sí, está bien. Vamos, date prisa antes de que se agoten.**
    Yes, that's fine. Come on, hurry up before they run out.

12. Agustín: **Perfecto. Tres para la de las diez por favor. ¿Empieza exactamente a las diez?**
    Perfect. Three for the ten o'clock showing, please. Does it start exactly at ten?

13. Empleado: **Sí, a las diez en punto, y les recomiendo que lleguen temprano. Es posible que haya mucha gente.**
Yes, at ten o'clock, and I recommend that you get here early. It's possible that it will be crowded.

Después de la película, en un café. After the movie, at a cafe.

14. Agustín: **¡Qué película tan entretenida!**
What an entertaining movie!

15. Mercedes: **Por los aplausos al finalizar la película, parece ser un gran éxito. A mí me ha gustado enormemente. Almodóvar siempre hace muy buenas películas. Siempre escoge tan buenos actores. ¿No les parece?**
Judging by the applause at the end of the movie, it seems to be a great success. I liked it a whole lot. Almodóvar always makes very good movies. He always picks such good actors. Don't you think so?

16. Natalia: **Es muy dramático y tiene unos diálogos estupendos. Me encanta también como usa los colores.**
He's very dramatic and has some terrific dialogues. I also love much how he uses color.

17. Agustín: **La interpretación fue estupenda. Se nota que la dirección fue de primera calidad.**
The acting was terrific. You can tell the direction was of the best quality.

18. Mercedes: **No hay nadie como Almodóvar.**
There's no one like Almodóvar.

19. Natalia: **También me han gustado mucho los decorados y el vestuario. . .**
I also really liked the sets and the costumes . . .

20. Mercedes: **Y, ¿qué te pareció el cine? Esa sala es nueva. Las butacas eran muy cómodas.**
And what did you think of the movie theater? The screening room is new. The chairs were so comfortable.

21. Natalia: **Sí, es verdad.**
Yes, that's true.

22. Mercedes: **¿Vieron su última película? No me acuerdo del título, pero tuvo muy buena crítica.**
Did you see his last film? I can't remember the title, but it got very good reviews.

23. Agustín: **¡Qué buena película!**
What a great movie!

24. Natalia: **¿Y ahora qué quieren hacer?**
And what do you want to do now?

25. Mercedes: **Pues no sé si se habrán dado cuenta que todavía hay entradas disponibles para las funciones de medianoche. Hay una excelente película. . . .**
Well, I don't know if you noticed that there are still tickets available for the midnight showings. There is a great movie . . .

B. NOTES

0. *chicos*: guys. This masculine term is used in Spanish, even when it is used to describe a group of mixed sexes. The term *chicos* is widespread through the Spanish speaking world. Synonyms for *chicos* are *muchachos* and *jóvenes*.

    película: means "movie" or "film." Other Spanish words are *filme* and *cinta*. When referring to "the movies" or to the movie theater itself you would need to use the word *cine*. *Voy al cine los sábados por la noche*. I go to the movies on Saturday nights.

Pedro Almodóvar is one of the most famous and original filmmakers that Spain has ever produced. Almodóvar never attended film school. He started making short films in the 1970s after buying his first camera with the money he saved from his job at a telephone company. During his early years as a filmmaker, he documented the underground *La Movida* (The Movement), the vibrant Spanish nightlife that emerged after decades under Franco's repressive dictatorship. Since the early days of Almodóvar's underground films, his work has matured, and he has since enjoyed worldwide success and appreciation. Almodóvar won the Academy Award in 2002 for his screenplay for *Hable con ella (Talk to Her)*.

1. *tanda*: The word is mostly used in Latin America to refer to a "session" or "showing." *No me gusta ir a la tanda de la medianoche*. I don't like to go to the midnight session. Another common word is *función* or *pase*. *Prefiero la primera función de la tarde*. I prefer the first showing in the afternoon. *No pude ir al pase de las seis*. I couldn't go to the six o'clock showing.

2. *boletos*: tickets. Other common words are *billetes* or *entradas* (literally, "entries"). Notice how they are used in the dialogue: *boletos* is more likely to be used when referring to the physical tickets.

3. *fila*: line. Another common word is *cola*. *Cola* also means "tail."

13. *en punto*: literally, "on the dot." It is normally used to denote the top of the hour. *Yo llegué a las once en punto*. I arrived at eleven o'clock.

15. *al finalizar la película*: Notice how the Spanish phrase differs from the English "at the end of the film." In Spanish, no extra "of" is necessary.

17. *de primera calidad*: the best; literally "of the first quality."

20. *butaca*: armchair. In theaters for live performances, the term *butaca de patio* refers to "orchestra seats."

C. GRAMMAR AND USAGE

1. Let's review some other uses of the prepositions *por* and *para*, two of the most common prepositions in the Spanish language.

Por means "along," "through," or "during" (approximate time).

Lo encontré andando por el parque.
   I ran into him walking through the park.

Vengan ustedes por aquí.
   Come this way (along here).

Espero verlo por la mañana.
   I hope to see him in the morning (anytime during the morning).

Nos gusta andar por las calles céntricas.
   We like to walk along the streets downtown.

The preposition *para* means "by" (a certain time limit) or "for" (a definite purpose).

Usted lo tendrá para las ocho.
   You'll have it by eight o'clock.

Lo necesito para las once.
   I need it by eleven o'clock.

¿Para qué necesita usted el dinero? Para pagar la cuenta.
What do you need the money for? To pay the bill.

2. The verbs *encontrar* (to find) and *entender* (to understand) are two examples of stem-changing verbs.

Encontrar: In this type of stem-changing verb, the *o* of the stem changes to *ue* when it is stressed (that is, in the first, second, and third persons singular and the third person plural). In unstressed syllables, the *o* remains an *o*. Similar verbs whose stems change from *o* to *ue* are: *poder* (to be able to), *mover* (to move), *contar* (to count), *acostarse* (to go to bed or lie down), *costar* (to cost), *acordar* (to agree), *probar* (to try), *almorzar* (to have lunch).

No encuentro el número.
I can't find the number.

A ver si lo encuentras aquí.
Let's see if you *(fam. sing.)* find it here.

Ella siempre lo encuentra.
She always finds it.

Ellos los encuentran fácilmente.
They find them easily.

No lo encontramos nunca.
We never find it.

Vosotros lo encontráis allí.
You'll *(fam. pl.)* find it there.

Entender: As with the change from *o* to *ue* in verbs like *encontrar*, in verbs like *entender* the *e* of the stem changes to *ie* under stress in the first, second, and third persons singular, and the third person plural forms. It remains an *e* in unstressed syllables. These changes occur in the present indicative and the present subjunctive. Other verbs with a similar stem change are: *sentar* (to sit), *cerrar* (to close), *comenzar* (to start), *despertar* (to wake up), *empezar* (to start), *pensar* (to think), *perder* (to lose), *defender* (to defend), *querer* (to want, to love).

Lo entiendo.
   I understand it.

¿Lo entiendes tú?
   Do you *(fam. sing.)* understand it?

Ella lo entiende.
   She understands it.

Ellos lo entienden.
   They understand it.

Nosotros lo entendemos.
   We understand it.

Vosotros lo entendéis.
   You *(fam. pl.)* understand it.

3. The word *qué* can be used to form an interjection when it is followed by a noun or an adjective.

   ¡*Qué* + Noun! = What a _____!

   ¡*Qué* + Adjective! = How _____!

   ¡Qué día!
      What a day!

   ¡Qué atleta!
      What an athlete!

   ¡Qué gusto!
      What a pleasure!

¡Qué bonito!
  How pretty!

¡Qué difícil!
  How difficult!

¡Qué tonto!
  How silly!

Notice that some words may be used as either a noun or an adjective, depending on whether they are followed by *ser* or *estar*:

¡Qué tonto eres!
  What a fool you are!

¡Qué tonto estás!
  How silly you are!

¡Qué listo eres!
  What a smartie you are!

¡Qué listo estás!
  How smart you are!

4. The English "to be" can be expressed by either *ser* or *estar* in Spanish.

Ser is used to express a permanent condition, a fixed state or existence.

Soy profesor.
  I am a teacher.

Juan es estudiante.
  Juan is a student.

La puerta es grande.
  The door is large.

Estar is used to express location, a transitory condition or a varying state.

Estoy en clase.
    I am in class.

Juan está cansado.
    Juan is tired.

La puerta está abierta.
    The door is open.

Some adjectives may be used with *ser* to denote a permanent, unchanging state or condition.

Es viejo.
    He's old (i.e., an old man).

Es aburrido.
    He's boring (i.e., dull, tiresome, a bore).

Es joven.
    He's young.

Contrast this with how *estar* is interpreted with the same adjectives:

Está viejo.
    He looks old. (He may not really be old.)

Está aburrido.
    He's bored.

Está joven.
    He looks young. (He could actually be old.)

EXERCISES

A. Substitute each of the words or expressions in parentheses for the underlined word or expression in the model sentence. Write the new sentence and say it aloud.

  1. *Lo vi andando por la calle.* (el centro, el parque, el pasillo, el campo, la carretera)

  2. *No tengo nada que hacer por la mañana.* (la tarde, la noche, el día, esta semana, el verano)

3. *Me lo tiene que entregar para las ocho.* (el fin de semana, esta noche, esta tarde, mediodía, la semana que viene)

4. *¡Qué hermosa está tu hermana hoy!* (cansada, vieja, fea, bonita, ocupada)

5. *¡Qué placer!* (gusto, pena, lástima, horror, problema)

6. *¿Cómo va tu hermano?* (está, se siente, se encuentra)

B. Change these sentences to the plural. Write the complete sentence and translate.

1. *Yo soy actor.*

2. *Él está en los Estados Unidos.*

3. *Usted es de México.*

4. *Tú estás cansado.*

5. *Ella está en la sala.*

C. Translate the following sentences into Spanish, then say them aloud.

1. What time does the performance begin?

2. What a pleasure to see you again!

3. I just bought this dress.

4. It's a very amusing comedy.

5. I saw a movie last Wednesday.

6. I don't remember the title.

7. It's going to start again.

8. A friend of mine went to see the comedy.

9. She liked it.

10. Let's go in right away.

D. From among the three choices given, choose the best equivalent of the English term (in parentheses) for each sentence, and translate it.

1. (How) ¡_____ hermosa es la vida!
   (a) *Cómo*
   (b) *Qué*
   (c) *Como*

2. (find) *Usted* _____ *las cosas siempre.*
   (a) *encontra*
   (b) *encuentras*
   (c) *encuentra*

3. (can) *Ellos dicen que* _____ *ir mañana.*
   (a) *pueden*
   (b) *poden*
   (c) *puden*

4. (What a) ¡_____ *día más agradable!*
   (a) *Qué un*
   (b) *Cómo*
   (c) *Qué*

5. (is) *Parece que él* _____ *un hombre muy importante.*
   (a) *es*
   (b) *está*
   (c) *ser*

6. (understand) *Yo lo* _____ *todo.*
   (a) *compriendo*
   (b) *entiendo*
   (c) *entendo*

7. (tells) *Juana les* _____ *una historia todos los días.*
   (a) *conta*
   (b) *cuentas*
   (c) *cuenta*

8. (can _____ be) *¿Dónde* _____ *el libro?*
   (a) *puede ser*
   (b) *estará*
   (c) *estar*

9. (was) *El hermano de Juan* _____ *el héroe.*
   (a) *estuvo*
   (b) *estaba*
   (c) *era*

10. (What a) *¡* _____ *placer me da verlos aquí!*
    (a) *Qué*
    (b) *Que un*
    (c) *Cómo*

Answer Key

B. 1. *Nosotros somos actores.*
We are actors.

2. *Ellos están en los Estados Unidos.*
They are in the United States.

3. *Ustedes son de México.*
You are from Mexico.

4. *Vosotros estáis cansados. Ustedes están cansados.*
You are tired.

5. *Ellas están en la sala.*
They are in the living room.

C. 1. *¿A qué hora empieza la función?*

2. *¡Qué gusto verlo (verte) otra vez!*

3. *Acabo de comprar(me) este vestido.*

4. *Es una comedia muy divertida.*

5. *Vi una película el miércoles pasado.*

6. *No me acuerdo del título.*

7. *Va a volver a empezar. Va a empezar otra vez.*

8. *Un amigo mío fue a ver la comedia.*

9. *A ella le gustó.*

10. *Entremos en seguida.*

D. 1. *¡Qué hermosa es la vida!*
How beautiful life is!

2. *Usted encuentra las cosas siempre.*
You always find things.

3. *Ellos dicen que pueden ir mañana.*
They say that they can go tomorrow.

4. *¡Qué día más agradable!*
   What a pleasant day!

5. *Parece que él es un hombre muy importante.*
   It seems that he is a very important man.

6. *Yo lo entiendo todo.*
   I understand it all.

7. *Juana les cuenta una historia todos los días.*
   Juana tells them a story every day.

8. *¿Dónde estará el libro?*
   Where can the book be?

9. *El hermano de Juan era el héroe.*
   Juan's brother was the hero.

10. *¡Qué placer me da verles aquí!*
    What a pleasure it is for me (gives me) to see you here!

LESSON 9

EN EL MUSEO DEL PRADO
IN THE PRADO MUSEUM

A. DIALOGUE

0. *Maruja y Gerardo están de visita en el Museo del Prado en Madrid. Ellos quieren ver varios cuadros en particular y están planificando la visita.*
   Maruja and Gerardo are visiting the Prado Museum in Madrid. They want to see some specific paintings and are planning their visit.

1. Empleada: **Son seis euros, por favor.**
   Six euros, please.

2. Gerardo: **Aquí tiene usted. Doce por dos entradas.** *(A Maruja)* **Debimos haber venido el martes. No cobran la entrada.**
   Here you are. Twelve euros for two tickets. *(To Maruja)* We should have come on Tuesday. They don't charge admission.

3. Maruja: **Sí, pero hay tanta gente que no se puede ver nada.**
   Yes, but there are so many people that you can't see anything.

4. Gerardo: **Tienes razón. Quiero verlo todo con calma. Es una de las colecciones más fabulosas del mundo. Me parece tan interesante esta visita, una de las mejores del viaje.**
   You're right. I want to take my time to see everything. It's one of the most fabulous collections in the world. I find this visit so interesting, one of the best of our trip.

5. Guía: **¿Quieren una guía, señores? Yo les puedo dar detalles sobre todas las obras y ayudarles a encontrar las que les interesan.**

   Do you want a guide? I can give you details about all the works and help you find the ones that interest you.

6. Maruja: **No, gracias, pero tenemos algunas preguntas.**

   No, thank you, but we have a few questions.

7. Gerardo: **Sí. Quiero aprender un poco porque me gusta pintar.**

   Yes. I'd like to learn a little because I like to paint.

8. Guía: **Usted encontrará inspiración aquí. Hay obras de todas las épocas, de todos los estilos, de antiguos a modernos.**

   You'll find inspiration here. There are works from every period, in every style, from ancient to modern.

9. Maruja: **¿Dónde está la Dama de Elche? Quiero verla primero. Se dice que es impresionante.**

   Where is the Dama de Elche? I want to see her first. They say she's impressive.

10. Guía: **El hermoso busto de la Dama de Elche no se encuentra aquí en este museo, señora. Está en el Museo Arqueológico Nacional. ¿Sabe usted que dicen que es una falsificación?**

    The beautiful bust of the Dama de Elche isn't here in this museum, ma'am. It's in the Museo Arqueológico Nacional. Do you know that they say it's a forgery?

11. Maruja: **¡No! ¿De veras? No lo sabía.**

    No! Really? I didn't know that.

12. Gerardo: **Interesante. Gracias, señora. Tenemos un plano del museo y sabemos lo que queremos ver hoy. Vamos, Maruja.**

Interesting. Thank you, ma'am. We have a map of the museum, and we know what we want to see today. Let's go, Maruja.

Más tarde. . . Later. . .

13. Gerardo: **Vamos a subir aquí, por esta escalera, a los salones de la pintura española. Es lo que me interesa más.**

Let's go up this stairway here to the rooms with Spanish paintings. That's what interests me most.

14. Maruja: **¡Ah! Aquí están las obras maestras de El Greco, Velázquez, Murillo, Goya, Zurbarán. . . Quiero ver "Las Meninas", "Las lanzas", "Los Borrachos" y. . .**

Oh! Here are the masterworks of El Greco, Velázquez, Murillo, Goya, Zurbarán . . . I want to see "The Meninas," "The Lances," "The Drunkards" and . . .

15. Gerardo: **¡Despacio! Espera un momento. No podemos verlo todo de un golpe. Vamos a empezar con este salón de las pinturas de El Greco.**

Slow down! Wait a minute. We can't see everything all at once. Let's begin with this room of paintings by El Greco.

16. Maruja: **¡Ay sí! Mira, allí delante está "La adoración de los pastores". ¡Qué hermosa es la figura de la Virgen! ¿Verdad que todo en este cuadro es luminoso y espiritual?**

Oh, yes! Look, there in front of us is "The Adoration of the Shepherds." How beautiful the figure of the

Virgin is! Isn't everything luminous and spiritual in this picture?

17. Gerardo: **Fíjate qué alargadas parecen todas las figuras. Es como si se las mirase desde abajo. Todo tiende a subir.**
Notice how elongated the figures look. It's as if we were looking at them from below. Everything seems to be rising.

18. Maruja: **¡Es verdaderamente una maravilla! Quiero ver el famoso cuadro "El entierro del conde Orgaz". ¿Dónde está? No lo veo por ninguna parte.**
It's really marvelous! I want to see the famous painting "The Burial of Count Orgaz." Where is it? I don't see it around here anywhere.

19. Gerardo: **Es que no está aquí, Maruja. Para eso tendremos que hacer un viaje a Toledo. Se encuentra en la Iglesia de Santo Tomé.**
That's because it's not here, Maruja. For that, we'll have to take a trip to Toledo. It's in the church of Santo Tomé.

20. Maruja: **A ver si podemos ir a Toledo a verlo. Se dice que es una ciudad encantadora. Allí podemos visitar el museo de El Greco. Es la casa en que vivió el pintor. Está restaurada y se encuentra ahora en las mismas condiciones del siglo XVII. ¿Cuándo podremos hacerlo? ¡Me entusiasma la idea!**
Let's see if we can go to Toledo to see it. They say it's a charming city. We can visit the El Greco Museum there. It's the house that the painter lived in. It's been restored and is in the same condition as in the seventeenth century. When can we do it? I'm excited about the idea!

21. Gerardo: **A mí también me gusta la idea. Miraremos nuestros planes para la semana que viene a ver si podemos organizarlo para algún día.** I like the idea, too. We'll look at our plans for next week to see if we can arrange it for some day.

22. Maruja: **¡Qué bien! Vamos a ver los cuadros de Velázquez. Quiero ver los famosos retratos del rey Felipe IV y el del príncipe don Baltasar Carlos.**
How wonderful! Let's see the paintings of Velázquez. I want to see the famous portraits of King Felipe IV and the one of Prince Baltasar Carlos.

23. Gerardo: **Mira, allí está "Las Meninas" con el famoso autorretrato. ¿Ves que el pintor está allí, a la izquierda, con el pincel en la mano como si estuviese pintando lo que tiene delante? Fíjate en la inocencia y belleza del retrato de la princesita.**
Look, there's "The Meninas" with the famous self-portrait. Do you see that the painter is there, on the left, with his brush on hand as if he were painting what is before him? Notice the innocence and beauty of the portrait of the little princess.

24. Maruja: **Velázquez era un maestro prodigioso. ¡Qué variedad de temas y estilos! No sé cuál de estos pintores me gusta más. ¡Todos me gustan tanto!**
Velázquez was a prodigious master. What a variety of themes and styles. I don't know which of these painters I like best. I like all of them so much.

25. Gerardo: **Pues tendremos que volver para ver lo demás. Es casi la hora de cerrar, y todavía no hemos visto nada de Zurbarán, ni de Murillo, ni de Goya, que te interesaba tanto. Las tres horas han pasado volando.**

We'll have to come back to see the rest. It's almost closing time, and we still haven't seen anything by Zurbarán, Murillo, or Goya that you were so interested in. The three hours flew by.

26. Maruja: **¡Qué lástima! ¡Cuando uno está pasándolo bien el tiempo sí que vuela!**
What a pity! Time really does fly when you're having fun!

B. NOTES

1. *Son seis euros*: Compare with the English, which omits the verb. Similar to "that'll be."

4. *con calma*: literally, "with calmness," used to indicated "taking one's time," "with patience."

9. *la Dama de Elche*: A polychrome bust of an idol or goddess, so-called because it was found in Elche, a small town on the Mediterranean coast, south of Alicante. It dates from the fifth century B.C. and is considered one of the most important, as well as one of the most beautiful, early Iberian works of art.
Se dice: In Spanish, reflexive expressions can be used to indicate the English pronoun "one." It is used in an impersonal sense. *Se dice que es impresionante*. They say/It is said/People say it is impressive.

13. *pintura*: painting. Another word for painting is *cuadro,* which we saw in the introduction to the dialogue. The Spanish word for painter is *pintor(a)*.

14. *El Greco*: Domenikas Theotokopoulos, born in Crete, lived in Spain from approximately 1577 until his death in 1614. He is generally known by the name El Greco ("The Greek").

Velázquez: Painter, born in Seville in 1599; court painter for Felipe IV. He left a rich gallery of portraits of the royal family and retainers, as well as a justly famed variety of paintings of mythological and historical subjects.

Murillo: Painter, also from Seville (c.1617–1682), known as "the Spanish Correggio."

Goya: Born in Fuendetodos, a small town in Zaragoza, in 1746; died in Bordeaux in 1828. One of the giants of Spanish art, his influence is felt to the present day. His work is considered a precursor to Expressionism.

Zurbarán: Born in Fuente de Cantos, Extremadura, in 1598. Studied and painted in Seville. Known for his monochromatic portraits of monks and nuns, he was a master of perspective and effects of light.

15. *todo de un golpe*: all at once. Literally, *todo de un golpe* means "all in one blow."

17. *tiende a*: seems to, tends to. The verb *tender* means "to have a tendency." In this case it refers to the impression one gets from looking at the painting with the elongated figures. "Everything seems to rise."

26. *Cuando uno está pasándolo bien el tiempo sí que vuela*: Contrast the construction of the Spanish expression to the English expression.

C. GRAMMAR AND USAGE

1. The verb *deber* followed by an infinitive means "must," "should," or "ought to." Notice that the verb *deber* is conjugated as a regular verb.

Juan debe tener las entradas.
Juan must have the tickets.

Deben estar por aquí.
They must be around here.

Debes estudiar la lección.
You ought to study the lesson.

2. The Spanish words *tanto* and *tan* are quantifiers.

   Tanto followed by a noun means "so much (*sing.*)" or "so many (*pl.*)."

   Hay tanta gente en el teatro.
   There are so many people in the theater.

   Nunca he visto tantas joyas.
   I have never seen so many jewels.

   No sabía que tenía tanto dinero.
   I didn't know that he had so much money.

   Tan followed by an adjective (or adverb) forms the equivalent of the English phrase "so _____."

   Teresa está tan ocupada.
   Teresa is so busy.

   Estaban tan enfermos que no podían ir.
   They were so sick they couldn't go.

   Me parece tan fácil.
   It seems so easy to me.

   Me habló tan lentamente que lo entendí todo.
   He spoke to me so slowly that I understood everything.

   No debes hacerlo tan de prisa.
   You shouldn't do it so quickly.

Tanto can be used on its own as an adverb.

¡Las obras de Velázquez me gustan tanto!
> I like the works of Velázquez so much!

¡Todo me interesa tanto!
> Everything interests me so much!

¡He comido tanto!
> I ate so much!

3. *No* (general negator), *nunca* (never), *nadie* (nobody), and *ninguno* (none, not any) are words that are used to express negative ideas. Unlike English, it is possible to use double or even triple negatives in the same sentence. Notice the examples below:

No veo a nadie.
> I don't see anyone.

No veo a nadie nunca.
> I never see anyone.

No voy nunca a ninguna parte.
> I never go anywhere.

A negative word may be placed before the verb, replacing the general negator, *no*. Compare the following sentences:

No veo nunca a nadie.
Nunca veo a nadie.
> I never see anyone.

No me habla nadie.
Nadie me habla.
> No one speaks to me.

No voy nunca a ninguna parte.
Nunca voy a ninguna parte.
> I never go anywhere.

Notice how *ninguna* is used in the last example with *parte* to mean "nowhere."

EXERCISES

A. Substitute each of the words or expressions in parentheses for the underlined word or expression in the model sentence. Write each new sentence and say it aloud.

1. *Juan debe estar en la biblioteca.* (el museo, la casa, la sala, el parque, el centro)

2. *Ellos deben haber estudiado.* (descansado, comido, ido, salido, terminado)

3. *Juana y yo debemos empezar.* (terminar, leer, practicar, hablar, salir)

4. *Hay tanta gente en el museo.* (tantos cuadros, tantas pinturas, tanto ruido, tantos niños, tantas señoras)

5. *Él lo hizo tan claramente.* (lentamente, rápidamente, de prisa, fácilmente, bien)

6. *Nunca he estado tan ocupado.* (cansado, enfermo, perezoso, contento, equivocado)

B. Rephrase the following sentences, placing "no" before the verb. Write the complete sentence and translate.

1. *Nunca le escribo a nadie.*

2. *Nadie me ayuda.*

3. *Nunca compramos nada.*

4. *Juan y José nunca van a ninguna parte.*

5. *Nunca he visto a tanta gente en el museo.*

C. Translate the following sentences into Spanish, then say them aloud.

1. There are so many people here.

2. He explained it so clearly that I understood everything.

3. I have never been so busy.

4. You must be tired.

5. Juan and María ought to study more.

6. I never want to see her.

7. How elongated all the figures look!

8. We have to take a trip to Toledo.

9. When can we do it?

10. I want to see the famous painting.

D. From among the three choices given, choose the best equivalent of the English term (in parentheses) for each sentence, and translate.

1. (so) *Es _____ difícil comprenderlo.*
   (a) *tanto*
   (b) *tanta*
   (c) *tan*

2. (ever) *No lo veo _____.*
   (a) *nunca*
   (b) *tanta*
   (c) *tan*

3. (everything that) *Creo _____ me dice Juan.*
   (a) *todo lo que*
   (b) *todos que*
   (c) *todas las*

4. (all the) *Juan ha comprado _____ libros que quería.*
   (a) *todos*
   (b) *todo el*
   (c) *todos los*

5. (so much) *¡Roberto tiene _____ tiempo libre!*
   (a) *tan mucho*
   (b) *tanto*
   (c) *tanto que*

6. (anything) *No quiero _____ ahora.*
   (a) *alguna cosa*
   (b) *nada*
   (c) *algo*

7. (ought to) *Me parece que (yo) _____ levantarme ahora.*
   (a) *debo*
   (b) *tengo que*
   (c) *hay que*

8. (so many) *No he tenido nunca _____ problemas.*
   (a) *tan muchos*
   (b) *tantos*
   (c) *tantas*

9. (anything) *No te debo _____.*
   (a) *algo*
   (b) *alguna cosa*
   (c) *nada*

10. (such) *Nunca ha leído libros _____ difíciles.*
    (a) *tan*
    (b) *tanto*
    (c) *tantos*

Answer Key

B. 1. *No le escribo nunca a nadie.*
    I never write to anyone.

    2. *No me ayuda nadie.*
    No one helps me.

    3. *No compramos nada nunca.*
    We never buy anything.

    4. *Juan y José no van nunca a ninguna parte.*
    Juan and José never go anywhere.

    5. *No he visto nunca a tanta gente en el museo.*
    I've never seen so many people in the museum.

C. 1. *Hay tanta gente aquí.*

    2. *Lo explicó tan claramente que lo comprendí todo.*

    3. *Nunca he estado tan ocupado.*

    4. *Usted (Tú) estará(s) cansado. Usted (Tú) debe(s) estar cansado.*

    5. *Juan y María deben estudiar más.*

    6. *No quiero verla nunca. Nunca quiero verla.*

    7. *¡Qué alargadas parecen todas las figuras!*

    8. *Tenemos que hacer un viaje a Toledo.*

    9. *¿Cuándo podemos hacerlo?*

    10. *Quiero ver la pintura famosa.*

D. 1. *Es tan difícil comprenderlo.*
    It's so difficult to understand.

    2. *No lo veo nunca.*
    I don't ever see him.

3. *Creo todo lo que me dice Juan.*
   I believe everything that Juan tells me.

4. *Juan ha comprado todos los libros que quería.*
   Juan bought all the books that he wanted.

5. *¡Roberto tiene tanto tiempo libre!*
   Roberto has so much free time!

6. *No quiero nada ahora.*
   I don't want anything now.

7. *Me parece que (yo) debo levantarme ahora.*
   It seems to me that I ought to get up now.

8. *No he tenido nunca tantos problemas.*
   I have never had so many problems.

9. *No te debo nada.*
   I don't owe you anything.

10. *Nunca ha leído libros tan difíciles.*
    He has never read such difficult books.

LESSON 10

LA ARTESANÍA ESPAÑOLA
SPANISH HANDCRAFTS

A. DIALOGUE

Una visita al Rastro de Madrid. A visit to the Rastro (Flea Market) in Madrid.

0. *Sara y Emilio son de Honduras y están visitando Madrid. Ellos deciden ir al Rastro en Madrid y llaman a Miguel para que los ayude con la visita.*
Sara and Emilio are from Honduras and are visiting Madrid. They decide to go to El Rastro in Madrid and they call Miguel to help them with the visit.

1. Sara: **Nos han hablado tanto del Rastro que deberíamos visitarlo. Tiene que ser interesante. No sé exactamente lo que es.**
People have talked to us so much about the Rastro that we should go see it. It must be interesting. I don't know exactly what it is.

2. Emilio: **Seguramente es una sección de calles donde hay muchas tiendas de antigüedades y vendedores de toda clase de cosas.**
It must be a section of streets where there are many antique shops and vendors of all kinds of things.

3. Sara: **Seguro que es más divertido los domingos por la mañana.**
I bet it's more fun on Sunday mornings.

4. Emilio: **Es cuando todo el mundo va. ¿Quieres ir hoy, cuando hay menos gente?**

That's when everyone goes. Do you want to go today, when there are fewer people?

5. Sara: **Sí, vamos. Miguel y Teresa me dijeron que querían ir también. Vamos a ver si pueden acompañarnos hoy. Seguro que pueden ayudarnos un poco.**

   Yes, let's go. Miguel and Teresa told me that they wanted to go, too. Let's see if they can come with us today. I am sure that they can help us a little.

6. Emilio: *(en el teléfono)* **¿Miguel? Hola, ¿cómo estás? Bien, bien, me alegro. Sara y yo estábamos hablando, y pensábamos ir al Rastro esta mañana. Como Sara me ha dicho que ustedes habían hablado de ir, llamo a ver si quieren venir. Nos gustaría muchísimo. ¡Ah, sí! ¡Estupendo! Entonces, pasaremos a buscarles, ya que están de camino. ¿Cuánto tiempo necesitan? ¿Una hora? Bien, Miguel, llegamos dentro de una hora. ¡Hasta pronto!**

   (on the telephone) Miguel? Hello, how are you? Fine, fine, I'm glad. Sara and I were talking, and we were thinking of going to the Rastro this morning. Sara told me that you had spoken of going, so I'm calling to find out if you want to come. We would like it very much. Oh, yes! Terrific! Then, we'll come by to pick you up, it's on the way. How much time do you need? An hour? Alright, Miguel, we'll be there in an hour. See you soon!

7. Sara: **¡Qué bien! Ellos vendrán con nosotros. Me alegro tanto. Teresa dice que hay que saber regatear, y ella ha prometido enseñarme la manera de hacerlo.**

   How nice! They're coming with us. I'm so pleased. Teresa says that you have to know how to bargain, and she promised to show me how to do it.

8. Emilio: **Eso es, hay que saber regatear. Y no debes dar la impresión de tener mucho dinero.**
That's right, you have to know how to bargain. And you shouldn't give the impression of having a lot of money.

En el Rastro. At the Rastro.

9. Emilio: **Vamos a entrar en esta tienda. ¡Hay tantos artículos de loza! Vean aquellos platos y tazas. ¡Todo lo que hay aquí es hermoso! Dígame, señora, ¿dónde hacen esos platos?**
Let's go into this store. There is so much china! Look at those plates and cups. Everything here is beautiful! Tell me, ma'am, where are those plates made?

10. Vendedora: **Son de Valencia, señor, de una de las fábricas más conocidas. Se puede reconocer la producción de esa fábrica por la extraordinaria fineza del trabajo. Estos platos son todos del siglo pasado.**
They're from Valencia, sir, from one of the best-known factories. You can recognize the products of that factory by the extraordinary quality of the work. These plates are all from the last century.

11. Sara: **Son preciosos. Me imagino que serán carísimos. Me gustaría tener algunos de los más grandes para colgar en la pared del comedor.**
They're beautiful. I imagine they must be very expensive. I would like to have some of the larger ones to hang on the wall in the dining room.

12. Miguel: **¿Cuánto valen los grandes, señora? Especialmente estos, en azul y amarillo, con el diseño de pájaros.**
How much are the large ones, ma'am? Especially these in blue and yellow, with the bird design.

13. Vendedora: **Esos son precisamente los más caros. Están pintados a mano y son de un estilo que no se encuentra muy a menudo.**

    Those are precisely the most expensive. They're hand painted and in a style that isn't found very often.

14. Emilio: **Bueno, de acuerdo. Pero, ¿cuánto valen?**

    All right, agreed. But how much do they cost?

15. Vendedora: **¿Cuántos quieren ustedes? Se los puedo dejar a muy buen precio.**

    How many do you want? I could let you have them for a very good price.

16. Emilio: **Depende de lo que quiere decir "muy buen precio". Queremos cuatro o cinco, ¿no te parece, Sara?**

    That depends on what "a very good price" means. We want four or five, don't you think, Sara?

17. Sara: **Sí. Y éstos son los que me gustan más. ¿Cuánto quiere usted por ellos?**

    Yes. And these are the ones that I like best. How much do you want for them?

18. Vendedora: **Bueno, para ustedes, les hago precio especial. Les dejo cinco en cuatrocientos euros.**

    All right, for you I'll do a special price. I'll let you have the five of them for four hundred euros.

19. Emilio: **Es demasiado. Por trescientos, me los llevo.**

    That's too much. For three hundred, I'll take them.

20. Vendedora: **Lo siento. Ya les he dado el mejor precio posible.**

    I'm sorry. I've already given you the best possible price.

21. Sara: **¡Ay, y me gustan tanto! ¿Qué le parece trescientos cincuenta?**
Oh, and I like them so much! What do you think of three hundred and fifty?

22. Vendedora: **Bueno, como ustedes son tan majos, se los dejo a ese precio.**
All right, since I like you, I'll let you have them for that price.

23. Emilio: **Bien, tome usted. Envuélvalos con cuidado y volveremos a buscarlos dentro de poco.**
Fine, here you are. Wrap them carefully and we'll come back for them in a little while.

24. Miguel: **Vamos a esa tienda de muebles antiguos. Tienen muchos arcones de madera labrada.**
Let's go to that antique furniture store. They have lots of chests of carved wood.

25. Sara: **¡Qué comedor! Mira esos sillones tan regios. ¿No los encuentras estupendos, Emilio?**
What a dining room set! Look at those big regal-looking chairs. Don't you think they're terrific, Emilio?

26. Emilio: **Desde luego. Pero ten en cuenta que no podemos cargar con cosas tan pesadas. Costaría una fortuna embalarlos y mandarlos.**
Of course. But bear in mind that we can't load ourselves down with such heavy things. It would cost a fortune to pack and send them.

27. Sara: **No te preocupes. Yo no estaba pensando en comprarlos.**
Don't worry. I wasn't thinking of buying them.

28. Miguel: **¿Qué os parece la idea de tomar algún refresco? Estoy cansado de andar.**

What do you think of having something to drink? I
am tired of walking.

29. Emilio: **¡Me parece muy bien! ¿Por qué no se
    sientan ustedes en la terraza de allí enfrente? Yo
    iré a buscar los platos. Los debe tener envueltos
    ya.**
    Sounds good. Why don't you sit down in that side-
    walk café across the street? I'll go get the plates. She
    ought to have them wrapped by now.

30. Sara: **¿Qué quieres tomar, Emilio? Te lo pido
    mientras tanto.**
    What are you having, Emilio? I'll order it in the
    meantime.

31. Emilio: **Me gustaría una cerveza bien fría. Tengo
    mucha sed.**
    I would like a cold beer. I'm very thirsty.

B. NOTES

1. *nos han hablado*: Note the third person plural used
   impersonally.
   El Rastro: an open-air market located in the old
   section of Madrid. There are restaurants and shops
   among the medieval-looking buildings of the neighborhood.

2. *Seguramente es*: surely it's, it must be, it probably is.
   You would use this expression whenever you want
   to express probability. Notice also *seguro que es* in
   the next line.

3. *los domingos*: on Sundays. Notice how the article is
   used with days of the week.

6. *buscarles*: from *buscar* (to look for). This may also
be used in the sense of "to stop by for someone," "to
pick them up."

   Ya que están de camino: Since you are already on
your way. The word *ya* means "already." Notice that
the word *ya* also appears in line 29. *Los debe tener
envueltos ya*. She must already have them wrapped.

11. *los más grandes:* the larger ones. Superlatives are
turned into nouns in Spanish when used with articles. There is no extra word for "ones" as there is in
English. See also *los grandes* (the large ones) in line
12, and *los más caros* (the most expensive ones) in
line 13. The article and adjective should match in
gender and number the noun they are describing.

28. *andar*: to walk. Notice the use of the infinitive as a
noun here.

29. *me parece muy bien:* sounds good. Literally, "[it]
seems very good to me."

   ya: Here, it means "by now" or "by this time." In
this final position *ya* often has this meaning.

C. GRAMMAR AND USAGE

1. The word *todos* or *todas* followed by an article means
"every" or "all."

Tenemos todos los estilos.
   We have every style (all the styles).

Hay pinturas de todas las épocas.
   There are paintings from every period (all the
   periods).

Quiero ver todos los muebles.
   I want to see all the furniture.

The word *todo* or *toda* followed by an article refers to "the whole" or "the entire."

Me gusta toda la ciudad.
   I like the whole city.

Él ha viajado por todo el país.
   He has traveled through the entire country.

Todo el mundo estaba allí.
   Everybody was there.

Notice that *todo el día* means "all day" or "the entire day" and *todos los días* means "every day" or "all the days."

2. The word *todo* is used in some other popular expressions:

Todo lo que means "everything (that)."

Ella quiere comprar todo lo que ve.
   She wants to buy everything (that) she sees.

Todo lo que hemos visto nos ha gustado.
   We have liked everything (that) we have seen.

Juan comió todo lo que le pusieron delante.
   Juan ate everything (that) they put in front of him.

Todo preceded by the word *lo*, whether attached to or preceding the verb, means "everything."

Quiero verlo todo.
   I want to see everything (see it all).

Me lo explicó todo.
   He explained everything to me.

Ellos querían comprarlo todo.
   They wanted to buy everything.

3. An article preceding the days of the week indicates an event that occurs "on" a specific day. *El* is used for a one

time event ("on Tuesday"), while *los* is used to indicate a recurring event ("on Tuesdays").

Estoy menos ocupada los sábados.
I am less busy (not so busy) on Saturdays.

Voy a verlo el lunes.
I am going to see him on Monday.

Hay corridas (de toros) los domingos por la tarde.
There are bullfights on Sundays in the afternoon.

4. The expression *pensar en* means "to think of" or "to think about."

¿En qué piensa usted?
What are you thinking about?

Estaba pensando en todo lo que tengo que hacer.
I was thinking about everything I have to do.

Ellos piensan en las dificultades que tienen.
They think about the difficulties they have.

EXERCISES

A. Substitute each of the words or expressions in the parentheses for the underlined word or expression in the model sentence. Write each new sentence and say it aloud.

1. *Juan quiere comprar todos los muebles.* (libros, zapatos, coches, cuadros, ceniceros)

2. *Ella ha visto todas las pinturas.* (blusas, casas, obras de teatro, bolsas, medias)

3. *Ellos han visto todo el país.* (museo, pueblo, centro, mercado, teatro)

4. *Lo vieron el martes.* (compraron, vendieron, visitaron, hicieron, terminaron)

5. *Me gusta <u>descansar</u> los domingos.* (pasear, ir al cine, leer, dormir hasta la tarde, jugar)

6. *Estaba pensando en <u>el trabajo</u>.* (el viaje, el tiempo, la comedia, el museo, la música)

B. Change these sentences to the negative. Write the complete sentence and translate.

1. *Siempre pienso en el viaje.*

2. *Vamos al museo el lunes.*

3. *(A él) Le gusta comprar todo lo que ve.*

4. *Los niños comieron todo el helado.*

5. *Es difícil comprenderlo.*

C. Translate the following sentences into Spanish, then say them aloud.

1. They have spoken to us so much about the museum.

2. It is said *(se dice)* that it's more amusing on Sundays.

3. We can go with you tommorrow.

4. You have to know how to bargain.

5. You shouldn't give the impression of being rich.

6. One can recognize all of the work of that factory by its style.

7. I can let you have it all at a very good price.

8. That depends on what you mean.

9. All the paintings are expensive.

10. He ought to have them (the plates) wrapped now.

D. From among the three choices given, choose the best equivalent of the English term (in parentheses) for each sentence, and translate.

1. (every) *Lo veo* _____ *martes.*
   - (a) *todas las*
   - (b) *todo el*
   - (c) *todos los*

2. (all) *He pasado* _____ *tarde en la piscina.*
   - (a) *todo el*
   - (b) *toda la*
   - (c) *toda*

3. (all day) *Juan estuvo leyendo* _____.
   - (a) *todo el día*
   - (b) *todo día*
   - (c) *toda la día*

4. (on) *Voy a verlo* _____ *domingo.*
   - (a) *en*
   - (b) *el*
   - (c) *por*

5. (everything) *Usted cree* _____ *él le dice.*
   - (a) *todos los que*
   - (b) *todo el que*
   - (c) *todo lo que*

6. (every) *Normalmente voy a visitarlo* _____ *sábados.*
   - (a) *cada*
   - (b) *todos los*
   - (c) *algunos*

7. (On) _____ *miércoles vamos a ir de compras.*
   - (a) *En*
   - (b) *El*
   - (c) *La*

8. (about her) *Nunca pienso* _____ *ahora.*
   - (a) *en ella*
   - (b) *sobre ella*
   - (c) *de ellas*

9. (all the news) *Siempre oigo* _____ *por radio.*
   (a) *todo la noticia*
   (b) *todas las noticias*
   (c) *todas noticias*

10. (of) *Yo no estaba pensando* _____ *comprarlo.*
    (a) *en*
    (b) *sobre*
    (c) *a*

Answer Key

B. 1. *No pienso nunca en el viaje.* Or, *Nunca pienso en el viaje.*
I don't ever think about the trip. Or, I never think about the trip.

2. *No vamos al museo el lunes.*
We are not going to the museum on Monday.

3. *No le gusta comprar todo lo que ve.*
He doesn't like to buy everything he sees.

4. *Los niños no comieron todo el helado.*
The children didn't eat all the ice cream.

5. *No es difícil comprenderlo.*
It's not difficult to understand it.

C. 1. *Nos han hablado tanto del museo.*

2. *Se dice que es más divertido los domingos.*

3. *Podemos acompañarte(lo) mañana. Podemos ir contigo (con usted) mañana.*

4. *Hay que saber regatear.*

5. *No debes dar la impresión de ser rico.*

6. *Se reconoce todo el trabajo de aquella fábrica por su estilo.*

7. *Se lo (Te lo) puedo dejar todo a muy buen precio.*

8. *Eso depende de lo que quiere(s) decir.*

9. *Todos los cuadros son caros.*

10. *Debe tenerlos envueltos ahora (ya).*

D. 1. *Lo veo todos los martes.*
I see him every Tuesday.

2. *He pasado toda la tarde en la piscina.*
   I spent all afternoon in the swimming pool.

3. *Juan estaba leyendo todo el día.*
   Juan was reading all day.

4. *Voy a verlo el domingo.*
   I am going to see him on Sunday.

5. *Usted cree todo lo que él le dice.*
   You believe everything that he tells you.

6. *Normalmente voy a visitarlo todos los sábados.*
   Usually I go to visit him every Saturday.

7. *El miércoles vamos a ir de compras.*
   On Wednesday, we are going to go shopping.

8. *Nunca pienso en ella ahora.*
   I never think about her now.

9. *Siempre oigo todas las noticias por radio.*
   I always hear all the news on the radio.

10. *Yo no estaba pensando en comprarlo.*
    I wasn't thinking of buying it.

LESSON 11

SAQUÉMONOS FOTOS
LET'S TAKE PICTURES

A. DIALOGUE

0. *Carlos y Rosa están visitando Ciudad de México.*
Han decidido pasarse el último día de las vaca-
ciones tomando fotos de sus sitios favoritos del
viaje.
Carlos and Rosa are visiting Mexico City. They have
decided to spend their last day of their vacation taking pictures of their favorite places from the trip.

En el hotel. At the hotel.

1. Carlos: **¿Recuerdas que hoy habíamos decidido**
volver a algunos de los sitios que nos gustaron
más para sacar más fotos?
Do you remember that today we had decided to go
back to some of the places we liked best to take
more pictures?

2. Rosa: **Claro que sí. Pero acuérdate que ya no tene-**
mos mucha memoria disponible en la cámara
digital.
Of course I do. But remember that we don't have a
lot of memory left in our digital camera.

3. Carlos: **Sí. Creo que solamente puedo tomar tres**
más, pero me gustaría ir a una tienda fotográfica
a comprar más memoria y a hacer unas preguntas.
Yes. I think I can only take three more, but I'd like
to go to a photo shop to buy more memory and ask
some questions.

4. Rosa: **Recuerda que nos hacen falta pilas para la cámara.**
Remember that we need batteries for the camera.

5. Carlos: **También quiero comprar postales de Ciudad de México.**
I also want to buy postcards of Mexico City.

6. Rosa: **Deberíamos comprar muchas, tienen un precio muy bueno.**
We should buy a lot of them; they have a very good price.

7. Carlos: **Tienes razón. Quiero recuerdos de todos los monumentos, ruinas y sitios históricos que hemos visitado.**
You're right. I want memories of all the monuments, ruins, and historical sites that we have visited.

8. Rosa: **Y a mí me gustaría tener un video de las plazas más hermosas, del Zócalo y de muchos otros sitios.**
And I would like to have a video of the prettiest squares, of the Zocalo, and of many other places.

En la tienda. In the shop.

9. Carlos: **¿Tiene usted tarjetas de memoria para esta cámara?**
Do you have memory cards for this camera?

10. Empleado: **¿Para ésta? Permítame verla, por favor. Sí, tengo de sesenta y cuatro megabytes o de ciento veintiocho.**
For this one? Let me see it, please. Yes, I have one with sixty-four megabytes and one with one hundred and twenty-eight.

11. Carlos: **La de ciento veintiocho, por favor.**
    The one with one hundred and twenty eight, please.

12. Empleado: **Aquí la tiene. Tiene usted una cámara muy buena.**
    Here you are. You have a very good camera.

13. Carlos: **Gracias. He tenido bastante suerte con ella, aunque no soy experto. ¿Podría darme también una cámara desechable?**
    Thanks. I have had good luck with it, although I'm no expert. Will you give me a disposable camera also, please?

14. Empleado: **¿De veinticuatro o de treinta y seis fotos?**
    Twenty-four or thirty-six exposures?

15. Carlos: **De treinta y seis, por favor. ¿Quiere usted revisar esta cámara de vídeo, por favor? Hay algo que no funciona bien.**
    Thirty-six, please. Can you take a look at this video camera? There's something that's not working well.

16. Empleado: **¿Qué es lo que no funciona?**
    What is it that isn't working?

17. Carlos: **A veces, cuando aprieto este botón, se congela la imagen.**
    Sometimes, when I press this button, the image freezes.

18. Empleado: **Conozco bien este modelo. Hay que apretarlo rápidamente, sin dejarlo demasiado tiempo. Una presión rápida y ligera, levantando el dedo en seguida.**
    I know this model well. You have to press it quickly, without leaving it for too long. Quick and light pressure, lifting the finger immediately.

19. Carlos: **Muchas gracias. Quiero también unas pilas.**
Thank you very much. I also want some batteries.

20. Empleado: **Muy bien, señor. ¿Desean ustedes algo más? Entonces voy a envolver todo esto. Buena suerte.**
Very well, sir. Do you want anything else? Then I'll wrap all this. Good luck!

En la Catedral Metropolitana. At the Metropolitan Cathedral.

21. Rosa: **Ah, la Catedral Metropolitana. Me gustaría tener una vista panorámica. Hay tantas cosas que ver por aquí. No te olvides de quitar la tapa del lente.**
Ah, the Metropolitan Cathedral. I'd like to get a panoramic view. There are so many things to see around here. Don't forget to take off the lens cap.

22. Carlos: **No te preocupes. Ponte delante de la estatua. Así estarás en la foto.**
Don't worry. Stand in front of the statue. That way you'll be in the picture.

23. Rosa: **Pero si vas a sacarla de tan lejos, nadie podrá reconocerme.**
But if you're going to take it from so far away, no one will be able to recognize me.

24. Carlos: **Pero nosotros sabremos que estás allí, y se lo podremos decir a todos: "¿No ves aquel puntito azul al pie de la estatua? Pues ese puntito es Rosa".**
But we'll know that you're there, and we can tell everyone: "Do you see that little blue dot at the foot of the statue? Well, that little dot is Rosa."

25. Rosa: **¡Qué chistoso eres! ¿No quieres sacar alguna otra vista del Palacio Nacional? Podemos hacer la foto con el teléfono móvil y mandársela inmediatamente a Gladys en Chicago.**
How funny you are! Don't you want to take some other view of the National Palace? We could take a picture with the cell phone and send it to Gladys in Chicago right away.

26. Carlos: **¡Lo contenta que se va a poner!**
She will be so happy!

27. Rosa: **Sí, y luego vamos al Bosque de Chapulte-pec. A esta hora de la tarde es tan bonito con tanta gente paseando.**
Yes, and then let's go to the Chapultepec Park. At this time of the afternoon it's so beautiful with all the people strolling around.

28. Carlos: **Quiero sacarte una foto sentada en nues-tra terraza preferida.**
I want to take a picture of you, sitting in our favorite café.

En el Palacio de Bellas Artes. At the Palace of Fine Arts.

29. Carlos: **Desde aquí podemos sacar unas fotos con el parque al fondo.**
From here we can take some shots with the park in the background.

30. Rosa: **Deberíamos tener algunas de Xochimilco, con los canales.**
We should have some of the Xochimilco, with the canals.

31. Carlos: **Espero que todas salgan bien. Tendremos una colección de fotos muy bonitas como recuerdo de nuestra visita en México.**

I hope they all turn out well. We'll have a collection of very pretty pictures as a souvenir of our visit to Mexico.

32. Rosa: **Saquemos unas de San Ángel.**
Let's take some of San Angel.

33. Carlos: **Claro que sí. Vamos, nos podemos pasar el resto de la tarde por allí.**
Of course. Let's go, we can spend the rest of the afternoon there.

34. Rosa: **Tenemos que sacar copias de las mejores para mandárselas a nuestros amigos.**
We'll have to make copies of the best ones to send to our friends.

35. Carlos: **Si es que salen bien.**
If they come out well.

36. Rosa: **Tú eres buen fotógrafo, Carlos. Siempre te salen bien.**
You're a good photographer, Carlos. They always come out well for you.

B. NOTES

0. *último*: last. It can also be used to mean "ultimate."
fotos: photographs, pictures. *Foto* is not used to refer to "movies." The Spanish word for "movies" is *película* or *filme*. *"Mujeres al borde de un ataque de nervios" es una buena película.* "Women on the Verge of a Nervous Breakdown" is a good movie. It can also be used when referring to the number of "exposures;" see line 14 for this usage.

2. *mucha memoria disponible*: literally, "a lot of available memory."
la cámara digital: digital camera.

4. *pilas*: batteries. Another word for battery is *batería,* which is mostly used to refer to large batteries such as the ones in cars.

8. *Zócalo*: The Zócalo is a massive plaza that houses many of the most important historical and religious buildings in Mexico City, including the Plaza de la Constitución. The Zócalo is in the middle of the Historic Center of Mexico City.

9. *tarjetas de memoria*: memory cards.

13. *una cámara desechable*: a disposable camera.

17. *congelarse*: to freeze. This verb is also used for computers.

21. *Catedral Metropolitana*: The Catedral Metropolitana is one of the most important historical buildings in Mexico City. The Catedral, which dominates el Zócalo, is the oldest and largest cathedral in Latin America. Construction started in the late 16th century and continued for three centuries. As a result, a variety of periods, from Spanish renaissance to French neoclassicism, are represented in the cathedral's stunning architecture.

   una vista panorámica: a panoramic view. Some other important camera terms: *enfocar* (to focus), *acercar* (to zoom in), *alejar* (to zoom out), *el flash* (flash), *el lente* (lens).

24. *¿No ves aquel puntito azul. . . ?*: In Spanish, the question is sometimes asked in the negative sense to act as a rhetorical question.

25. *Palacio Nacional*: The *Palacio Nacional,* or "National Palace," is also in the Zócalo. The palace,

apart from housing the Mexican government, is home to many astonishing murals by Diego Rivera, Mexico's famed muralist. Rivera's portrayal of the history of Mexican civilization is on display on the second floor.

27. *Bosque de Chapultepec*: This huge urban park in the middle of Mexico City is a much-needed oasis of green. The park is popular with families, providing multiple activities, including a former Aztec zoo, the Parque Zoológico de Chapultepec.

28. *Palacio de Bellas Artes*: The Palacio de Bellas Artes, or Palace of Fine Arts, with its white marble exterior, is considered one of Mexico City's most beautiful buildings. It was designed in 1905 as a national theater, and today serves as a concert hall and center of Mexican and international art. The palace houses some of Mexico's finest murals by renowned artists such as Diego Rivera, Rufino Tamayo, and David Alfaro Siqueiros.

30. *Xochimilco*: Famous for its canals as well as the colorful gondolas that navigate through them, the name *Xochimilco* means "place where flowers grow" in Nahuatl. It is 12 miles south of Mexico City. The semi-floating flower and vegetable gardens were built by the Aztecs. In Xochimilco there is also a popular crafts market.

32. *San Ángel*: The suburb of San Ángel is popular with writers and artists; Frida Kahlo, Diego Rivera, and Leon Trotsky are some of this neighborhood's most famous former residents. The cobblestone streets and colonial houses make the neighborhood a treat to visit, as does the popular flower market in the Plaza San Jacinto, which attracts large crowds every Saturday.

C. GRAMMAR AND USAGE

1. The demonstrative adjectives, *este*, *ese*, and *aquel* in their various forms have a written accent to denote their use as pronouns. Remember that the pronouns must agree in number and gender with the noun they are replacing.

éste/ésta(s): this (near the speaker)

¿El libro? No me gusta éste.
   The book? I don't like this one.

¿Los cuadros? Me gustan éstos.
   The pictures? I like these.

¿La máquina fotográfica? Quiero ver ésta.
   The camera? I want to see this one.

¿Las pinturas? Podría venderle éstas.
   The paintings? I could sell you these.

ése/ésa(s): that (near the listener)

Me gusta este libro pero no me gusta ése que estás leyendo.
   I like this book but I don't like that one you're reading.

Voy a llevar estos paquetes y usted puede mandar ésos al hotel.
   I'm going to carry these packages and you can send those to the hotel.

Esta foto es preciosa pero ésa que miras no salió bien.
   This photograph is beautiful but the one you're looking at didn't turn out well.

Estas blusas son preciosas pero ésas no me gustan.
   These blouses are pretty but I don't like those.

aquél/aquélla(s): that (removed from both speaker and listener)

Ese disco compacto que tienes en la mano es muy caro pero es mejor que aquél que escuchamos ayer.
That CD (you have in your hand) is very expensive but it's better than that one we listened to yesterday.

Esos cuadernos son muy buenos pero no tan buenos como aquéllos de la otra tienda.
Those notebooks are very good, but they're not as good as those in the other store.

Esa mesa es demasiado grande, pero aquélla en el rincón es demasiado pequeña.
That table is too large but that one in the corner is too small.

Esas lámparas son muy prácticas pero aquéllas que vimos en Segovia eran más bonitas.
Those lamps are very practical but those that we saw in Segovia were prettier.

2. The following forms of the personal pronoun are used with prepositions for emphasis or clarification.

mí, ti, usted, él, ella, nosotros, ustedes, ellos, ellas

A mí me gusta este helado. ¿Y a ti?
I like this ice cream. Do you?

A mí también me gusta.
I like it too.

A él no le gusta. ¿Y a ella?
He doesn't like it. Does she?

A ella le gusta mucho.
She likes it very much.

- These forms are used with all prepositions with the exception of the forms *conmigo* (with me) and *contigo* (with you).

Este regalo es para mí.
    This gift is for me.

Pablo lo ha hecho para ti.
    Pablo did it for you.

¿Quieres venir conmigo?
    Do you want to come with me?

Juan hablará contigo mañana.
    Juan will speak with you tomorrow.

Dice que estaba pensando en mí.
    She says she was thinking of me.

Siempre pienso en ti.
    I always think of you.

Another exception is *entre tú y yo* (between you and me).

3. The expression *hay que* means "one must/has to" or "you must/have to (impersonal)."

Al llegar a la esquina hay que doblar a la derecha.
    When you reach the corner, you must turn right.

Hay que estudiar mucho para comprenderlo.
    One has to study a lot to understand it.

Hay que comprar las entradas en la taquilla.
    You have buy the tickets at the box office.

4. The expression

Hay + noun + *que* + infinitive

is equivalent to the English expression

There are + noun + infinitive.

Hay muchos libros que leer.
There are many books to read.

Hay unas películas interesantes que ver.
There are some interesting movies to see.

Hay muchas cosas que comprar.
There are many things to buy.

Compare the following sentences:

Hay que comprar muchas cosas.
You (One) must buy many things.

Hay muchas cosas que comprar.
There are many things to buy.

EXERCISES

A. Substitute each of the words or expressions in parentheses for the underlined word or expression in the model sentence. Write each new sentence and say it aloud.

1. *Este cuadro es muy bonito pero no me gusta aquél.*
   (edificio, mueble, libro, color, cenicero)

2. *Aquellas pinturas que vimos ayer me gustaron.*
   (obras, blusas, lámparas, mesas, camisas)

3. *¿Dónde compraste esa camisa?* (máquina, pluma, silla, papelera, chaqueta)

4. *Hay que comprar el libro.* (vender, leer, escribir, mandar, estudiar)

5. *Se dice que hay muchas cosas que ver.* (muchos cuadros, muchas estatuas, muchas fuentes, muchos monumentos, muchas pinturas)

6. *Juan lo ha escrito para ti.* (El poeta, El señor Hernández, María, Mi amigo, Aquel señor)

B. Change these sentences to the present tense. Write the complete sentence and translate.

  1. *Lo compraste para él.*

  2. *Los señores Andrade hicieron el viaje conmigo.*

  3. *No lo he visto jamás contigo.*

  4. *Ellos me lo regalaron a mí.*

  5. *El cuadro era para usted.*

C. Translate the following sentences into Spanish; then say them aloud.

  1. I prefer to buy that camera in the other shop.

  2. We ought to buy more batteries.

  3. We can take some wonderful pictures of that park.

  4. Do you like the view with that building in the background?

  5. They want to take a picture of you.

  6. Don't forget to take off the lens cap

  7. We have to make copies for our friends.

  8. They wanted to go to that museum on Sunday.

  9. We have to buy more black-and-white film.

  10. Do you think he likes that suit?

D. From among the three choices given, choose the best equivalent of the English term (in parentheses) for each sentence, and translate.

  1. (with me) *Van a ir* _____.
     (a) *con mí*
     (b) *conmigo*
     (c) *con me*

2. (to him) *Déselo* _____.
   (a) *a ella*
   (b) *a él*
   (c) *a ello*

3. (these) *No me gustan aquellas lámparas. Déme dos de* _____.
   (a) *éstos*
   (b) *éstas*
   (c) *estos*

4. (that one) *La novela que más me gusta es* _____ *que tienes en la mano.*
   (a) *eso*
   (b) *sea*
   (c) *ésa*

5. (that one) *Esta alfombra es muy bonita pero, ¿recuerdas* _____ *que vimos ayer?*
   (a) *aquel*
   (b) *aquélla*
   (c) *ésa*

6. (one must) *Dicen que* _____ *estudiar mucho.*
   (a) *debes*
   (b) *hay que*
   (c) *uno tiene*

7. (all these) *Tenemos que llevar* _____ *papeles a casa.*
   (a) *estos todos*
   (b) *todos estos*
   (c) *todo esto*

8. (all that) *La historia es muy interesante. Pablo no me contó* _____.
   (a) *todo eso*
   (b) *todos esos*
   (c) *toda esa*

9. (many things) *Hay* _____ *leer*.
   (a) *muchas cosas*
   (b) *muchas cosas que*
   (c) *mucha cosa*

10. (the whole) *Juan no me explicó* _____ *pro-blema*.
    (a) *toda la*
    (b) *todo el*
    (c) *el todo*

Answer Key

B. 1. *Lo compras para él.*
        You buy it for him.

    2. *Los señores Andrade hacen el viaje conmigo.*
        Mr. and Mrs. Andrade are making the trip with me.

    3. *No lo veo jamás contigo.*
        I never see him with you.

    4. *Ellos me lo regalan a mí.*
        They are giving it to me.

    5. *El cuadro es para usted.*
        The picture is for you.

C. 1. *Prefiero comprar aquella máquina (cámara) en la
        otra tienda.*

    2. *Debemos comprar más pilas.*

    3. *Podemos sacar unas fotos maravillosas de aquel
        parque.*

    4. *¿Le (Te) gusta la vista con aquel edificio en el
        fondo?*

    5. *Quieren sacarle una foto (a usted or a ti).*

    6. *No se (te) olvide(s) de quitar la tapa del lente.*

    7. *Tenemos que hacer copias para nuestros amigos.*

    8. *Querían ir a aquel museo el domingo.*

    9. *Tenemos que comprar más rollos de película en
        blanco y negro.*

    10. *¿Cree(s) usted (tú) que le guste ese traje?*

D. 1. *Van a ir conmigo.*
        They are going to go with me.

2. *Déselo a él.*
Give it to him.

3. *No me gustan aquellas lámparas. Déme dos de
éstas.*
I don't like those lamps. Give me two of these.

4. *La novela que más me gusta es ésa que tienes en
la mano.*
The novel that I like best is that one that you have
in your hand.

5. *Esta alfombra es muy bonita pero, ¿recuerdas
aquélla que vimos ayer?*
This carpet is very pretty, but do you remember
that one that we saw yesterday?

6. *Dicen que hay que estudiar mucho.*
They say that one must study a great deal.

7. *Tenemos que llevar todos estos papeles a casa.*
We have to take all these papers home.

8. *La historia es muy interesante. Pablo no me contó
todo eso.*
The story is very interesting. Pablo didn't tell me
all that.

9. *Hay muchas cosas que leer.*
There are many things to read.

10. *Juan no me explicó todo el problema.*
Juan didn't explain the whole problem to me.

LESSON 12

LA AGENCIA DE VIAJES
THE TRAVEL AGENCY

A. DIALOGUE

0. *Leonardo y Carmen están de visita en España.*
   Están en una agencia de viajes para planificar
   excursiones.
   Leonardo and Carmen are visiting Spain. They are
   in a travel agency planning some sightseeing tours.

En la agencia. In the agency.

1. Empleada: **Buenos días. ¿En qué puedo servirles?**
   Good morning. How can I help you?

2. Leonardo: **Nos gustaría viajar un poco por**
   España, especialmente por los alrededores de
   Madrid. ¿Puede usted sugerirnos algunos itine-
   rarios?
   We would like to travel a little through Spain, especially the area around Madrid. Could you suggest
   some itineraries?

3. Empleada: **Desde luego. Tenemos muchos viajes**
   de un día a sitios de interés cerca de Madrid: a
   Toledo, al Escorial, al Valle de los Caídos, a
   Segovia y muchos otros lugares de gran interés
   turístico. Los viajes son en autobús de lujo, con
   guía, a un precio fijo, con todos los gastos inclui-
   dos.
   Of course. We have many one-day trips to places of
   interest near Madrid: to Toledo, to the Escorial, to
   the Valley of the Fallen, to Segovia and many other

places of great interest to tourists. The trips are by luxury bus, with a guide, at a set price with all costs included.

4. Leonardo: **Queremos ver tantas cosas. ¿Qué piensa usted de la idea de alquilar un coche? Queremos crear un buen itinerario.**
We want to see so many things. What do you think of the idea of renting a car? We want to come up with a good itinerary.

5. Empleada: **El coche les permite mucha más libertad de movimiento. Este folleto les da detalles sobre gastos y servicios.**
A car gives you much greater freedom of movement. This pamphlet gives you details on costs and services.

6. Leonardo: **¿A qué hora salen los autobuses para Toledo?**
What time do the buses leave for Toledo?

7. Empleada: **Hay varias salidas todos los días. A las ocho, a las diez y a la una.**
There are several departures every day. At eight, at ten, and at one o'clock.

8. Carmen: **Leonardo, ¿qué te parece la idea de ir mañana a Toledo? Tengo tantas ganas de verlo. Ya que hemos visto algunas obras de El Greco, quiero ver dónde vivía y trabajaba.**
Leonardo, what do you think of the idea of going to Toledo tomorrow? I really want to see it. Now that we've seen some of the works of El Greco, I want to see where he lived and worked.

9. Empleada: **Yo podría arreglarlo todo ahora, si quieren. Podría reservarles asientos en el autobús**

de las ocho. Claro que la comida en Toledo va incluida en el precio.

I could arrange it all now, if you want. I could reserve seats for you on the eight o'clock bus. Of course, your meal in Toledo is included in the price.

10. Leonardo: **Bien. Eso es lo que haremos mañana. Ahora nos interesan también algunos informes sobre el sur de España. Queremos ir a Sevilla, a Córdoba y a Jerez de la Frontera, y tal vez podríamos hacer una breve visita a Gibraltar.**

    Fine. That's what we'll do tomorrow. Now we're also interested in some information on the south of Spain. We want to go to Seville, Córdoba, Jerez de la Frontera, and perhaps we could make a brief visit to Gibraltar.

11. Empleada: **Todo eso es muy fácil de arreglar. Si quieren, les doy varios folletos, mapas, horarios de tren y de autobuses, y algunas sugerencias sobre posibles itinerarios.**

    All of that is very easy to arrange. If you wish, I can give you several pamphlets, maps, train and bus schedules, and some suggestions on possible itineraries.

12. Leonardo: **Perfecto. Así podremos pensarlo un poco esta noche y darle nuestra decisión mañana.**

    Perfect. That way we can think about it a little tonight and give you our decision tomorrow.

13. Empleada: **Muy bien. Ahora les preparo una lista de todo lo que necesitan. Permítanme que los recomiende el alquiler de un coche para visitar los sitios cerca de Madrid antes de hacer el viaje por el sur.**

    Very well. I'll prepare a list now of everything you need. Allow me to recommend renting a car to visit the places near Madrid before you make the trip through the south.

14. Leonardo: **Me parece muy buena idea. Mañana podremos arreglarlo todo. ¿A qué hora dijo usted que sale el autobús para Toledo?**
That sounds like a very good idea to me. Tomorrow we can arrange everything. What time did you say the bus leaves for Toledo?

15. Empleada: **A las ocho en punto, señores. La agencia estará abierta a las siete y media.**
At eight o'clock sharp. The agency will be open at seven-thirty.

16. Leonardo: **Bien. Así vendremos un poco antes de la hora de salida.**
Good. So we'll come a little before the departure time.

Al día siguiente. The following day.

17. Empleada: **Muy buenos días, señores. ¿Qué han decidido?**
Good morning. What have you decided?

18. Leonardo: **Pensamos ir a Segovia mañana y queremos ir en tren. Nos han dicho que es un viaje muy agradable. Así podemos ver el acueducto y el Alcázar.**
We plan to go to Segovia tomorrow and we want to go by train. We have heard it is a very pleasant trip. That way we can see the aqueduct and the Alcázar.

19. Empleada: **Muy bien. Yo les prepararé los billetes y los tendrán aquí al volver de Toledo esta tarde. Les recomiendo que coman en el Mesón de Cándido, el segoviano. Es famoso por el "tostón", el**

cochinillo asado; además, tendrán a la vista el acueducto mientras estén comiendo. ¿Quieren que llame para reservar una mesa? Siempre está lleno.

Very well. I'll prepare the tickets for you and you will have them here upon returning from Toledo this afternoon. And I recommend that you eat at the Mesón de Cándido, el Segoviano. It's famous for its "tostón," roast suckling pig, and you will have a view of the aqueduct while you're eating. Do you want me to call and reserve a table for you? It's always full.

20. Carmen: **Sí, por favor. Vamos a pasar un día espléndido en Toledo. Tendremos que hablar de hoteles y otros detalles del viaje por el sur, también.**

    Yes, please. We're going to have a wonderful day in Toledo. We'll have to talk about hotels and other details of our trip through the south, too.

21. Empleada: **Desde luego. ¿Han decidido si quieren ir en tren, en autobús o en coche?**

    Of course. Have you decided whether you want to go by train, by bus, or by car?

22. Leonardo: **Por el momento habíamos pensado hacer el viaje de Madrid a Sevilla en tren, y luego ir en autobús de allí a Córdoba y a Jerez de la Frontera.**

    For the moment we had thought about making the trip from Madrid to Seville by train, and then going by bus from there to Córdoba and Jerez de la Frontera.

23. Empleada: **Está bien. ¿Y luego?**

    That's fine. And then?

24. Leonardo: **Queríamos saber si podemos alquilar un coche en Cádiz para seguir el viaje por la costa a Málaga y luego, en Motril, tomar la carretera que va a Granada.**
    We wanted to know if we could rent a car in Cádiz in order to continue the trip along the coast to Málaga and then, in Motril, take the highway that goes to Granada.

25. Empleada: **Sí, nuestra sucursal en Cádiz puede ayudarles. Pero necesitan fijar las fechas en cada sitio para la reserva de habitaciones. Me imagino que también querrán pasar unos días en Marbella y Torremolinos, ¿no?**
    Yes, our branch in Cádiz can help you. But you have to fix the dates in each place for room reservations. I imagine that you'll want to spend a few days in Marbella and Torremolinos too, won't you?

26. Leonardo: **¡Claro que sí! Esa parte de la costa es muy bonita. Nos gustaría reservar habitaciones que dan a la playa en esos pueblos de la costa.**
    By all means! That part of the coast is very pretty. We would like to reserve rooms that look out on the beach in those coastal towns.

27. Empleada: **Podemos arreglarlo todo a su gusto. Cuando regresen podemos aclarar el resto de los detalles. Espero que tengan un buen viaje.**
    We can arrange it all to your liking. Upon your return we can discuss the rest of the details. I hope it will be a good trip.

B. NOTES

2. *los alrededores de Madrid*: the area around Madrid. *Alrededores* literally means "environs" or "surroundings." It can also mean "outskirts."

3. *El Escorial*: Most visitors to Madrid take a day trip
to see the magnificent palace of El Escorial, 41 km
(approximately 25 miles) from the capital of Spain.
When King Felipe II ordered the construction of
this palace he had several purposes in mind. It was
to serve as a royal palace, a monastery, and the
final resting place of Spain's royals. It was built
between 1563 and 1584 by Spanish architect Juan
de Herrera.

   Valle de los Caídos: The Valley of the Fallen. This
controversial monument was built by former Spanish dictator Francisco Franco. His official intention
was to honor those who died in the Spanish Civil
War, but many see it as a monument that he built for
himself as his resting place. In fact the only two
names commemorated are his and that of the
founder of the Falange Party. The grandiose monument built on top of a hill on the Guadarrama Mountains is topped by a huge 500-foot cross that weighs
more than 200,000 tons. It was built by many pris-
oners of the Civil War.

   Segovia: Capital of the province of Segovia, the
city is known for its still-functioning Roman aqueduct and for the Alcázar de Segovia, one of Spain's
most beautiful castles.

   de gran interés turístico: of great interest to
tourists. Notice the use of the adjective *turístico*
where the accusative is used in the English sentence.
Also notice the shortened form *gran* used before the
noun, which we'll discuss in this lesson.

10. *Sevilla*: Sevilla is the most important city in southern
Spain's Andalucía. Its key monuments are the
Giralda Tower, the Alcázar de Sevilla, and the cathe-
dral. Sevilla also hosts one of the most interesting
Holy Week festivals in the world, where hooded pen-
itents carry huge floats from one church to another.

Another popular festival is La Feria de Abril, a week-long celebration of drink, dance, and music.

Córdoba: Another beautiful city in Andalucía. The impact of the Moorish culture in southern Spain could not be more evident than it is in Córdoba. For years it was the seat of an Arabic caliphate. The beautiful *Mezquita* (mosque) is a great example of this Moorish influence.

Jerez de la Frontera: The name of this Andalusian town means "sherry from the frontier." This town lies in the center of Spain's sherry and brandy region. It is also known for its good flamenco.

13. *el alquiler de un coche*: car rental. Compare with the verb form in line 4: *alquilar un coche* (to rent a car).

19. *cochinillo asado*: roast suckling pig.

24. *Cádiz*: Columbus set sail from this important seaport on the southern coast of Spain. It is considered one of the country's oldest settlements and was built by the Phoenicians.

Málaga: Málaga is north of Cádiz along Spain's Mediterranean coast. It is a beautiful port city.

Motril: Motril is a small coastal town not far from Granada. From its beautiful beaches you can see the snow-capped mountain range of Sierra Nevada.

Granada: In Granada you will find the Alhambra, a Moorish palace surrounded by gardens and fountains. Many consider the Alhambra to be Spain's most beautiful tourist attraction.

25. *sucursal*: branch.

Marbella: This town on Spain's *Costa del Sol* (sunny coast) attracts international residents and tourists year-round. It is where many jet-setters and "beautiful people" spend their summers.

Torremolinos: This resort town south of Málaga has grown from a small fishing village into an international tourist center. You will find popular crowded beaches, pubs, and many shopping arcades in Torremolinos. The massive development of the town in recent years has been spectacular for some but detrimental according to others.

26. *habitaciones que dan a la playa*: rooms that look out on the beach.

27. *buen viaje*: good trip. This can be used on its own to say "Have a nice trip!": *¡Buen viaje!*

C. GRAMMAR AND USAGE

1. Certain adjectives have a shortened form when they appear before a masculine singular noun: *buen, mal, primer, tercer, ningún, algún.*

Hace muy buen tiempo.
    The weather is nice.

Hace mal tiempo.
    The weather is bad.

Es el primer libro.
    It's the first book.

Es el tercer capítulo.
    It's the third chapter.

Ningún libro lo dice.
    No book says it.

Algún amigo me lo ha dicho.
    Some friend told it to me.

In other positions these adjectives agree in the regular way.

Es un buen hombre.
He's a good man.

Es un hombre muy bueno.
He's a very good man.

Es un mal hombre.
He's a bad man.

Es un hombre muy malo.
He's a very bad man.

Es un buen director.
He's a good director.

Es un director muy bueno.
He's a very good director.

Las buenas novelas son pocas.
The good novels are very few. (There are few good novels.)

La primera novela que leí fue muy mala.
The first novel I read was very bad.

2. The shortened forms *gran* and *cualquier* are used when these adjectives come before either a masculine or a feminine singular noun.

Se me ha ocurrido una gran idea.
I've had a great idea.

Es un gran hombre.
He's a great man.

Cualquier libro es bueno.
Any book is good.

En cualquier tienda se encuentra eso.
You find that in any store.

Note:

- *Gran* before the noun usually has the figurative meaning of "great." After the noun, it has its literal meaning of "large" or "big."

Compare:

Es un gran hombre.
   He's a great man.

Es un hombre grande.
   He's a big/large man.

- *Cualquier* (used before either masculine or feminine singular nouns) has the singular form *cualquiera* and the plural form *cualesquiera* when used elsewhere.

No es un hombre cualquiera.
   He's not just any man.

No son mujeres cualesquiera.
   They are not just any women.

No son películas cualesquiera.
   They're not just any movies.

3. The subjunctive mood follows verbs of emotion when there is a change of subject in the sentence.

Espero que ustedes hayan tenido buen viaje.
   I hope you have had a good trip.

Temo que se haya equivocado.
   I'm afraid you've made a mistake.

Me alegro de que te guste la habitación.
   I'm happy that you like the room.

4. You must also use the subjunctive after verbs of volition.

Quieren que lo hagamos ahora.
   They want us to do it now.

Juan prefiere que no lo leamos.
Juan prefers that we not read it.

Él recomienda que vayamos hoy al museo.
He recommends that we go to the museum today.

EXERCISES

A. Substitute each of the words or expressions in parentheses for the underlined word or expression in the model sentence. Write each new sentence and say it aloud.

1. *Es un buen libro.* (cuadro, hotel, hombre, parque, restaurante)

2. *No me ha dado ningún regalo.* (número, problema, horario, periódico, billete)

3. *Me dijeron que es un(a) gran hombre.* (poeta, idea, escritor, amigo, novela)

4. *Espero que ellos estudien.* (escriban, vengan, salgan, coman, lleguen)

5. *Se alegran de que hayamos comido bien.* (dormido, llegado, estudiado, oído, estado)

6. *Los señores Fernández quieren que estudiemos.* (descansemos, comamos, bebamos, nos vayamos, entremos)

B. Change the sentences to the plural. Write each complete sentence and translate.

1. *Él no quiere ningún coche.*

2. *Ella no ha comprado ningún regalo.*

3. *Espero que Juan llegue a tiempo.*

4. *Ella quiere que Teresa estudie esta noche.*

5. *Yo prefiero que usted se vaya.*

C. Translate the following sentences into Spanish, then say them aloud.

   1. They want us to see the movie.

   2. We hope you have a good trip.

   3. Juan wants you to buy color film.

   4. There isn't any money in this jacket.

   5. It is said that it's a great hotel.

   6. He was a great poet.

   7. Don't give me just any book.

   8. Do you want them to do it?

   9. He was a great friend.

  10. I'm afraid you can't go now.

D. From among the three choices given, choose the best equivalent of the English term (in parentheses) for each sentence, and translate.

   1. (nice) *Me alegro de que haga tan _____ tiempo.*
     (a) *bueno*
     (b) *buen*
     (c) *buena*

   2. (the first) *¿Ha terminado usted _____ capítulo?*
     (a) *la primera*
     (b) *el primer*
     (c) *los primeros*

   3. (some) *Espero que nos veamos _____ día.*
     (a) *algún*
     (b) *alguna*
     (c) *algo*

4. (any) *Juan no tiene* _____ *dinero.*
   - (a) *nada de*
   - (b) *ninguna*
   - (c) *ningún*

5. (good) *Es un hombre muy* _____.
   - (a) *bueno*
   - (b) *buen*
   - (c) *buenamente*

6. (any) *No me compres un regalo* _____.
   - (a) *cualquier*
   - (b) *cualquiera*
   - (c) *cualesquiera*

7. (great) *Es una* _____ *idea.*
   - (a) *grande*
   - (b) *gran*
   - (c) *grandes*

8. (like) *Espero que te* _____ *las habitaciones.*
   - (a) *gustan*
   - (b) *gusten*
   - (c) *guste*

9. (do) *Prefieren que nosotros lo* _____ *ahora.*
   - (a) *hacemos*
   - (b) *hagamos*
   - (c) *hacen*

10. (us to go) *Juan quiere* _____.
   - (a) *que vayamos*
   - (b) *que vamos*
   - (c) *para nosotros ir*

Answer Key

B. 1. *Ellos no quieren ningún coche.*
       They don't want any car.

    2. *Ellas no han comprado ningún regalo.*
       They didn't buy any gift.

    3. *Esperamos que Juan llegue a tiempo.*
       We hope that Juan arrives on time.

    4. *Ellas quieren que Teresa estudie esta noche.*
       They want Teresa to study tonight.

    5. *Preferimos que usted se vaya.*
       We prefer that you leave/go away.

C. 1. *Quieren que veamos la película.*

    2. *Deseamos/Esperamos que tengan un buen viaje.*

    3. *Juan quiere que usted (tú) compre(s) una película
       de fotos a color.*

    4. *No hay dinero en esta chaqueta.*

    5. *Se dice que es un gran hotel.*

    6. *(Él) Era un gran poeta.*

    7. *No me dé (des) (usted/tú) un libro cualquiera.*

    8. *¿Quiere(s) (usted/tú) que ellos lo hagan?*

    9. *(Él) Era un gran amigo.*

    10. *Temo que no pueda(s) irse (irte) ahora.*

D. 1. *Me alegro de que haga tan buen tiempo.*
       I am glad that the weather is so nice.

    2. *¿Ha terminado usted el primer capítulo?*
       Have you finished the first chapter?

3. *Espero que nos veamos algún día.*
   I hope that we see each other some day.

4. *Juan no tiene nada de dinero.*
   Juan doesn't have any money.

5. *Es un hombre muy bueno.*
   He's a very good man.

6. *No me compres un regalo cualquiera.*
   Don't buy me just any gift.

7. *Es una gran idea.*
   It's a great idea.

8. *Espero que te gusten las habitaciones.*
   I hope that you like the rooms.

9. *Prefieren que nosotros lo hagamos ahora.*
   They prefer that we do it now.

10. *Juan quiere que vayamos.*
    Juan wants us to go.

LESSON 13

ALQUILAR UN COCHE
RENTING A CAR

A. DIALOGUE

0. *Roberto Cánovas y Javier Martínez son ejecutivos en viaje de negocios en Santiago de Chile. En el aeropuerto deciden alquilar un coche.*
   Roberto Canovas and Javier Martinez are executives on a business trip in Santiago, Chile. While at the airport, they decide to rent a car.

1. Empleada: **Buenos días, señores. ¿En qué puedo ayudarles?**
   Good morning. How can I help you?

2. Roberto: **Estábamos pensando en alquilar un coche. ¿Quiere usted decirme los precios y gastos? Me imagino que varían bastante, ¿verdad?**
   We were thinking of renting a car. Would you explain the prices and costs? I imagine that they vary a good deal, right?

3. Empleada: **Así es, señor. Depende del modelo que escojan. ¿Es para ustedes dos?**
   That's right, sir. It depends on the model that you choose. Is it for the two of you?

4. Javier: **Sí, pero tenemos bastante equipaje también. Hemos traído mucho material de promoción.**
   Yes, but we have quite a lot of baggage, too. We brought a lot of promotional material.

5. Empleada: **Me parece que el Renault Clio sería ideal para ustedes. Hay sitio para cuatro, para que estén cómodos, y tiene cuatro puertas.**
I think the Renault Clio would be ideal for you. There's room for four so that you'd be comfortable, and it has four doors.

6. Javier: **¿Se puede incluir un portaequipajes sin cargo adicional?**
Can you include a luggage rack for no extra charge?

7. Empleada: **No, señor, pero no cuestan mucho. Y en cuanto al alquiler, se necesita un depósito a menos que usen tarjeta de crédito.**
No, sir, but they don't cost much. And, as for the rates, a deposit is needed unless you use a credit card.

8. Roberto: **¿Qué se incluye en el precio?**
What's included in the price?

9. Empleada: **Está incluido el seguro y todos los impuestos.**
It includes insurance and all taxes.

10. Javier: **¿Están incluidos la gasolina y el kilometraje?**
Are gas and mileage included?

11. Empleada: **No hay límite en el kilometraje, señor. En cuanto a la gasolina, le pedimos que nos devuelva el tanque lleno; si no, se le cobrará cuatrocientos pesos chilenos por litro.**
There's no limit on mileage, sir. As for gas, we ask that you please return the tank full; otherwise we will charge you four hundred Chilean pesos per liter.

12. Roberto: **¿Y cuántos litros necesita este coche por cada cien kilómetros?**

And how many liters does this car need per hundred kilometers?

13. Empleada: **Sólo siete, señor. Como ve, este coche es económico.**
Only seven, sir. As you see, this car is economical.

14. Roberto: **¿Pagamos al devolver el coche?**
Do we pay when we return the car?

15. Empleada: **Sí, señor. Se paga cuando se devuelva el coche; también nos quedamos con una impresión de su tarjeta.**
Yes, sir. You pay when you return the car; we will also keep an imprint of your credit card.

16. Javier: **¿Cobran ustedes por entregar y recoger el coche?**
Do you charge to deliver and pick up the car?

17. Empleada: **Sí, señor; si es aquí en Santiago, se lo podemos entregar en el hotel y mandar a alguien a buscarlo si ustedes nos llaman al volver.**
Yes, sir; if it is here in Santiago we can deliver it to your hotel and send someone to pick it up if you call us when you return.

18. Roberto: **Pero, ¿qué pasa si decidimos dejarlo en otro sitio, por ejemplo en Valparaíso?**
But what happens if we decide to leave it somewhere else, for example in Valparaiso?

19. Empleada: **Si deciden dejarlo en una ciudad donde tengamos sucursal, lo pueden entregar en la sucursal sin pagar extra. En cambio, si quieren dejarlo en algún sitio donde no hay sucursal, tendrán que pagar los gastos para ir a recogerlo.**
If you decide to leave it in a city where we have a branch, you can deliver it to the branch office with-

out paying anything extra. On the other hand, if you want to leave it in someplace where there is no branch office, you will have to pay the expenses of going to pick it up.

20. Javier: **¿Qué documentos necesitamos?**
What documents do we need?

21. Empleada: **Necesitan el carnet de conducir, los pasaportes y la tarjeta de crédito. Nosotros les daremos todos los documentos del coche.**
You need a driver's license, your passports, and the credit card. We will give you all the documents for the car.

Más tarde. . . Later . . .

22. Roberto: **Pienso que nos ha dado un precio estupendo. ¿Qué piensas?**
I think she has given us a great price. What do you think?

23. Javier: **Estoy de acuerdo, nos ha salido bien la jugada.**
I agree, we got a good deal.

24. Roberto: **Pues, me alegro mucho por mi informe de gastos.**
Well, I am happy for my expense report.

25. Javier: **¡Yo sé que el jefe se sentirá todavía más contento!**
I know the boss will be even happier!

B. NOTES

0. *ejecutivos*: executives, businessmen. The adjective *ejecutivo(a)* means "urgent."
   viaje de negocios: business trip.

Santiago: Santiago is the capital of Chile, one of South America's leading economic powers. Located between the Andes and the Coastal Mountain Range, surrounded by the San Cristóbal and Santa Lucía hills, Santiago is home to 5 million people. The city was founded by Pedro de Vadivia in 1541 along the Río Mapocho, which crosses the city east to west. Santiago has a privileged location: less than an hour away on each side are world-class ski resorts and beautiful beaches.

2. *varían bastante*: vary a great deal. *Bastante*: enough, fairly, rather.

4. *material de promoción*: promotional material.

5. *Renault Clio*: The Clio is a very popular car in South America and Europe. Cars in South America tend to be more compact than in the United States.

6. *Se puede incluir*: Can you include. Notice the use of the impersonal *se puede*. This is preferable when asking general questions such as these.

10. *kilometraje*: Distance in South America is measured in kilometers. A kilometer is about five-eights of a mile.

11. *litro*: liter, liquid measure. A little over a quart. The metric system is used throughout South America.

16. *entregar/recoger*: to deliver/to pick up. Make sure not to attach the object to *entregar*; *entregarla* means "to die."

18. Note the punctuation in this sentence: the "¿" comes after *pero*.

Valparaíso: Valparaíso is Chile's second-largest city and most important port. Located only 112 km

northwest of Santiago, the city lies on a large bay
facing the Pacific Ocean. The city of Valparaíso was
built on a narrow strip of land perched on the edge
of steep drops and hills.

23. *salir bien la jugada*: literally "the move/trick came
out well," *salir bien* means "to turn out well";
jugada means "move," "throw," or "trick."

24. *informe de gastos*: expense report.

C. GRAMMAR AND USAGE

1. The expression *en cuanto a* means "as for" or "as far as
_____ is concerned."

En cuanto al alquiler, eso se puede arreglar mañana.
As far as the rental is concerned, it can be arranged
tomorrow.

En cuanto a la gasolina, no gasta mucho.
As for the gasoline, it doesn't use much.

En cuanto a los precios, son económicos.
As for the prices, they are affordable.

2. When the word *cuando* is used to mean "whenever," it
should be followed by the subjunctive form of the verb.

Cuando lleguen, vamos a decírselo.
When they arrive, we're going to tell them (it).

Usted puede marcharse cuando quiera.
You can go whenever you want.

Lo haremos cuando venga el cartero.
We'll do it when the mail carrier comes.

3. *Por* means "per" and is used to indicate the rate of something.

¿Cuánto cobra usted por sus cuadros?
How much do you charge for your paintings?

¿Cuántos kilómetros hace por hora?
How many kilometers per hour does it go?

El veinte por ciento de los problemas es imposible.
Twenty percent of the problems are impossible.

4. The expression *para que* followed by a subjunctive means "in order that" or "so that."

Se lo compro para que se ponga contenta.
I'll buy it for her so that she'll be happy.

Se lo digo para que lo sepa.
I'm telling you so (that) you'll know.

Hay que ayudarles para que terminen pronto.
One must help them so (that) they'll finish soon.

EXERCISES

A. Substitute each of the words or expressions in parentheses for the underlined word or expression in the model sentence. Write each new sentence and say it aloud.

1. *En cuanto al <u>alquiler</u>, podemos arreglarlo.* (precio, problema, viaje, hotel, coche)

2. *Lo podemos hacer cuando vengan <u>los invitados</u>.* (los señores Andrade, los estudiantes, nuestros amigos, María y José)

3. *No sé cuánto cobran por <u>hora</u>.* (día, semana, mes, clase, cada viajero)

4. *Voy a dárselo para que lo <u>tengan</u>.* (estudien, lean, aprendan, envíen, envuelvan)

5. *Hablaremos de eso cuando usted lo haya <u>terminado</u>.* (visto, leído, mandado, comprado, arreglado)

6. *En cuanto a Juan, puede pagar cuando quiera.* (tu amigo, María, su peluquero, nuestro profesor, la empleada)

B. Change these sentences to the present tense. Write the complete sentence and translate.

1. *Se lo pediremos cuando lleguen.*

2. *Me cobraron trescientos pesos por hora.*

3. *Ellos me lo darán para que lo estudie.*

4. *No habrá fiesta mañana.*

5. *Juan lo compró para dármelo.*

C. Translate the following sentences into Spanish, then say them aloud.

1. I recommend that you go pick up the car at the factory.

2. As for the money, I'll give it to him when he comes.

3. When they arrive, Juan will tell them.

4. María may leave whenever she wishes.

5. They'll include a luggage rack.

6. How much does the gasoline cost per liter?

7. Take as many pamphlets as you want.

8. When you have chosen the model you want, go to the factory.

9. There are no taxes on factory prices, are there?

10. Do you want to meet a great friend of mine?

D. From among the three choices given, choose the best equivalent of the English term (in parentheses) for each sentence, and translate.

1. (As for) _____ *la gasolina, hay suficiente.*
   (a) *Como por*
   (b) *Cuanto*
   (c) *En cuanto a*

2. (they arrive) *Cuando* _____, *vamos a darles el regalo.*
   (a) *llegan*
   (b) *lleguen*
   (c) *llegaron*

3. (whenever you want) *Usted puede hacerlo* _____.
   (a) *cuando quieres*
   (b) *cuando quiera*
   (c) *como quiere*

4. (per hour) *Hace ciento viente kilómetros* _____.
   (a) *por hora*
   (b) *por la hora*
   (c) *para hora*

5. (he'll know) *Voy a decirle el número a Juan, para que lo* _____.
   (a) *sabe*
   (b) *sepa*
   (c) *sabrá*

6. (tell it to them) *Hay que* _____ *para que vengan pronto.*
   (a) *decírleslo*
   (b) *les lo decir*
   (c) *decírselo*

7. (so that) *Escríbale los detalles* _____ *lo comprenda bien.*
   (a) *para que*
   (b) *para*
   (c) *porque*

8. (study) *Hay que anunciarles el examen para que*

   _____.

   (a) *estudian*
   (b) *estudien*
   (c) *estudiaron*

9. (read) *Dásela a María para que la* _____.
   (a) *lee*
   (b) *lea*
   (c) *leerá*

10. (whenever they are) *Yo siempre los trato bien*
    _____ *aquí.*
    (a) *cuandoquiera sean*
    (b) *cuando están*
    (c) *cuando sean*

Answer Key

B. 1. *Se lo pedimos cuando lleguen.*
We are going to ask them for it when they arrive.

2. *Me cobran trescientos pesos por hora.*
They are charging me 300 pesos per hour.

3. *Ellos me lo dan para que lo estudie.*
They are giving it to me so that I will study it.

4. *No hay fiesta mañana.*
There is no party/holiday tomorrow.

5. *Juan lo compra para dármelo.*
John is buying it to give it to me.

C. 1. *Le (Te) recomiendo que vaya(s) a buscar el coche a la fábrica.*

2. *En cuanto al dinero, se lo daré (a él) cuando venga.*

3. *Cuando lleguen, Juan se lo dirá.*

4. *María puede marcharse cuando quiera.*

5. *Incluirán un portaequipajes.*

6. *¿Cuánto cuesta la gasolina por litro?*

7. *Llévese (Llévate) todos los folletos que quiera(s).*

8. *Cuando haya(s) escogido el modelo que quiera (quieras), vaya (ve) a la fábrica.*

9. *No hay impuestos sobre los precios de fábrica, ¿verdad?*

10. *¿Quiere(s) usted (tú) conocer a un gran amigo mío?*

D. 1. *En cuanto a la gasolina, hay suficiente.*
As for the gasoline, there is enough.

2. *Cuando lleguen, vamos a darles el regalo.*
When they arrive, we are going to give them the gift.

3. *Usted puede hacerlo cuando quiera.*
You can do it whenever you want.

4. *Hace ciento veinte kilómetros por hora.*
It does 120 kilometers per hour.

5. *Voy a decirle el número a Juan, para que lo sepa.*
I am going to tell the number to Juan so that he'll know it.

6. *Hay que decírselo para que vengan pronto.*
One must tell it to them so that they will come at once.

7. *Escríbale los detalles para que lo comprenda bien.*
Write him the details so that he will understand it well.

8. *Hay que anunciarles el examen para que estudien.*
One must announce the examination to them so they will study.

9. *Dásela a María para que la lea.*
Give it to María so she will read it.

10. *Yo siempre los trato bien cuando están aquí.*
I always treat them well whenever they are here.

LESSON 14

EN LA ESTACIÓN DE SERVICIO
AT THE SERVICE STATION

A. DIALOGUE

0. *César vive en San José, Costa Rica. Está planificando un viaje por la costa durante el fin de semana. Pero de repente, se da cuenta de que tiene un problema. . .*
   César lives in San José, Costa Rica. He is planning to go on a weekend trip along the coast. But suddenly he realizes he has a problem . . .

1. Empleado: **¿En qué le puedo servir, señor?**
   What can I do for you, sir?

2. César: **No sé exactamente. Hay algo que no funciona bien. Al encender el coche oigo unos ruidos bastante raros en el motor. Me tienen preocupado. ¡Este coche es de mi amigo!**
   I don't know exactly. There's something that's not working well. When I turn the ignition I hear some pretty strange noises in the engine. It has me worried. This is my friend's car!

3. Empleado: **¿No será que el tanque está vacío? ¿Lo ha mirado usted?**
   Could it be that the tank is empty? Did you check it?

4. César: **Creo que el tanque todavía está por la mitad.**
   I think the tank is still half full.

5. Empleado: **¿Se lo lleno de todas maneras?**
   Should I fill it up anyway?

6. César: **Sí, llénelo, por favor. Y hágame el favor de llenar este bote también, por si acaso. Voy a hacer un viaje bastante largo.**
Yes, fill it up, please. And please fill this can too, just in case. I'm going to take a rather long trip.

7. Empleado: **Es buena idea. A veces no se encuentran gasolineras.**
That's a good idea. Sometimes you don't find gas stations.

8. César: **¿Puede revisar las llantas? A ver si necesitan aire.**
Will you check the tires? To see if they need air.

9. Empleado: **Con mucho gusto. Pero, ¿qué es eso? Parece que ésta de adelante tiene un pinchazo.**
With pleasure. But what's that? It looks as if this front tire has a puncture.

10. César: **¿Qué dice? No puede ser.**
What are you saying? It can't be.

11. Empleado: **Habrá sido un clavo o algo parecido. ¿No ha notado usted nada? ¿Ningún movimiento?**
It must have been a nail, or something similar. Didn't you notice anything? No movement?

12. César: **Hace un momento, en la carretera, parecía patinar un poco.**
A little while ago, on the highway, it seemed to skid a little.

13. Empleado: **Fue eso entonces. Voy a cambiársela.**
That was it, then. I'm going to change it for you.

14. César: **Hay una llanta de repuesto allí atrás.**
There's a spare tire back there.

15. Empleado: **Bien. Cambiaré la pinchada y luego la voy a reparar.**
Good. I'll change the flat tire and then I'm going to repair it.

16. César: **Estupendo.**
Terrific.

17. Empleado: **Como hace un viaje tan largo, hay que ver si las bujías y la batería están en buenas condiciones.**
Since you're taking such a long trip, we have to see if the spark plugs and the battery are in good shape.

18. César: **Por favor. Y échele un poco de agua al radiador. Hace poco se estaba calentando el motor.**
Please. And put a little water in the radiator. The engine was heating up a little while ago.

19. Empleado: **Muy bien, señor. ¿Quiere usted que lo engrase, o que le cambie el aceite?**
Very well, sir. Do you want me to do a lube job or change the oil?

20. César: **No, gracias.**
No, thank you.

21. Empleado: **Veo algunas cosas que necesitan atención.**
I see some things that need attention.

22. César: **¡Mi amigo no me dijo que tiene un cacharro!**
My friend didn't tell me he has a piece of junk!

23. Empleado: **De ningún modo, señor. Estos problemas ocurren siempre. Más vale repararlos en seguida.**

Not at all, sir. These problems always happen. It's better to take care of them right away.

24. César: **Tiene razón. ¿Tendré que dejarlo en el garaje?**
    You're right. Will I have to leave it in the garage?

25. Empleado: **Por lo menos tres horas si quiere que lo deje en buenas condiciones.**
    At least three hours if you want me to leave it in good shape.

26. César: **Pero necesito el coche sin falta hoy mismo. Salgo para la costa mañana por la mañana.**
    But I definitely need the car today. I leave for the coast tomorrow morning.

27. Empleado: **No se preocupe. Estoy seguro de que no hay que pedir piezas nuevas.**
    Don't worry. I'm sure it won't be necessary to order any new parts.

28. César: **Haga solamente lo necesario.**
    Do only what's necessary.

29. Empleado: **Bien. Si usted quiere volver a las cinco, todo estará listo.**
    All right. If you want to come back at five o'clock, everything will be ready.

30. César: **De acuerdo. Hasta las cinco, entonces.**
    OK. Until five o'clock, then.

B. NOTES

2. *encender el coche*: literally, "to ignite/turn on the car."

   Me tienen preocupado: It has me worried.

3. *tanque*: tank. The same word is used for the military vehicle.

6. *bote*: Here used as "can" or "container," this word is more commonly used for "boat." The word for "can" in Latin America is *lata*.

7. *gasolinera*: gas station. In other Latin American countries the term for "gas station" is *estación de gasolina*.

8. *llantas*: tires. Another word for "tire" is *neumático*.

12. *patinar*: literally, "to skate," but it is often used to describe a motion such as skidding or slipping.

15. *la pinchada*: the flat tire. Literally, "the punctured one." Another word for "flat tire" is *desinflado*.

17. *bujías*: spark plugs. *Las bujías* can also mean "candles."

22. *cacharro*: literally, "an earthenware pot." Often used as a synonym for a worthless object.

23. *en seguida*: right away.

26. *sin falta*: definitely. Literally, *sin falta* means "without fail."

C. GRAMMAR AND USAGE

1. The words *unos* and *unas* mean "some" or "a few."

Oigo unos ruidos muy raros.
   I hear some very strange noises.

Hay unas tiendas muy buenas en esta calle.
   There are some very good stores on this street.

2. The word *algún* also means "some." Notice that its plural form is *algunos*, and its feminine forms are *alguna* (singular) and *algunas* (plural). *Algún* has a more concrete, numeric meaning than *unos*.

Algún día vamos a visitarlo.
   Someday we're going to visit him.

Algunos amigos vinieron ayer.
   Some friends came yesterday.

Algunas personas no lo creen.
   Some people don't believe it.

Se lo ha dicho alguna chica.
   Some girl told him that.

Alguna señora lo ha dejado aquí.
   Some woman left it here.

3. Look at the use of *ninguno* in these negative sentences. Notice its ending changes depending on the gender of the noun that follows it:

No diría eso ningún amigo. Ningún amigo diría eso.
   No friend would say that.

No quedaba ninguna mesa libre en el restaurante.
   There wasn't a free table in the restaurant.

No tengo ningún prejuicio.
   I don't have any prejudice.

Ninguno is also used as a pronoun in response to questions.

¿Tiene usted alguna novela interesante?
   Do you have an interesting novel?

No, no tengo ninguna.
   No, I don't have any.

¿Ha visto usted una parada de autobús por aquí?
> Have you seen a bus stop along here?

No, no he visto ninguna.
> No, I haven't seen any.

4. The expression *unos cuantos* is used to refer to an indefinite small amount or "a few, some."

¿Le gustan a usted estos dulces?
> Do you like these candies?

Sí, deme unos cuantos por favor.
> Yes, give me some, please.

¿Te quedan algunos pesos?
> Do you have any pesos left?

Sí, aún me quedan unos cuantos.
> Yes, I still have some left.

5. The word *lo* followed by an adjective denotes an abstract noun.

Lo difícil es hacerlo bien.
> The difficult thing (part) is to do it well.

Lo malo del caso es que no se comprenden.
> The bad part of the matter is that they don't understand each other.

Lo bueno es que vienen todos.
> The good thing is that they're all coming.

Lo extraño es que el coche no funciona.
> The strange thing is that the car doesn't work.

Notice that the adjectives may be in the superlative form.

lo más difícil	the most difficult thing
lo mejor	the best thing (part)
lo más extraño	the strangest thing

EXERCISES

A. Substitute the words or expressions in parentheses for the underlined word or expression in the model sentence. Write each new sentence and say it aloud.

    1. *Me mandaron unos <u>cuadros</u>.* (retratos, libros, sellos, folletos, lápices)

    2. *¿Tiene usted algunas <u>revistas</u>?* (novelas, amigas, casas, noticias, entradas, llantas)

    3. *No he visto ninguna <u>película</u> interesante.* (comedia, ciudad, tienda, pintura, obra)

    4. *Juan ha comprado unos cuantos <u>dulces</u>.* (libros, planos, pañuelos, sobres, sellos)

    5. *<u>Lo bueno</u> es comprenderlo bien.* (Lo mejor, Lo interesante, Lo fácil, Lo difícil, Lo imposible)

    6. *¿Quiere usted mandarme unas <u>revistas</u>?* (cartas, noticias, tarjetas, fotos, direcciones)

B. Change these sentences to the negative. Write the complete sentence and translate.

    1. *Me quedan algunas fotos.*

    2. *¿Quiere usted algún periódico?*

    3. *Ellos tienen algunas dificultades.*

    4. *Queríamos comprar algunas revistas.*

    5. *Me dieron unos cuantos papeles.*

C. Translate the following sentences into Spanish, then say them aloud.

    1. I think I left a few letters there.

    2. He heard some strange noises.

3. Put a little water in the radiator.

4. I just bought some stamps.

5. Do you want to come back at five?

6. Do only what is necessary (the necessary thing).

7. We'll do everything we can.

8. The good thing is that we arrived early.

9. I'm sure you'll like the car.

10. The bad part of the matter is that they don't know us.

D. From among the three choices given, choose the best equivalent of the English term (in parentheses) for each sentence, and translate.

1. (some) *Les voy a enviar* _____ *programas del concierto.*
   (a) *unas*
   (b) *algunas*
   (c) *unos*

2. (any) *No me ha dado* _____ *dinero.*
   (a) *ninguno*
   (b) *algún*
   (c) *nada de*

3. (any) *Me gustan las novelas románticas. ¿Tiene usted* _____?
   (a) *algunas*
   (b) *ninguna*
   (c) *ningunas*

4. (some) *Voy a decírselo* _____ *día.*
   (a) *alguna*
   (b) *algún*
   (c) *algo*

5. (the impossible part) *Eso precisamente es* _____ *del caso.*
   - (a) *lo imposible*
   - (b) *los imposibles*
   - (c) *imposible*

6. (none) *No se lo ha dicho a* _____ *de sus amigos.*
   - (a) *alguno*
   - (b) *ninguno*
   - (c) *ninguna*

7. (some) *Querían vender* _____ *vestidos.*
   - (a) *algunas*
   - (b) *unos cuantos*
   - (c) *unas*

8. (the best thing) *Me gustó la comedia. Las primeras escenas fueron* _____ *de la obra.*
   - (a) *la mejor*
   - (b) *lo mejor*
   - (c) *los mejores*

9. (any) *¿Le has dado* _____ *dinero?*
   - (a) *alguno*
   - (b) *algo de*
   - (c) *ningúno*

10. (the most difficult part) *Les he explicado* _____ .
    - (a) *lo difícil*
    - (b) *lo más difícil*
    - (c) *los difíciles*

Answer Key

B. 1. *No me quedan ningunas fotos.*
I don't have any photos left.

2. *¿No quiere usted ningún periódico?*
Don't you want any newspapers?

3. *Ellos no tienen ningunas dificultades.*
They don't have any difficulties.

4. *No queríamos comprar ningunas revistas.*
We didn't want to buy any magazines.

5. *No me dieron ningunos papeles.*
They didn't give me any papers.

C. 1. *Creo que dejé unas cuantas cartas allí.*

2. *Él oyó unos ruidos raros.*

3. *Eche(a) un poco de agua en el radiador.*

4. *Acabo de comprar algunos sellos.*

5. *¿Quiere(s) usted (tú) volver a las cinco?*

6. *Haga (Haz) sólo lo necesario.*

7. *Haremos todo lo que podamos.*

8. *Lo bueno es que llegamos temprano.*

9. *Estoy seguro que le (te) gustará el coche.*

10. *Lo malo del caso es que ellos no nos conocen.*

D. 1. *Les voy a enviar unos programas del concierto.*
I am going to send them some concert programs.

2. *No me ha dado nada de dinero.*
He didn't give me any money.

3. *Me gustan las novelas románticas. ¿Tiene usted
   algunas?*
   I like romantic novels. Do you have any?

4. *Voy a decírselo algún día.*
   I am going to tell (it to) him someday.

5. *Eso precisamente es lo imposible del caso.*
   That is precisely the impossible part of the matter.

6. *No se lo ha dicho a ninguno de sus amigos.*
   He didn't tell it to any of his friends.

7. *Querían vender unos cuantos vestidos.*
   They wanted to sell some (a few) dresses.

8. *Me gustó la comedia. Las primeras escenas fueron
   lo mejor de la obra.*
   I liked the comedy. The first scenes were the best
   (thing) in the play.

9. *¿Le has dado algo de dinero?*
   Have you given him any money?

10. *Les he explicado lo más difícil.*
    I have explained the most difficult part to them.

LESSON 15

LA FRONTERA
THE BORDER

A. DIALOGUE

0. *Paola y Álvaro son ciudadanos estadounidenses de origen mexicano residentes en San Diego. Ellos han decidido pasar el fin de semana en el norte de México cerca de la frontera con California para visi-tar parientes.*
   Paola and Alvaro are American citizens of Mexican origin who live in San Diego. They have decided to spend the weekend in the north of Mexico close to the Californian border to visit relatives.

Al acercarse a la frontera con los Estados Unidos.
Approaching the United States border.

1. Paola: **Mira, ¡qué cantidad de coches haciendo cola delante de la aduana!**
   Look. What a huge amount of cars lined up before the customs station!

2. Álvaro: **Lo esperaba. ¡Hay siempre tanto tráfico por la frontera!**
   I expected it. There is always so much traffic crossing the border!

3. Paola: **¡Claro! Pero yo creía que los viernes el tráfico sería mejor. Sin duda tendremos que esperar un poco.**
   Of course! But I thought on Friday traffic would be better. Undoubtedly, we will have to wait a little.

4. Álvaro: **Dicen que si te mantienes a la izquierda pasas bastante rápido.**
They say that if you stay to your left, you go through pretty fast.

5. Paola: **¡Ojalá! No quiero estar mucho tiempo parada en tráfico.**
I hope so! I don't want to spend too much time stuck in traffic.

6. Álvaro: **Mira, algunos coches, como el azul de allí, pasan muy fácilmente.**
Look, some cars, like the blue one over there, go through really easily.

7. Paola: **Ya estamos en la frontera. ¡No puedo creerlo! ¡Van a pararnos! ¡Qué suerte que tenemos! Viene el inspector.**
We are already at the border. I can't believe it! They're going to stop us! What luck we have! Here comes the inspector.

8. Inspector: **Buenos días, señores. ¿Piensan quedarse mucho tiempo en México?**
Good morning. Do you intend to stay very long in Mexico?

9. Álvaro: **No, señor. Solamente el fin de semana. Vamos a visitar familiares nuestros.**
No, sir. Only the weekend. We're going to visit our relatives.

10. Inspector: **Permítame ver los documentos del coche y su carnet de conducir.**
Let me see the documents for the car and your driver's license.

11. Álvaro: **Aquí los tiene.**
Here you are.

12. Inspector: **El coche tiene matrícula de Nevada, ¿y el carnet de conducir es de California?**
The car has a license plate from Nevada, and the driver's license is from California?

13. Álvaro: **Sí, señor. Nos mudamos recientemente.**
Yes, sir. We moved recently.

14. Paola: **Compramos el coche en Nevada y no hemos tenido tiempo para cambiar la matrícula.**
We bought the car in Nevada and we haven't had time to change the license plate.

15. Inspector: **¿Me permiten ustedes ver sus pasaportes, por favor?**
May I see your passports, please?

16. Paola: **Ah, sí. Pero, ¿donde estarán? Los tenía en la bolsa, ¡y ahora no los veo por ninguna parte!**
Oh, yes. But, where did they go? I had them in this bag and now I don't see them anywhere!

17. Álvaro: **Los sacaste hace poco. Deben de estar en el asiento.**
You took them out a little while ago. They must be on the seat.

18. Paola: **Dile que espere un momento. Deben haberse caído al suelo. ¡Ah! Los encontré. Se habían caído.**
Tell him to wait a minute. They must have fallen on the floor. Ah! I've found them. They had fallen.

19. Álvaro: **Aquí los tiene, señor.**
Here you are, sir.

20. Inspector: **Muchas gracias. ¿Ustedes tienen algo que declarar?**

Thank you very much. Do you have anything to declare?

21. Álvaro: **Nada que yo sepa.**
Nothing that I know of.

22. Inspector: **Muy bien. ¡Que tengan buen viaje!**
Very well. Have a good trip!

23. Álvaro: **Gracias.**
Thank you.

24. Paola: **Ya estamos de camino a México. Espero que no haya mucho tráfico.**
Now we're on our way to Mexico. I hope that there isn't too much traffic.

25. Álvaro: **¿En cuánto tiempo crees que vamos a llegar a casa de tu madre?**
How long will it take us to get to your mother's house?

26. Paola: **Al menos cuatro horas; depende del tráfico.**
At least four hours, depending on traffic.

27. Álvaro: **Yo creo que el domingo deberíamos salir temprano. No podemos llegar tarde a casa, tenemos que levantarnos temprano el lunes para ir al trabajo.**
I think that Sunday we should leave early. We can't get home late, we have to get up early on Monday to go to work.

B. NOTES

0. *parientes*: The English meaning of the word is "relatives." Many students of Spanish incorrectly

assume that the meaning of the word is "parents." Note that the Spanish word for "parents" is *padres*.

1. *hacer cola*: to get in line, to form a line, to wait in line.

2. *Lo esperaba*: I expected it. *Esperar* means "to expect," "to hope," or "to wait." *Esperar* is used with the latter definition in line 3.

5. *estar parada en tráfico*: to be stuck in traffic. The verb *parar* means "to stop," while the adjective *parado(a)* means "idle" or "slow."

10. *carnet de conducir*: driver's license. *Carnet* can be used to refer to a general I.D. card, or it can mean "notebook."

12. The word *matrícula* has several meanings. In this case it refers to the license plate. It can also mean "register," "list," "enrollment," and "registration fee."

16. *no los veo por ninguna parte*: Notice the use of the negative *ninguna* after a verb in the negative. The affirmative equivalent would be *alguna*: *¿Los ve usted por alguna parte?* Do you see it anywhere?

21. *Nada que yo sepa.*: Nothing that I know of. Notice that the verb *saber* (to know) is used in the present subjunctive form.

C. GRAMMAR AND USAGE

1. Use the preterit followed by *hace* and a time expression to convey that an action occurred some time ago.

   Los sacaste hace poco.
   You took them out a while ago.

Ellos llegaron hace una semana.
   They arrived a week ago.

Juan salió hace una hora.
   Juan left an hour ago.

2. To give an indirect command, use the verb *decir* with the appropriate direct object pronoun followed by *que* and the subjunctive form of the verb.

Dile que espere.
   Tell him to wait.

Les dijeron que vinieran en seguida.
   They told them to come at once.

Dígale a ella que saque su pasaporte.
   Tell her to take out her passport.

3. To form an adverb, add *-mente* to the feminine form of an adjective.

Se lo dije claramente.
   I told it to him clearly.

Le acusaron injustamente.
   They accused him unjustly.

Le preguntó amablemente.
   He asked him nicely.

Note:

• Adjectives that have only one singular form take the *-mente* ending without any other change. Adjectives with written accents retain the accents in the adverbial form.

Lo puedes hacer fácilmente.
   You can do it easily.

Normalmente, no lo hacemos así.
   Normally, we don't do it that way.

Posiblemente está aquí todavía.
Possibly he's still here.

4. Nouns may be formed from adjectives by preceding it with the proper article.

Estoy buscando un vestido azul. No me gusta el rojo.
I'm looking for a blue dress. I don't like the red one.

Estos libros no valen nada. Los buenos están allí.
These books aren't worth anything. The good ones are there.

Los malos siempre sufren.
The bad always suffer.

Me gusta ayudar a los pobres.
I like to help the poor.

EXERCISES

A. Substitute the words or expressions in parentheses for the underlined word or expression in the model sentence. Write each new sentence and say it aloud.

1. *Juan y José llegaron hace <u>una semana</u>.* (una hora, un año, cuatro meses, mucho tiempo, poco)

2. *Ellos lo <u>compraron</u> hace tres días.* (vendieron, escribieron, hicieron, mandaron, recibieron)

3. *Dígale a Juana que <u>venga</u>.* (escriba, llame, entre, trabaje, coma)

4. *Ya lo escribí <u>claramente</u>.* (mala-, fácil-, difícil-, inútil-, inmediata-)

5. *María es la <u>rubia</u>.* (buena, morena, inteligente, fuerte, tímida)

6. *Los <u>buenos</u> son siempre los primeros.* (malos, inteligentes, perezosos, imposibles, interesantes)

B. Rewrite these sentences following the example. Write the complete sentence and translate.

Example: *Juan llegó la semana pasada.*
Juan llegó hace una semana.

1. *Ellos vinieron el año pasado.*

2. *Ella me escribió el mes pasado.*

3. *Jorge se casó anteayer.*

4. *Hoy es el quince de agosto. María se marchó el doce.*

5. *Me mandaron el libro el año pasado.*

C. Translate the following sentences into Spanish; then say them aloud.

1. There are so many tourists that go through the border.

2. Are you *(plural)* going to stay in California very long?

3. I thought it would be better on Tuesday.

4. You *(impersonal)* don't have to open the suitcases.

5. All the papers are in order.

6. Tell him to wait a minute.

7. I hope I see you on the return trip.

8. It was much quicker than the last time.

9. He came a year ago.

10. We're on our way to Mexico.

D. From among the three choices given, choose the best equivalent of the English term (in parentheses) for each sentence, and translate.

1. (called) *Juan* _____ *hace una hora.*
   - (a) *llama*
   - (b) *llamó*
   - (c) *llamaba*

2. (ago) *Nuestros amigos llegaron* _____ *unas horas.*
   - (a) *hace*
   - (b) *hacen*
   - (c) *hizo*

3. (to wait) *Dígale que* _____.
   - (a) *espera*
   - (b) *espere*
   - (c) *esperar*

4. (easily) *Él dice que lo puede hacer* _____.
   - (a) *fácilmente*
   - (b) *facilmente*
   - (c) *fácil*

5. (did) *Lo* _____ *Juan hace mucho tiempo.*
   - (a) *hace*
   - (b) *hizo*
   - (c) *haces*

6. (to come) *Dígales* _____.
   - (a) *venir*
   - (b) *vienen*
   - (c) *que vengan*

7. (some days ago) *Los señores Andrade llegaron*
   _____.
   - (a) *hizo unos días*
   - (b) *hace unas días*
   - (c) *hace unos días*

8. (clearly) *El jefe me lo dijo* _____.
   - (a) *clara*
   - (b) *claros*
   - (c) *claramente*

9. (to write) *Dígale a María que* _____.
   (a) *escribe*
   (b) *escriba*
   (c) *escribir*

10. (to declare) *¿Tienen ustedes algo que* _____?
    (a) *declarar*
    (b) *declare*
    (c) *declaran*

Answer Key

B.   1. *Ellos vinieron hace un año.*
   They came a year ago.

     2. *Ella me escribió hace un mes.*
   She wrote me a month ago.

     3. *Jorge se casó hace dos días.*
   Jorge got married two days ago.

     4. *Hoy es el quince de agosto. María se marchó hace tres días.*
   Today is the fifteenth of August. María left three days ago.

     5. *Me mandaron el libro hace un año.*
   They sent me the book a year ago.

C.   1. *Hay tantos turistas que pasan por la frontera.*

     2. *¿Van a quedarse en California mucho tiempo?*

     3. *Creía (Pensé) que sería mejor el martes.*

     4. *No hay que abrir las maletas.*

     5. *Todos los papeles están en orden.*

     6. *Dígale (Dile) que espere un momento.*

     7. *Espero verlo (verte) en el viaje de vuelta.*

     8. *Fue mucho más rápido que la última vez.*

     9. *Él vino hace un año.*

     10. *Estamos en camino a México.*

D.   1. *Juan llamó hace una hora.*
   Juan called an hour ago.

     2. *Nuestros amigos llegaron hace unas horas.*
   Our friends arrived a few hours ago.

3. *Dígale que espere.*
   Tell her (him) to wait.

4. *Él dice que lo puede hacer fácilmente.*
   He says that he can do it easily.

5. *Lo hizo Juan hace mucho tiempo.*
   Juan did it a long time ago.

6. *Dígales que vengan.*
   Tell them to come.

7. *Los señores Andrade llegaron hace unos días.*
   Mr. and Mrs. Andrade arrived a few days ago.

8. *El jefe me lo dijo claramente.*
   The boss told it to me clearly.

9. *Dígale a María que escriba.*
   Tell María to write.

10. *¿Tienen ustedes algo que declarar?*
    Do you have anything to declare?

LESSON 16

EN EL BANCO
AT THE BANK

A. DIALOGUE

0. *Carlos es de Montevideo, Uruguay. Él no está contento con su banco actual y decide abrir una cuenta con otro banco.*
   Carlos is from Montevideo, Uruguay. He is not happy with his current bank and decides to open an account with another bank.

En el vestíbulo de la sucursal. At the reception area of the bank.

1. Carlos: **Estoy interesado en abrir una cuenta corriente.**
   I am interested in opening a checking account.

2. Empleado: **Claro que sí. Tiene que llenar los formularios y mostrar identificación.**
   Of course. You'll have to fill out the applications and show identification.

3. Carlos: **¿Piensa que me va a tomar mucho tiempo?**
   Do you think it will take me a long time?

4. Empleado: **Dudo que tome más de quince minutos. ¿Ha traído su documento de identidad?**
   I doubt it will take more than fifteen minutes. Did you bring your identification card?

5. Carlos: **Ah, claro. Aquí tiene el pasaporte y mi documento nacional de identidad.**
   Of course. Here you have my passport and my identification card.

6. Empleado: **Voy a empezar a tomar sus datos en la computadora mientras usted termina de llenar los formularios. ¿Es ésta la dirección correcta?**
   I'll start entering your information in the computer while you finish filling out those forms. Is this the right address?

7. Carlos: **Sí, es la más reciente. Es increíble lo fácil que es abrir una cuenta.**
   Yes, it's my most recent. It's incredible how easy it is to open an account.

8. Empleado: **Pues ya ve, señor. La computadora ya me ha dado su número de cuenta.**
   As you can see, sir, the computer has already given me your account number.

9. Carlos: **Me gusta el número, es muy fácil de recordar.**
   I like the number, it's very easy to remember.

10. Empleado: **¿Cómo piensa hacer el primer ingreso a su cuenta?**
    How do you plan to make your first deposit?

11. Carlos: **He traído un cheque para depositarlo.**
    I brought a check to deposit.

12. Empleado: **También puede hacer una transferencia electrónica si todavía mantiene un balance con su banco anterior.**
    You can also make an electronic transfer if you still maintain a balance with your previous bank.

13. Carlos: **Perfecto. ¿Es muy complicado?**
    Perfect. Is it very complicated?

14. Empleado: **No, muy fácil. Solamente tiene que llenar este formulario. Lo puede mandar por correo si no tiene tiempo hoy.**

No, very easy. You just have to fill out this form. You can send it by mail if you don't have time today.

15. Carlos: **Gracias. ¿Hay alguien que pueda ayudarme a crear un perfil para hacer mis transacciones por computadora?**
Thank you. Is there someone who can help me create a profile to perform online transactions?

16. Empleado: **Yo le puedo ayudar con eso, señor.**
I can help you with that, sir.

17. Carlos: **Bueno. Necesito hacer la mayoría de mis pagos electrónicamente.**
Fine. I need to make most of my payments electronically.

18. Empleado: **Yo le daré un folleto informativo. Además le daré el número de servicio al cliente. El servicio es completamente gratis.**
I'll give you an informational brochure. I will also give you the customer service phone number. The service is absolutely free.

19. Carlos: **¿De verdad? Cuando llamé por teléfono, la persona de servicio al cliente me dijo que había un pequeño cargo mensual.**
Really? When I called on the phone, the person from customer service told me there would be a small monthly charge.

20. Empleado: **Sí, pero tenemos una promoción especial para nuevos clientes.**
Yes, but we have a special promotion for new clients.

21. Carlos: **Muchas gracias.**
Thank you very much.

B. NOTES

0. The Spanish word *actual* means "current," not "actual." The Spanish equivalent of "actual" is *real* or *verdadero*.

1. *una cuenta corriente*: a checking account.

2. *los formularios*: This word means "applications," not "formulas." The word for "formula" is *fórmula*.

5. *Documento Nacional de Identidad*: often referred to as simply *DNI*. It is a national identification card used in many Spanish speaking countries. DNI cards are issued by national governments, have an identification number similar to a social security number, and have a picture of the bearer.

7. *lo fácil que es*: how easy it is. The construction is always followed by a verb in the infinitive; here, *abrir* (to open).

9. *es muy fácil de recordar*: it's very easy to remember. Notice how *es muy fácil* is followed by the preposition *de*.

10. *cómo piensa*: how do you plan (to), how are you thinking (of).

19. Note that *la persona* is always feminine, whether it refers to a man or a woman.

C. GRAMMAR AND USAGE

1. The subjunctive is used after verbs or expressions of disbelief, doubt, denial, or impossibility.

    Dudo que Juan esté aquí.
    I doubt that Juan is here.

Es imposible que María haga tal cosa.
>It's impossible that María would do such a thing.

Niego que sea verdad.
>I deny that it's true.

No creo que ellos vengan.
>I don't believe they'll come.

2. The subjunctive is also used in an adjective clause when the noun or pronoun referred to is undetermined or nonexistent.

No conozco a nadie que pueda ayudarnos.
>I don't know anyone who can help us.

No tenemos nada que sea tan interesante.
>We have nothing that is so interesting.

Voy a buscar una agencia que tenga una sucursal en Nueva York.
>I'm going to look for an agency that has a branch in New York.

¿Conoce usted a alguien que sepa el precio?
>Do you know anyone who knows the price?

No conocen a nadie que tenga este modelo.
>They don't know anyone who has this model.

¿Dónde puedo encontrar un guía que hable inglés?
>Where can I find a guide who speaks English?

3. Conjunctions referring to the future or to an indeterminate time trigger the subjunctive.

Voy a esperar hasta que llegue Juan.
>I'm going to wait until Juan arrives.

Vamos a trabajar mucho mientras estemos aquí.
>We are going to work hard while we're here.

Se lo diré tan pronto como lleguen.
 I'll tell them as soon as they arrive.

En cuanto lo tenga, voy a mandártelo.
 As soon as I have it, I'm going to send it to you.

4. The reflexive is used for reciprocal actions: one another, each other.

Nos saludamos cada día.
 We greet each other every day.

Ellos se conocieron en Madrid.
 They met each other in Madrid.

No creo que nos veamos otra vez.
 I don't think we'll see each other again.

María y Teresa siempre se hablan.
 María and Teresa always talk to each other.

EXERCISES

A. Substitute each of the words or expressions in parentheses for the underlined word or expression in the model sentence. Write each new sentence and say it aloud.

  1. *No creo que ellos lo sepan.* (compren, vendan, escriban, manden, conozcan)

  2. *Es imposible que ellos lleguen ahora.* (hablen, duerman, se levanten, vayan, entren)

  3. *Busco una casa que sea bastante grande.* (cómoda, económica, pequeña, bonita, nueva)

  4. *No conocemos a nadie que hable ruso.* (italiano, inglés, alemán, griego, árabe)

  5. *Vamos a esperar hasta que vengan.* (llamen, lleguen, se levanten, escriban, coman)

6. *En cuanto Juan lo <u>compre</u>, se lo dirá usted.* (vea, venda, reciba, tenga, mande)

B. Change the following sentences to the interrogative. Write the complete sentence and translate.

1. *Juan y José se alegrarán cuando se vean.*

2. *Rafael está buscando una secretaria que hable inglés.*

3. *Ellos van a esperar hasta que lleguemos.*

4. *Usted conoce a alguien que trabaja rápidamente.*

5. *María lo dirá en cuanto lo sepa.*

C. Translate the following sentences into Spanish, then say them aloud.

1. I'm going to look for a book that I (will) like.

2. They don't know anyone who writes poetry.

3. Juan will wait until we arrive.

4. Do you always see each other in Paris?

5. Will you write to me when you arrive in New York?

6. I doubt that they are here.

7. We don't believe Juan knows it.

8. Juan doesn't think María will come.

9. He's looking for a bank that has a branch in Madrid.

10. As soon as I buy it, I will show it to you.

D. From among the three choices given, choose the best equivalent of the English term (in parentheses) for each sentence, and translate.

1. (is) *No creo que María* _____ *aquí.*
   (a) *está*
   (b) *esté*
   (c) *es*

2. (do) *Es imposible que ellos* _____ *tal cosa.*
   (a) *hacen*
   (b) *hagan*
   (c) *harán*

3. (can) *No hay ninguno que* _____ *hacerlo.*
   (a) *puede*
   (b) *pueda*
   (c) *podrá*

4. (has) *Quiero encontrar una casa que* _____
   siete habitaciones.
   (a) *tiene*
   (b) *tener*
   (c) *tenga*

5. (believe) *Es imposible que ella* _____ *la historia.*
   (a) *cree*
   (b) *crea*
   (c) *creerá*

6. (it is) *Niegan que* _____ *verdad.*
   (a) *es*
   (b) *ser*
   (c) *sea*

7. (speaks) *Tenemos que esperar hasta que Juan*
   _____.
   (a) *habla*
   (b) *hable*
   (c) *hablará*

8. (have) *En cuanto ellos lo* _____, *se lo man-darán a usted.*
   (a) *tengan*
   (b) *tienen*
   (c) *tendrán*

9. (Each other) _____ *vemos todos los días.*
   (a) *Cada uno*
   (b) *Nos*
   (c) *Cada otro*

10. (is) *Busco una bolsa que* _____ *bastante grande.*
    (a) *sea*
    (b) *está*
    (c) *ser*

Answer Key

B. 1. *¿Se alegrarán Juan y José cuando se vean?*
Will Juan and José be happy when they see each other?

2. *¿Está buscando Rafael una secretaria que hable inglés?*
Is Rafael looking for a secretary who speaks English?

3. *¿Van a esperar ellos hasta que lleguemos?*
Are they going to wait until we arrive?

4. *¿Conoce usted a alguien que trabaje rápidamente?*
Do you know anyone who works fast?

5. *¿Lo dirá María en cuanto lo sepa?*
Will María say it as soon as she knows it?

C. 1. *Voy a buscar un libro que me guste.*

2. *No conocen a nadie que escriba poesía.*

3. *Juan esperará hasta que lleguemos.*

4. *¿Se ven siempre ustedes en París?*

5. *¿Me escribirá(s) usted (tú) cuando llegue(s) a Nueva York?*

6. *Dudo que estén aquí.*

7. *No creemos que Juan lo sepa.*

8. *Juan no cree que María venga.*

9. *Él busca un banco que tenga sucursal en Madrid.*

10. *En cuanto lo compre, se (te) lo enseñaré.*

D. 1. *No creo que María esté aquí.*
I don't think María is here.

2. *Es imposible que ellos hagan tal cosa.*
   It's impossible that they would do such a thing.

3. *No hay ninguno que pueda hacerlo.*
   There is no one who can do it.

4. *Quiero encontrar una casa que tenga siete habitaciones.*
   I want to find a house that has seven rooms.

5. *Es imposible que ella crea la historia.*
   It's impossible that she would believe the story.

6. *Niegan que sea verdad.*
   They deny that it's true.

7. *Tenemos que esperar hasta que Juan hable.*
   We have to wait until Juan speaks.

8. *En cuanto ellos lo tengan, se lo mandarán a usted.*
   As soon as they have it, they will send it to you.

9. *Nos vemos todos los días.*
   We see each other every day.

10. *Busco una bolsa que sea bastante grande.*
    I am looking for a purse that is large enough.

LESSON 17

EN LA OFICINA DE CORREOS
AT THE POST OFFICE

A. DIALOGUE

0. *Verónica está en la oficina de correos. Tiene que comprar sellos, enviar una carta urgente, mandar un paquete a España y recoger su correo.*
   Veronica is in the post office. She has to buy stamps, send an express letter, ship a package to Spain, and pick up her mail.

En la ventanilla de sellos. At the stamp window.

1. Verónica: **Perdone, señora. Quiero mandar estas tres cartas a España. ¿Cuánto cuesta, por favor?**
   Excuse me, ma'am. I want to send these three letters to Spain. How much is it, please?

2. Empleada: **Tengo que pesarlas. Vamos a ver... son sesenta céntimos cada una, señora.**
   I have to weigh them. Let's see . . .they're sixty cents each, ma'am.

3. Verónica: **Y quiero mandar ésta urgente. ¿Cuánto es?**
   And I want to send this one rush delivery. How much is it?

4. Empleada: **Si es para España, son solamente seis pesos, y será entregada en dos días.**
   If it's for Spain, it's only six pesos, and it will be delivered in two days.

5. Verónica: **¿Cuánto le debo?**
   How much do I owe you?

6. Empleada: **Vamos a ver. Contemos los sellos, uno, dos, tres. . . Son nueve pesos en total.**
Let's see. Let's count the stamps, one, two, three . . . It's nine pesos total.

7. Verónica: **Gracias. Tengo que mandar un paquete también. ¿Adónde hay que ir para mandar paquetes?**
Thank you. I have to send a package too. Where do you have to go to mail a package?

8. Empleada: **Está en la sección de atrás. Pase por aquella puerta a la izquierda y la verá usted.**
It's in the back section. Go through that door on the left, and you'll see it.

En la ventanilla de la lista de correos. At the general delivery window.

9. Verónica: **¿Hay algo para mí? Recibí una nota que dice que mi buzón está lleno.**
Is there anything for me? I received a notice that says that my mailbox is full.

10. Empleado: **A ver. . .¿Me permite su identificación? Sí, señora. Hay varias postales, una carta certificada y un paquete pequeño. Tendrá que firmar el recibo aquí.**
Let's see . . .May I see your ID? Yes, ma'am. There are several postcards, a registered letter, and a small package. You'll have to sign the receipt here.

11. Verónica: **Por supuesto. ¿Dónde hay que firmar?**
Of course. Where do I have to sign?

12. Empleado: **En esta línea, por favor. Y por el paquete hay que pagar ocho pesos de aduana.**
On this line, please. And for the package, you'll have to pay eight pesos of customs duties.

13. Verónica: **Gracias. ¿Qué será? No esperaba ningún paquete. Tengo que mandar un paquete también. ¿Dónde puedo hacerlo?**
Thank you. What can it be? I wasn't expecting any packages. I have to send a package too. Where can I do that?

14. Empleado: **Para eso hay que ir a aquella ventanilla de enfrente, la número veintiuno.**
For that, you'll have to go to that window in front, number twenty-one.

En la ventanilla de paquetes. At the package window.

15. Verónica: **Quiero mandar este paquete a España.**
I want to send this package to Spain.

16. Empleado: **A ver. . . Señora, pesa muchísimo. Lo siento, pero si quiere usted mandarlo, tendrá que pagar mucho dinero.**
Let's see . . . It weighs a lot, ma'am. I am sorry, if you want to send it, you'll have to pay a lot of money.

17. Verónica: **No importa, es un paquete importante.**
It doesn't matter, it's an important package.

18. Empleado: **¿Lo quiere mandar por correo normal?**
Do you want to send it by regular mail?

19. Verónica: **No, por el correo más lento por favor. Si no pesara tanto, lo mandaría por correo normal.**
No, slower freight, please. If it didn't weigh so much, I would send it by regular mail.

20. Empleado: **Llene estas dos declaraciones para la aduana, por favor.**
Please fill out these two customs declarations.

21. Verónica: **¡Ya está!**
    Done!

22. Empleado: **¿Quiere asegurarlo también? Si quiere asegurarlo, tendrá que pagar más.**
    Would you like to insure it too? If you want to insure it, you will have to pay more.

23. Verónica: **Depende ¿Cuánto me va a costar?**
    It depends, how much will it cost me?

24. Empleado: **Todo depende del valor del artículo.**
    It all depends on the value of the item.

25. Verónica: **Quisiera asegurarlo por quinientos pesos.**
    I would like to insure it for 500 pesos.

26. Empleado: **Bueno, pues es quince pesos.**
    Well, it's fifteen pesos.

27. Verónica: **No lo hagamos, no merece la pena.**
    Let's not do it, it's not worth it.

28. Empleado: **Pase usted a la caja con este papel y vuelva aquí con el recibo.**
    Go to the cashier with this note, and come back here with your receipt.

B. NOTES

3. *urgente*: urgent. In Latin America it is also common to say *para entrega inmediata* or *por mensajero especial* ("for immediate delivery" or "by special messenger").

6. *Vamos a ver*: Let's see. Notice how this expression is shortened to just *a ver* in line 10.

13. *No esperaba ningún paquete*: I wasn't expecting any packages/a package.

14. Numbers from sixteen to twenty-nine have alternative spellings. For example, "eighteen" can be *dieciocho* or *diez y ocho*.

21. *¡Ya está!* In an exclamation of this kind, concepts such as *hecho* (done, finished) or *listo* (ready) are understood, as in *¡Ya estoy!* (I'm ready!).

27. *No merece la pena*: It's not worth it. Literally, "it's not worth the trouble."

C. GRAMMAR AND USAGE

1. When *si* (if) introduces a contrary-to-fact condition, the verb is in the imperfect subjunctive, and the result is expressed by the conditional.

Si yo fuera rica, viajaría mucho.
    If I were rich, I would travel a lot.

Si los señores Andrade estuvieran aquí, podríamos decírselo.
    If Mr. and Mrs. Andrade were here, we could tell them (it).

Si estuviéramos en Londres ahora, podríamos ver la comedia.
    If we were in London now, we could see the comedy.

Si trabajara más, usted ganaría más dinero.
    If you worked harder, you would earn more money.

2. When *si* (if) introduces a possible condition, the indicative can follow it.

Si puedo encontrarlo, te lo daré.
   If I can find it, I'll give it to you.

Si ellos me lo dicen, lo creo.
   If they tell me (it), I'll believe it.

Si llueve, no salgo.
   If it rains, I'm not going out.

Si ella llega a tiempo, podemos ir.
   If she arrives on time, we can go.

3. The English expression "let's" is expressed either by
   vamos a followed by the infinitive, or by the first person
   plural of the present subjunctive.

Vamos a hablar del viaje.
Hablemos del viaje.
   Let's talk about the trip.

Vamos a acostarnos temprano esta noche.
Acostémonos temprano esta noche.
   Let's go to bed early tonight.

Vamos a salir enseguida.
Salgamos enseguida.
   Let's leave at once.

Vamos a comprarlo.
Comprémoslo.
   Let's buy it.

Vamos a levantarnos a las siete.
Levantémonos a las siete.
   Let's get up at seven o'clock.

Note:

• When the reflexive *nos* is added to the first person
  plural form, the final *s* of the verb form is dropped.

Levantémonos.
   Let's get up.

Sentémonos.
> Let's sit down.

• *ss* is reduced to *s*:

Comprémoselo.
> Let's buy it for him.

In the negative "let's not," the pronoun is not attached to the verb.

No lo compremos.
> Let's not buy it.

No nos levantemos.
> Let's not get up.

No se lo compremos.
> Let's not buy it for him.

EXERCISES

A. Substitute each of the words or expressions in parentheses for the underlined word or expression in the model sentence. Write each new sentence and say it aloud.

1. *Si Juan fuera rico, lo podría hacer.* (norteamericano, dentista, médico, profesor, millonario)

2. *Si tuviéramos el libro, lo (la) podríamos leer.* (el diccionario, la revista, el periódico, la novela, la carta)

3. *Si veo a Juan, se lo digo.* (María, los señores Andrade, tu amigo, los estudiantes, mi hermano)

4. *Si llegan hoy, yo voy (iré) a verlos.* (mañana, la semana que viene, el martes, esta mañana, pronto)

5. *Compremos las entradas.* (el libro, los periódicos, la revista, el billete, los guantes)

6. *Levantémonos pronto.* (a las ocho, más tarde, en seguida, ahora, después)

B. Rewrite these sentences following the example. Write the complete sentence and translate.

Example: *Vamos a decírselo.*
         Digámoselo.

   1. *Vamos a acostarnos.*

   2. *Vamos a comprarlo.*

   3. *No vamos a decirlo.*

   4. *Vamos a llegar a tiempo.*

   5. *Vamos a estudiarlo.*

C. Translate the following sentences into Spanish, then say them aloud.

   1. If Juan were here, I would give him the book.

   2. If they had the time, they would go to Barcelona.

   3. If María were in Paris, she would buy the dress.

   4. If it rains, we won't go to the theater.

   5. If they see us, we'll talk to them.

   6. If you had your car, we would arrive on time.

   7. Let's go to the store.

   8. Let's not get up early tomorrow.

   9. Let's look for the book next week.

   10. Let's not give it (the book) to Juan.

D. From among the three choices given, choose the best equivalent of the English term (in parentheses) for each sentence, and translate.

   1. (were) *Si yo _____ usted, no lo haría.*
      (a) *fui*

(b) *fuera*
(c) *estuve*

2. (worked) *Juan ganaría mucho más si* _____
más.
(a) *trabajará*
(b) *trabajó*
(c) *trabajara*

3. (were) *Yo se lo daría a los señores Andrade si*
_____ *aquí.*
(a) *estuvieron*
(b) *estuvieran*
(c) *estan*

4. (read) *Si ellos* _____ *el periódico sabrían lo*
que ha pasado.
(a) *leen*
(b) *lean*
(c) *leyeran*

5. (Let's get up) _____ *temprano mañana.*
(a) *Vamos a levantar*
(b) *Levantémonos*
(c) *Levantémosnos*

6. (Let's not read) _____ *el periódico esta*
mañana.
(a) *No leemos*
(b) *No leamos*
(c) *No leeremos*

7. (arrive) *No les diremos nada si* _____ *tarde.*
(a) *lleguen*
(b) *llegan*
(c) *llegaran*

8. (rains) *No quiere ir al campo si* _____.
(a) *llueva*
(b) *lloverá*
(c) *llueve*

9. (Let's talk) _____ *de lo que tenemos que hacer.*
   (a) *Hablamos*
   (b) *Hablemos*
   (c) *Hablaremos*

10. (Let me) _____ *contar las palabras.*
    (a) *Permítame*
    (b) *Permitamos*
    (c) *Me permitamos*

Answer Key

B.   1. *Acostémonos.*
        Let's go to bed.

     2. *Comprémoslo.*
        Let's buy it.

     3. *No lo digamos.*
        Let's not say it.

     4. *Lleguemos a tiempo.*
        Let's arrive on time.

     5. *Estudiémoslo.*
        Let's study it.

C.   1. *Si Juan estuviera aquí, le daría el libro.*

     2. *Si ellos tuvieran tiempo, irían a Barcelona.*

     3. *Si María estuviera en París, compraría el vestido.*

     4. *Si llueve, no iremos al teatro.*

     5. *Si ellos nos ven, les hablaremos.*

     6. *Si usted(tú) tuviera(s) el coche, llegaríamos a tiempo.*

     7. *Vamos a la tienda.*

     8. *No nos levantemos temprano mañana.*

     9. *Busquemos el libro la semana que viene.* Or, *Vamos a buscar el libro la semana que viene.*

    10. *No se lo demos a Juan.*

D.   1. *Si yo fuera usted, no lo haría.*
        If I were you, I wouldn't do it.

     2. *Juan genaría mucho más si trabajara más.*
        Juan would earn a lot more if he worked more.

3. *Yo se lo daría a los señores Andrade si estuvieran aquí.*
   I would give it to Mr. and Mrs. Andrade if they were here.

4. *Si ellos leyeran el periódico, sabrían lo que ha pasado.*
   If they read the newspaper, they would know what has happened.

5. *Levantémonos temprano mañana.*
   Let's get up early tomorrow.

6. *No leamos el periódico esta mañana.*
   Let's not read the newspaper this morning.

7. *No les diremos nada si llegan tarde.*
   We won't say anything to them if they arrive late.

8. *No quiere ir al campo si llueve.*
   He/She doesn't want to go to the country if it rains.

9. *Hablemos de lo que tenemos que hacer.*
   Let's talk about what we have to do.

10. *Permítame contar las palabras.*
    Let me count the words.

LESSON 18

EN LA TIENDA DE MUEBLES
IN THE FURNITURE STORE

A. DIALOGUE

0. *Pilar acaba de comprarse su primera casa. Como
   siempre ha vivido en un apartamento pequeño, tiene
   que comprar muebles para su nueva casa más
   grande. Ha decidido pasarse el día buscando muebles para su hogar. Para empezar ha ido a una
   tienda que se especializa en toda clase de muebles.*
   Pilar has just purchased her first home. Since she has
   always lived in a small apartment, she has to buy furniture for her new bigger house. She has decided to
   spend the day looking for furniture for her new
   home. She is in a store that specializes in all kinds
   of furniture.

1. Empleada: **Buenos días, señora. ¿Necesita ayuda?**
   Good morning, ma'am. Do you need help?

2. Pilar: **Buenos días. Pues sí, tengo una lista bastante larga. Para empezar, estoy buscando un
   colchón nuevo.**
   Good morning. Well, yes, I have a rather long list.
   To begin with, I am looking for a new mattress.

3. Empleada: **Pues está en el departamento correcto.
   Tenemos muchísimos tipos de colchón. ¿De qué
   tamaño lo quiere?**
   Well, you are in the right department. We have many
   types of mattresses. What size are you looking for?

4. Pilar: **Necesito un colchón para una cama doble.**
   I need one for a queen-sized bed.

5. Empleada: **Muy bien, tengo éste que está reba-jado.**
All right, I have this one that is on sale.

6. Pilar: **Muy bien. Necesito también almohadas.**
All right. I also need pillows.

7. Empleada: **Seguro que éstas le gustarán, señora. Éstas son de pluma ciento por ciento. Son mucho más cómodas que las de espuma. Pero también son mucho más caras.**
I'm sure you'll like these, ma'am. They are 100% down. They are much more comfortable than the ones filled with foam. But they are also much more expensive.

8. Pilar: **No me importa el precio. ¿Tiene también mesitas de noche?**
I don't care about the price. Do you also have night-stands?

9. Empleada: **Sí, señora. ¿Qué le parece ésta? Es de madera de primera calidad.**
Yes, ma'am. What do you think of this one? It is made with first rate wood.

10. Pilar: **Prefiero una más grande.**
I prefer a bigger one.

11. Empleada: **Esta otra tiene un tamaño perfecto, es ideal para una cama doble.**
This one is the perfect size, it is ideal for a queen-sized bed.

12. Pilar: **Ésta sí me gusta. Me la llevo.**
This one I do like. I'll take it.

13. Empleada: **De acuerdo. ¿Qué más necesita?**
Very well. What else do you need?

14. Pilar: **Necesito un juego de comedor.**
    I need a dining set.

15. Empleada: **Está en el departamento de al lado,
    pero yo puedo ir con usted. ¿De cuántas sillas lo
    quiere?**
    It's in the department next door, but I can go with
    you. How many do you want it to seat?

16. Pilar: **Me hace falta uno de no menos de seis
    plazas, entre seis y ocho está bien.**
    I need to buy one that seats no less than six, between
    six and eight is fine.

17. Empleada: **Esta mesa es muy elegante, es de
    caoba.**
    This is a very elegant table. It's mahogany.

18. Pilar: **Sí, pero estoy buscando una más informal.
    Yo tengo niños y además invito a amigos a mi
    casa con frecuencia.**
    Yes, but I'm looking for something more casual. I
    have children and I also invite friends to my house
    frequently.

19. Empleada: **Es cierto; cuando se tiene niños hay
    que tener cuidado con lo que uno compra. ¿Qué
    le parece ésta?**
    It's true; when you have kids you have to be careful
    with what you buy. What do you think of this one?

20. Pilar: **Mejor. El color es más bonito y parece ser
    más resistente. Aunque a decir la verdad tam-
    poco me vuelve loca.**
    Better. The color is prettier and it seems to be more
    resistant. Although, to tell you the truth, I'm not too
    crazy about it.

21. Empleada: **Ésta es más contemporánea, ¿qué cree? Además, este juego está rebajado. Es el más barato que tengo.**
This is more modern, what do you think? Besides, this set is on sale. It's the cheapest one we have.

22. Pilar: **Éste sí. Es el que más me gusta. Me lo llevo.**
This is it. It's the one I like best. I'll take it.

23. Empleada: **¿Quiere alguna otra cosa?**
Would you like anything else?

24. Pilar: **Necesito una alfombra nueva para la sala.**
I need a new rug for the living room.

25. Empleada: **Hay gran variedad; las tenemos persas, turcas, modernas, de lana... ¿De qué tamaño la quiere?**
We have a large variety, we have Persian, Turkish, modern, wool . . . What size are you looking for?

26. Pilar: **Pues, realmente no tengo la medida exacta.**
Well, I don't have the exact measurement.

27. Empleada: **Con las alfombras yo recomiendo que se tengan las medidas exactas; no es bueno comprar una que sea demasiado grande para la habitación.**
With rugs I recommend that you have the exact measurements; it's not a good idea to buy something too big for the room.

28. Pilar: **Además, quiero que mi esposo venga a ver los colores. Él es muy quisquilloso. ¿Están abiertos mañana?**
Besides, I want my husband to come with me to take a look at the colors. He is very fussy. Are you open tomorrow?

29. Empleada: **Sí, abrimos hasta las ocho de la noche.**
    Yes, we are open until eight o'clock.

30. Pilar: **Pues nos vemos mañana.**
    So I'll see you tomorrow.

B. NOTES

0. Notice the difference between *hogar, casa,* and *apartamento. Hogar* is the Spanish word for "home," while *casa* refers to a "house." *Apartamento* is the most common word used for "apartment." However, in Spain, *piso* (flat) is used more commonly than *apartmento.*

5. *rebajado*: on sale. *Rebajas* is the word for "sale."

7. *ciento por ciento*: one hundred percent.
    de pluma, de algodón, de espuma, de caoba: made of down/feathers, made of cotton, made of foam, made of mahogany. Notice the use of the preposition *de* to indicate the material that the item is made of.

8. *mesita de noche:* literally, "little table for the night."

14. *juego de comedor:* dining set. The word *juego,* besides meaning "set," is also generally used to refer to a "game."

15. *¿De cuántas sillas lo quiere?*: Literally, "of how many chairs do you want it?" In English, this expression would equate to "How many do you want it to seat?"

16. *plaza:* In this case it indicates "seats." *Ella se ha comprado un deportivo de dos plazas.* She has bought a two seater sports car. It can also be used to refer to an open job position or vacancy, or to a town square.

20. *volver loco*: to drive crazy. It can also be used figuratively. *La comida italiana no me vuelve loco.* Italian food doesn't drive me crazy (doesn't excite me much).

21. *contemporáneo:* this term is used as frequently as its synonym *moderno.*

24. *alfombra:* In most Spanish speaking countries you use the same word for "carpet" and "rug." In Spain, the word for "carpet" is *moqueta.*

28. *quisquilloso*: finicky, fussy, or touchy. *Es muy quisquilloso con la comida, no sé si le va a gustar lo que preparé.* He is very finicky with food, I don't know if he will like what I prepared.

C. GRAMMAR AND USAGE

1. The comparative and superlative can be formed simply using *más* (more) or *menos* (less) with nouns, verbs, adjectives, or adverbs.

No puedo andar más.
   I can't walk (any)more.

Tengo más tiempo.
   I have more time.

Juan está menos cansado.
   Juan is less tired.

Este libro es más interesante.
   This book is more interesting.

Ellos hablan más fuerte.
   They speak louder.

Ella vendrá más tarde.
   She will come later.

2. Some comparatives are formed without *más* and *menos*:

mejor = better, best
peor = worse, worst
mayor = older, oldest; greater, greatest; bigger, biggest
menor = younger, younger; smaller, smallest; lesser, least

Mis hermanos escriben mejor.
    My brothers write better.

Este coche es mejor.
    This car is better.

Es la mejor chaqueta.
    It's the best jacket.

Yo soy el hermano menor.
    I'm the younger (youngest) brother.

Él es mi hermano mayor.
    He is my older (oldest) brother.

Note:

• *Más grande* and *más pequeño* are used when physical size is emphasized.

3. In Spanish, an article and a prepositional phrase or adjective clause may be added to distinguish adequately between the comparative and superlative. Usually *que* is used with a comparative construction, while an article and *de* are used to denote a superlative statement.

Pedro es mejor que usted.
    Pedro is better than you.

Pedro es el mejor del mundo.
    Pedro is the best in the world.

Ella es más bonita que Juana.
    She's prettier than Juana.

Ella es <u>la</u> más bonita <u>de</u> la ciudad.
She's the prettiest in the city.

Esta lección es más difícil.
This lesson is more difficult.

Ésta es la lección más difícil del libro.
It's the most difficult lesson in the book.

Roberto es más fuerte que Juan.
Roberto is stronger than Juan.

Roberto es el más fuerte del equipo.
Roberto is the strongest on the team.

Este libro es más interesante.
This book is more interesting.

Es el libro más interesante que jamás he leído.
It's the most interesting book that I've ever read.

Ella es más inteligente.
She's more intelligent.

Ella es más inteligente que nadie.
She's more intelligent than anyone.

4. "Than" is translated by *de* with numbers or degrees in comparisons.

Hay más de veinte alumnos.
There are more than twenty students.

Él tiene más de cuarenta dólares.
He has more than forty dollars.

Ellos vieron más de cien aviones.
They saw more than a hundred airplanes.

Note:

• In the negative, *que* is used before numbers to mean "only"; *de* is used to mean "no more than."

No tengo más que veinte dólares.
I have only twenty dollars.

No vieron más de cien aviones.
They saw no more than a hundred planes.

EXERCISES

A. Substitute the words or expressions in parentheses for the underlined word or expression in the model sentence. Write each new sentence and say it aloud.

1. *Roberto es más <u>fuerte</u> que tú.* (ambicioso, inteligente, pobre, rico, lento)

2. *Ellos tienen el restaurante más <u>típico</u> de Madrid.* (caro, económico, bonito, divertido, antiguo)

3. *Lo siento. No puedo <u>andar</u> más.* (estudiar, hablar, escribir, mandar, pedir)

4. *Mi hermano menor <u>canta</u> mejor que yo.* (baila, escribe, juega, lee, contesta)

5. *Es el coche más <u>moderno</u> del mundo.* (caro, peligroso, rápido, bonito, pequeño)

6. *Ellos me dieron más de cuarenta <u>libros</u>.* (dólares, números, folletos, sellos, nombres)

B. Rewrite these sentences in the negative. Write the complete sentence and translate.

1. *Tengo más de tres hermanos.*

2. *Me cobraron más de cien pesos.*

3. *Hay más de cinco sastres.*

4. *Compraron más de cinco maletas.*

5. *Murieron más de veinte soldados.*

C. Translate the following sentences into Spanish, then say them aloud.

   1. They have a better car.

   2. We are older than they are.

   3. This suit is more expensive.

   4. This soap washes better.

   5. The cloth that I bought is softer.

   6. Juana is the prettiest girl in the class.

   7. He is my youngest son.

   8. It's the best magazine in the world.

   9. I can't write (any) more.

   10. He is more intelligent than his older brother.

D. From among the three choices given, choose the best equivalent of the English term (in parentheses) for each sentence, and translate.

   1. (anymore) *No quiero estudiar* _____.
      (a) *alguna más*
      (b) *más*
      (c) *algo más*

   2. (stronger) *Juan es mucho* _____ *que José.*
      (a) *mas fuerte*
      (b) *más fuerte*
      (c) *fuerte*

   3. (bigger) *Este edificio es bastante* _____.
      (a) *grande*
      (b) *más*
      (c) *más grande*

   4. (biggest) *Es el edificio* _____ *de la ciudad.*
      (a) *menos grande*
      (b) *más grande*
      (c) *mas grande*

5. (than) *No creo que tenga más* _____ *veinte euros.*
   (a) *que*
   (b) *de*
   (c) *de los*

6. (only) *No me dieron más* _____ *treinta dólares.*
   (a) *de*
   (b) *que*
   (c) *de las*

7. (easier than) *Esta lección es* _____ *la otra.*
   (a) *más fácil de*
   (b) *menos fácil*
   (c) *más fácil que*

8. (than her sister) *Ella es más inteligente* _____ .
   (a) *de su hermana*
   (b) *que su hermana*
   (c) *su hermana*

9. (louder) *El profesor les dijo que hablaran* _____ .
   (a) *alto*
   (b) *fuerte*
   (c) *más fuerte*

10. (younger) *Es mi hermana* _____ .
    (a) *menor*
    (b) *más menor*
    (c) *la menor*

Answer Key

B. 1. *No tengo más que tres hermanos.*
    I only have three brothers.

    2. *No me cobraron más que (de) cien pesos.*
    They charged me only (no more than) 100 pesos.

    3. *No hay más que cinco sastres.*
    There are only five tailors.

    4. *No compraron más que (de) cinco maletas.*
    They bought only (no more than) five suitcases.

    5. *No murieron más que (de) veinte soldados.*
    Only (No more than) twenty soldiers died.

C. 1. *Tienen un coche mejor.*

    2. *Somos mayores que ellos.*

    3. *Este traje es más caro.*

    4. *Este jabón lava mejor.*

    5. *La tela que compré es más suave.*

    6. *Juana es la muchacha más bonita de la clase.*

    7. *Él es mi hijo menor.*

    8. *Es la mejor revista del mundo.*

    9. *No puedo escribir más.*

    10. *Él es más inteligente que su hermano mayor.*

D. 1. *No quiero estudiar más.*
    I don't want to study anymore.

    2. *Juan es mucho más fuerte que José.*
    Juan is much stronger than José.

    3. *Este edificio es bastante más grande.*
    This building is quite a bit bigger.

4. *Es el edificio más grande de la ciudad.*
   It's the biggest building in the city.

5. *No creo que tenga más de veinte euros.*
   I don't think I have more than twenty euros.

6. *No me dieron más que treinta dólares.*
   They only gave me thirty dollars.

7. *Esta lección es más fácil que la otra.*
   This lesson is easier than the other one.

8. *Ella es más inteligente que su hermana.*
   She is more intelligent than her sister.

9. *El profesor les dijo que hablaran más fuerte.*
   The professor told them to speak louder.

10. *Es mi hermana menor.*
    She is my younger sister.

LESSON 19

LA DENTISTA, EL MÉDICO Y LA FARMACÉUTICA
THE DENTIST, THE DOCTOR, AND THE PHARMACIST

A. DIALOGUE

0. *Esperanza y Diego están de vacaciones en Cancún cuando de repente a Esperanza le da un fuerte dolor de muelas.*
Esperanza and Diego are on vacation in Cancun when suddenly Esperanza gets a strong toothache.

La dentista. The dentist.

1. Recepcionista: **Buenos días. ¿En qué puedo servirle, señora?**
Good morning. What can I do for you, ma'am?

2. Esperanza: **Tengo un dolor de muelas terrible. Es un dolor punzante. ¿Puedo ver a la dentista?**
I have a terrible toothache. It's a very sharp pain. Could I see the dentist?

3. Recepcionista: **Claro. Un momento, por favor.**
Of course. Just a minute, please.

4. Dentista: **A ver, señora. ¿Quiere sentarse? Muy bien. ¿Qué es lo que le pasa?**
Let's see, ma'am. Would you like to sit down? Okay. What is the matter?

5. Esperanza: **La encía está un poco hinchada y hasta sangra a veces.**
The gum is a little swollen and it even bleeds at times.

6. Dentista: **Más vale tomar una radiografía. Eche usted la cabeza un poco para atrás y abra la boca, por favor. Muerda esto.**
Better take an X-ray. Tilt your head back a little. And open your mouth, please. Bite on this.

7. Esperanza: **¿Tardará mucho?**
Will it take long?

8. Dentista: **No. La radiografía estará en seguida. Mientras tanto, déjeme examinarle el diente.**
No. The X-ray will be ready right away. Meanwhile, let me examine the tooth.

9. Esperanza: **¡Ay! ¡Cómo me duele!**
Ouch! How painful!

10. Dentista: **Tendré que ponerle una inyección.**
I'll have to give you an injection.

11. Esperanza: **Sí, por favor. No aguanto el dolor.**
Yes, please. I can't stand this pain.

12. Dentista: **Ya veo lo que es. Tiene una caries en la muela aquí a la izquierda. No me parece muy serio el asunto.**
Now I see what it is. You have a cavity in the molar on the left. It doesn't look very serious.

13. Esperanza: **Menos mal. Espero que no tenga usted que sacármela.**
Good. I hope you don't have to pull it out.

14. Dentista: **Vamos a ver la radiografía. No, no hay que sacarla, pero hay que reparar esa caries.**
Let's look at the X-ray. No, it won't have to come out, but I have to fill the cavity.

15. Esperanza: **¿Me lo puede arreglar, entonces?**
You can fix it for me, then?

16. Dentista: **Será cosa de unos minutos y no sentirá nada, señora. No se preocupe.**
It will be a matter of a few minutes, and you won't feel anything, ma'am. Don't worry.

A Esperanza se le pasa el dolor de muelas, pero al llegar al hotel, se encuentra con Diego que no se siente muy bien.
Esperanza's toothache is gone, but when she returns to the hotel, she finds that Diego doesn't feel so good.

El médico. The doctor.

17. Diego: **Esperanza, no estoy nada bien. Tengo dolores por todo el cuerpo. Me duele la cabeza, el estómago, hasta me duele la garganta.**
I'm not well at all, Esperanza. I have aches all over my body. My head aches, my stomach aches, even my throat is sore.

18. Esperanza: **Desde luego, tienes mal aspecto. Voy a llamar al médico del hotel. Mientras tanto, acuéstate.** *(Llama.)*
You sure don't look well. I'm going to call the hotel doctor. Meanwhile, go to bed. *(She calls.)*

19. Médico: *(más tarde)* **A ver, señor, ¿qué le pasa? Abra la boca, por favor. Tosa. . . usted tiene fiebre y la garganta está bastante irritada.**
(later) Let's see, sir. What seems to be the problem? Open your mouth, please. Cough . . . You have a fever and your throat is quite irritated.

20. Esperanza: **¿Qué hay que hacer?**
What should we do?

21. Médico: **Su marido tendrá que guardar cama dos o tres días, señora, hasta que le pase la fiebre.**
Your husband will have to stay in bed for two or three days, ma'am, until the fever goes away.

22. Esperanza: **¿Puede comer de todo?**
    Can he eat anything?

23. Médico: **No, señora. Sopa o caldos. Bastante
    líquido. Jugos de frutas o cosas parecidas, y debe
    tomar estas píldoras que le voy a recetar. Dele
    una cada cuatro horas hasta que le baje la tem-
    peratura. Si no mejora esta noche, vuelva a lla-
    marme.**
    No, ma'am. Soups or broths. Plenty of liquids. Fruit
    juices, or something similar, and he ought to take
    these pills that I'm going to prescribe. Give him one
    every four hours until his temperature goes down. If
    he doesn't get better by tonight, call me again.

24. Diego: **¡Qué lástima! Ahora tenemos que aplazar
    el viaje a las pirámides.**
    What a shame! Now we have to postpone the trip to
    the pyramids.

25. Médico: **Ya lo creo. Tendrá que descansar.**
    I certainly think so. He'll have to rest.

26. Esperanza: *(La mañana siguiente)* **¿Cómo te
    sientes hoy, querido? ¿Has dormido bien?**
    (The following day) How do you feel today, dear?
    Did you sleep well?

27. Diego: **Mucho mejor, gracias. Me parece que no
    tengo tanta fiebre como antes. Y no me duele
    tanto la garganta.**
    Much better, thanks. I don't think I have as much of
    a fever as before. And my throat isn't so sore.

28. Esperanza: **Me alegro. Creo que es la misma
    enfermedad que yo tuve el mes pasado. Aquí está**

el periódico de hoy si lo quieres leer. Voy a la farmacia. Vuelvo enseguida.

I'm glad. I think it's the same illness that I had last
month. Here's today's paper if you want to read it.
I'm going to the pharmacy. I'll be right back.

En la farmacia. At the pharmacy.

29. Esperanza; **Por favor, ¿quiere prepararme esta
receta?**

    Will you prepare this prescription, please?

30. Farmacéutica: **No se preocupe, señora. Estará
dentro de un momento. ¿Quiere alguna otra
cosa?**

    Don't worry, ma'am. It will be ready in a moment.
    Do you want anything else?

31. Esperanza: **Ah, sí. Por poco se me olvida. ¿Tiene
usted un buen protector solar?**

    Oh, yes. I almost forgot. Do you have a good sun-
    screen lotion?

32. Farmacéutica: **Sí, en la parte de enfrente. Lo
preparamos en los laboratorios aquí; no hay
ninguna loción tan buena como la nuestra.**

    Yes, in the front of the store. We make it in our lab-
    oratories here, there's none that's as good as ours.

33. Esperanza: **Voy a probarla. ¿ Y dónde están las
hojas de afeitar y la crema dentífrica?**

    I'm going to try it. And where are the razor blades
    and the toothpaste?

34. Farmacéutica: **También al frente. Cerca de los
jabones.**

    Also in the front. Next to the soap.

B. NOTES

0. *El (La) dentista:* dentist. The same ending is used for either a male or female dentist.

2. *dolor de muelas*: toothache. "Headache" in Spanish is *dolor de cabeza*.

5. *hasta sangra*: it even bleeds. From the verb *sangrar* (to bleed). *Hasta*: in this case it means "even," though it is generally used to mean "until." *Estuve en la fiesta hasta las once.* I was in the party until eleven o'clock.

7. *¿Tardará mucho?*: Will it take long? The Spanish verb *tardar* means "to be long" or "to be slow."

11. *No aguanto el dolor*: I can't stand the pain. The verb *aguantar* (to bear) is followed by a noun with its appropriate article.

17. *Me duele la cabeza*: My head hurts. Notice the difference between this expression and the noun form, "headache", or *dolor de cabeza*. The verb form is *doler*, which means "to hurt." *Me duele* means "it hurts me."

21. *guardar cama*: to stay in bed.

23. *jugos de frutas:* fruit juice. *Zumos* is the term commonly used in Spain.

31. *por poco se me olvida*: Notice the present tense for an idea that is usually expressed by the past tense in English "I almost forgot." *Por poco* is used in this manner quite frequently. *Por poco se me cae el plato*. I almost dropped the plate. *Por poco se pierde Juan*. Juan almost got lost.

32. *en la parte de enfrente*: in the front. *Parte*, meaning "part," is used frequently when describing location in Spanish.

C. GRAMMAR AND USAGE

1. The Spanish expression *el mismo que* means "the same as."

Rafael tiene el mismo disco que yo.
   Rafael has the same record as I do.

Ellos estudian los mismos libros que nosotros.
   They are studying the same books as we are.

Teresa lleva la misma blusa que ayer.
   Teresa is wearing the same blouse as yesterday.

Todos tienen las mismas preocupaciones que él.
   They all have the same worries as he does.

2. To form the possessive pronoun, use the appropriate form of the article with the long form of the possessive adjective.

Juan dice que este coche es mejor que el suyo.
   Juan says this car is better than his.

Aquí está tu pluma. ¿Dónde está la mía?
   Here's your pen. Where's mine?

La clase de Rafael empieza a las cuatro.
¿Cuándo empieza la nuestra?
   Rafael's class begins at four o'clock.
   When does ours begin?

Los zapatos de María son nuevos.
Me gustan tanto como los tuyos.
   Maria's shoes are new.
   I like them as much as yours.

Préstame tu libro, por favor.
He perdido el mío.
> Lend me your book, please.
> I lost mine.

¿Las maletas? Las mías están aquí.
> The suitcases? Mine are here.

¿Los abrigos? El mío está allí y éste es el tuyo.
> The coats? Mine is there and this one is yours.

¿El de Juan? Dile que el suyo está aquí también.
> Juan's? Tell him that his is here, too.

3. You can use *poco, mucho, otro, alguno,* and *ninguno* as nouns.

¿Flores? Me quedan muy pocas.
> Flowers? I have very few left.

¿Botones? ¿Quiere usted muchos?
> Buttons? Do you want many?

Sí, quiero algunos grandes.
> Yes, I want some big ones.

No tengo ninguno.
> I don't have any.

¿Tiene usted otro más barato?
> Do you have another cheaper one?

EXERCISES

A. Substitute the words or expressions in parentheses for the underlined word or expression in the model sentence. Write each new sentence and say it aloud.

1. *Esteban ha comprado el mismo <u>modelo</u> que yo.*
   (coche, abrigo, sombrero, reloj, traje)

2. *Ella siempre compra los mismos <u>libros</u> que su amiga.* (zapatos, vestidos, periódicos, cuadernos, vinos)

3. *Creo que esta <u>casa</u> es más bonita que la mía.* (blusa, máquina, lámpara, mesa, revista)

4. *¿Cuadros? Tenemos <u>unos</u> más bonitos.* (algunos, pocos, muchos, otros)

5. *¿Computadora? ¿Quiere usted ver una <u>portátil</u>?* (nueva, barata, bonita, práctica, moderna, japonesa)

6. *No veo mis <u>zapatos</u> pero aquí están los tuyos.* (libros, lápices, papeles, cuadernos, guantes)

B. Change these sentences to the present tense. Write the complete sentence and translate.

1. *Ellos siempre mandaron los mismos periódicos.*

2. *Él compró la misma crema de afeitar que Juan.*

3. *Tú recibiste el mismo premio que yo.*

4. *Cuando mi padre recibió su nueva máquina de escribir, me dio la vieja.*

5. *Juan no escuchó el mismo programa que yo.*

C. Translate the following sentences into Spanish, then say them aloud.

1. I like your car but mine is better.

2. We bought the same record as María.

3. Juan always goes to the same school as his brother.

4. When he lost his book, I gave him mine.

5. They bought tickets in the same row as ours.

6. Juan and I went to the same theater as you.

7. I had my umbrella but Juan lost his.

8. I bought some candy. Do you want some?

9. Will you give me a few dollars?

10. Where are yours (dollars)?

D. From among the three choices given, choose the best equivalent of the English term (in parentheses) for each sentence, and translate.

1. (the same) *Estos discos son* _____ *que tengo yo.*
   (a) *los mismos*
   (b) *la misma*
   (c) *mismos*

2. (mine) *Me gusta este coche más que* _____.
   (a) *la mía*
   (b) *el mío*
   (c) *míos*

3. (yours) *Esta es mi pluma. ¿Dónde está* _____?
   (a) *el tuyo*
   (b) *los tuyos*
   (c) *la tuya*

4. (Ours) *Me gusta esta casa.* _____ *es más pequeña.*
   (a) *La nuestra*
   (b) *Las nuestras*
   (c) *El nuestro*

5. (his) *Me pidió el libro porque había perdido* _____.
   (a) *la suya*
   (b) *lo suyo*
   (c) *el suyo*

6. (few) *Puedes llevarte estos lápices, aunque me quedan muy* _____.
   (a) *pocas*
   (b) *pocos*
   (c) *unos pocos*

7. (some) *Veo que hay muchas revistas. Voy a comprar* _____.
   (a) *alguno*
   (b) *algunas*
   (c) *algunos*

8. (the same) *Tengo* _____ *preocupaciones que tú.*
   (a) *el mismo*
   (b) *los mismos*
   (c) *las mismas*

9. (yours) *Aquí están mis maletas. ¿Dónde están* _____?
   (a) *el tuyo*
   (b) *las tuyas*
   (c) *la tuya*

10. (hers) *Tu sombrero es muy bonito y me gusta* _____ *también.*
    (a) *la suya*
    (b) *el suyo*
    (c) *las suyas*

Answer Key

B. 1. *Ellos siempre mandan los mismos periódicos.*
      They always send the same newspapers.

   2. *Él compra la misma crema de afeitar que Juan.*
      He buys the same shaving cream as Juan.

   3. *Tú recibes el mismo premio que yo.*
      You receive the same prize as I do.

   4. *Cuando mi padre recibe su nueva máquina de escribir, me da la vieja.*
      When my father receives his new typewriter, he gives me the old one.

   5. *Juan no escucha el mismo programa que yo.*
      Juan doesn't listen to the same program as I do.

C. 1. *Me gusta tu coche pero el mío es mejor.*

   2. *Compramos el mismo disco que María.*

   3. *Juan siempre va a la misma escuela que su hermano.*

   4. *Cuando perdió su libro, le di el mío.*

   5. *Compraron entradas en la misma fila que la nuestra.*

   6. *Juan y yo fuimos al mismo teatro que tú.*

   7. *Yo tenía mi paraguas pero Juan perdió el suyo.*

   8. *Compré unos dulces. ¿Quieres algunos?*

   9. *¿Quiere(s) usted (tú) darme algunos dólares?*

   10. *¿Dónde están los suyos (tuyos)?*

D. 1. *Estos discos son los mismos que tengo yo.*
      These records are the same ones that I have.

   2. *Me gusta este coche más que el mío.*
      I like this car better than mine.

3. *Ésta es mi pluma. ¿Dónde está la tuya?*
   This is my pen. Where is yours?

4. *Me gusta esta casa. La nuestra es más pequeña.*
   I like this house. Ours is smaller.

5. *Me pidió el libro porque había perdido el suyo.*
   He asked me for the book because he had lost his.

6. *Puedes llevarte estos lápices, aunque me quedan muy pocos.*
   You can take these pencils, although I have very few left.

7. *Veo que hay muchas revistas. Voy a comprar algunas.*
   I see that there are many magazines. I am going to buy some.

8. *Tengo las mismas preocupaciones que tú.*
   I have the same worries as you do.

9. *Aquí están mis maletas. ¿Dónde están las tuyas?*
   Here are my suitcases. Where are yours?

10. *Tu sombrero es muy bonito y me gusta el suyo también.*
    Your hat is very pretty, and I like hers too.

LESSON 20

LA POLÍTICA
POLITICS

A. DIALOGUE

0. *Juan y Luis están hablando de política. Es un tema muy interesante para los dos, sobre todo unas semanas antes de las elecciones.*
   Juan and Luis are talking about politics. It is a very interesting topic for both of them, especially a few weeks before the elections.

1. Juan: **Estas elecciones van a ser muy reñidas.**
   These elections are going to be very tight.

2. Luis: **Los dos candidatos principales presentan unas alternativas interesantes a los problemas actuales. Sin embargo, no sé por quién votar.**
   The two main candidates present some interesting alternatives to the current problems. However, I don't know which one to vote for.

3. Juan: **Yo creo que ambos candidatos han sido bastante honestos, pero todavía no han sido muy específicos con los detalles.**
   I think both candidates have been quite honest, but they haven't been too specific with the details.

4. Luis: **Estoy de acuerdo. Realmente me cuesta mucho trabajo decidir por quién votar.**
   I agree. I find it really difficult to decide who I'm going to vote for.

5. Juan: **A mí me ocurre exactamente lo mismo. Hay tantas cosas que valorar: el medio ambiente, la economía, la educación, la política internacional.**

The exact same thing is happening to me. There are so many things to consider: the environment, the economy, education, and international policy.

6. Luis: **De cualquier forma, me parece que vamos a estar mejor que con el actual presidente.**
In any case, I think we'll be better off than with the current president.

7. Juan: **Estoy de acuerdo. Yo me alegro mucho de que haya decidido dejar la política.**
I agree. I am so happy that he decided to leave politics.

8. Luis: **Sí, el actual presidente es una persona que prometió mucho pero no cumplió con sus promesas.**
Yes, the current president is someone who promised a lot but didn't deliver on his promises.

9. Juan: **También creo que no supo cómo manejar las protestas estudiantiles. Los estudiantes querían que él bajara los precios de la matrícula.**
I also think that he didn't know how to deal with the student protests. The students wanted him to lower the price of tuition.

10. Luis: **Él no reaccionó de la manera correcta. Estoy de acuerdo.**
He didn't respond the right way. I agree.

11. Juan: **Fue una situación muy violenta en las universidades. Los heridos fueron muchos en las protestas.**
The situation turned violent in the universities. There were many people injured in the protests.

12. Luis: **Bueno, ojalá que el próximo presidente pueda tener una mejor comunicación con estudiantes y sindicatos.**
Well, I hope the next president can maintain better communication with the students and the unions.

13. Juan: **Yo creo que sí. Me parece que los dos candidatos nuevos tienen un mejor temperamento. Parecen ser bastante calmados y sensatos.**
I think so. Both new candidates seem to have a better temper. They seem calm and sensible enough.

14. Luis: **¿Quién es el preferido en este momento?**
Who is the favorite now?

15. Juan: **Las encuestas le dan una ligera ventaja a Mayoral, pero Calderón está pisándole los talones.**
The polls give Mayoral a slight lead, but Calderon is close behind.

16. Luis: **Pues sí que van a ser unas elecciones muy interesantes.**
They will certainly be very interesting elections.

17. Juan: **¿Qué te parece la política internacional de los dos candidatos?**
What do you think of the candidates' international policies?

18. Luis: **La política internacional de Calderón me gusta más que la de Mayoral. Sin embargo, Mayoral ha sugerido muy buenas propuestas econó-micas.**
I like Calderon's international policies better than Mayoral's. However, Mayoral has suggested some good economic proposals.

19. Juan: **El desempleo es uno de los problemas más importantes que tenemos en este momento.**
Unemployment is one of the most important problems we have at this time.

20. Luis: **Lo que no me convence mucho de ninguno de los dos candidatos es su política ambiental.**
What hasn't convinced me much about the two candidates are their environmental policies.

21. Juan: **Yo estoy de acuerdo; el último gobierno no hizo mucho para proteger el medio ambiente y los candidatos no están hablando mucho del tema.**
I agree, the previous government didn't do much to protect the environment, and the candidates aren't talking much about the issue.

22. Luis: **¡Que lo expliquen bien antes de las elecciones!**
Let them explain it before the elections!

23. Juan: **Sí, y la gente parece muy apática.**
Yes, and people seem very apathetic.

24. Luis: **Estoy de acuerdo. Ojalá que la gente prestara más atención a los problemas actuales.**
I agree. I wish that people would pay more attention to current problems.

25. Juan: **¿Y cuándo van a televisar los debates?**
And when are they going to broadcast the debates?

26. Luis: **La semana que viene hay uno.**
There's one next week.

27. Juan: **Yo creo que a raíz de los debates vamos a tener una idea más clara de los candidatos.**

I think that as a result of the debates we are going to
have a clearer idea about the candidates.

28. Luis: **Mientras tanto solo tenemos que esperar...
    ¡y esperar que gane el mejor!**
    In the meantime we just have to wait . . . and hope
    that the best wins!

B. NOTES

1. *reñidas*: contested. *Reñir*: to fight.

2. *Sin embargo*: however, nonetheless.

8. *cumplir*: to deliver or to fulfill. It is also used for
   birthdays. *Yo cumplo años en octubre.* I turn a year
   older in October. (My birthday is in October). *¡Feliz
   cumpleaños!* Happy birthday!

14. *el preferido*: the favorite, the preferred one.

15. *pisándole los talones*: literally, "stepping on the
    heels."

19. *desempleo*: unemployment. The term *paro* (stop-
    page) is also common.

20. *Lo que no me convence mucho de ninguno de los dos
    candidatos es su política ambiental.*: Literally,
    "That which doesn't convince me much about either
    of the two candidates is their environmental policy."

21. *el medio ambiente*: the environment. *Ambiente* can
    also mean "atmosphere;" *medio* in other contexts
    indicates "the middle" or "half."
        tema: topic, theme. In this case it translates into
    "issue." *Es un tema importante para los políticos.* It
    is an important issue for the politicians.

25. *televisar*: to broadcast on television, to televise. From *televisión* (television).

26. *la semana que viene*: next week. Literally, "the week that is coming."

27. *raíz*: root. *A raíz de*: As a result of, as a consequence of.

28. *esperar*: Notice the play of words in the expression. The verb *esperar* has two meanings, "to wait for" and "to hope for." *Llevo veinte minutos esperando el autobús.* I have been waiting for the bus for twenty minutes. *Espero que el vuelo llegue a tiempo.* I hope that the flight arrives on time.

C. GRAMMAR AND USAGE

1. The past participle may be used as a noun:

El invitado fue muy simpático.
   The guest was very nice.

Los heridos fueron muchos.
   The wounded were many.

Los más avanzados llegaron.
   The most advanced arrived.

La más informada nos habló del asunto.
   The most informed (one) spoke to us about the matter.

Juan es el menos preparado para el trabajo.
   Juan is the one least prepared for the job.

El preferido fue un hombre mayor.
   The preferred one was an older man.

La casada no habló.
   The married one didn't speak.

El más conocido era don Juan Satrústegui.
> The best known one was Don Juan Satrústegui.

2. Indirect commands or wishes are formed using the subjunctive with *que.*

   Que ellos lo compren.
   > Have them buy it.

   Que él lo diga.
   > Let him say it.

   Que ella lo mande.
   > Have her send it.

   Note:

   • In these indirect commands, the subject, if expressed, may precede or follow the verb form.

   Que lo diga Juan.
   > Let Juan say it.

   Que lo hagan ellos.
   > Have them do it.

3. Use the past imperfect subjunctive in a dependent clause when the main clause is in the past (whether it is in the preterit, imperfect, or conditional).

   Me dijo que fuera a misa.
   > He told me to go to Mass.

   Querían que él lo hiciera.
   > They wanted him to do it.

   Fue imposible que ellos llegaran tan temprano.
   > It was impossible for them to arrive so early.

   Esperaban que Juan los invitara.
   > They were hoping that Juan would invite them.

Nos pidió que mandáramos los paquetes.
He asked us to send the packages.

Era necesario que ustedes lo leyeran.
It was necessary for you to read it.

El jefe sentía que ella tuviera que marcharse.
The boss was sorry that she had to leave.

Ella se alegró de que no oyéramos las noticias.
She was happy that we didn't hear the news.

4. The word *ojalá* followed by the imperfect subjunctive is used to express a wish.

Ojalá que estuvieran aquí.
If only [I wish that] they were here!

Ojalá que lo encontrara usted.
If only [I wish that] you would find it!

Ojalá que ella lo supiera.
If only [I wish that] she knew it!

Note:

• *Ojalá* may be used alone in exclamation.

¿Que yo soy muy rico? ¡Ojalá!
Am I very rich? I wish (I were)!

¿Se casó ella? ¡Ojalá!
Did she get married? I wish (she had)!

EXERCISES

A. Substitute the words or expressions in parentheses for the underlined word or expression in the model sentence. Write each new sentence and say it aloud.

  1. *El desconocido llegó muy tarde.* (La casada, El invitado, La acusada, El herido, La más querida)

2. *Que él lo haga.* (diga, compre, mande, escriba, lea)

3. *Ojalá que ellos lo supieran.* (vendieran, vieran, sintieran, dudaran, dijeran)

4. *Era imposible que yo llegara a las seis y treinta.* (saliera, viniera, me levantara, hablara, llamara)

5. *Era difícil que ellos me creyeran.* (imposible, increíble, necesario, fantástico, probable)

6. *El jefe dijo que mandáramos las cartas en seguida.* (rogó, mandó, pidió, se alegró de, quiso)

B. Change these sentences to the past tense. Write the complete sentence and translate.

1. *Es posible que vengan Juan y José.*

2. *Lo dice para que lo sepamos.*

3. *Espero que lo hagan inmediatamente.*

4. *Dudo que Juan lo oiga.*

5. *María siente que ellos lo crean.*

C. Translate the following sentences into Spanish, then say them aloud.

1. I'm sorry he's here.

2. He was sorry that I did it.

3. If only he were here!

4. Let them do it!

5. The best informed (one) spoke to us.

6. They said it so that he would know (it).

7. It's impossible for them to believe it.

8. He doubted that we knew it.

9. They wanted us to buy the book.

10. The boss told me to do it.

D. From among the three choices given, choose the best equivalent of the English term (in parentheses) for each sentence, and translate.

1. (the best-informed woman) *Me gustaría hablar con* _____.
   - (a) *el más informado*
   - (b) *la más informada*
   - (c) *las más informadas*

2. (the wounded) *Tenían que ayudar* _____.
   - (a) *los heridos*
   - (b) *herido*
   - (c) *a los heridos*

3. (Let) _____ *él lo escriba.*
   - (a) *Tenga*
   - (b) *Que*
   - (c) *Dígale*

4. (sell) *Fue imposible que ellos* _____ *el coche.*
   - (a) *vendiera*
   - (b) *vendieron*
   - (c) *vendieran*

5. (couldn't) *Sentía que Juan* _____ *venir a la boda.*
   - (a) *no puede*
   - (b) *no podrá*
   - (c) *no pudiera*

6. (go) *Yo quería que ellos* _____ *al cine.*
   - (a) *van*
   - (b) *fueran*
   - (c) *fueron*

7. (do) *Que lo _____ Juan.*
   (a) *haga*
   (b) *hace*
   (c) *hagan*

8. (the favorite) *De todos los empleados, Rafael es*
   _____.
   (a) *el preferido*
   (b) *lo preferido*
   (c) *la preferida*

9. (say) *Querían que el jefe lo _____.*
   (a) *dice*
   (b) *dijera*
   (c) *dijo*

10. (I wish I were) *Dicen que soy muy inteligente*
    ¡_____!
    (a) *Quiero estar*
    (b) *Quería*
    (c) *Ojalá*

Answer Key

B. 1. *Era posible que vinieran Juan y José.*
      It was possible that Juan and José would come.

   2. *Lo dijo para que lo supiéramos.*
      He said it so that we would know it.

   3. *Esperaba que lo hicieran immediatamente.*
      I hoped that they would do it immediately.

   4. *Dudaba que Juan lo oyera.*
      I doubted that Juan heard it.

   5. *María sentía que ellos lo creyeran.*
      María was sorry that they believed it.

C. 1. *Siento que él esté aquí.*

   2. *Él sintió que yo lo hiciera.*

   3. *¡Ojalá él estuviera aquí!*

   4. *¡Que lo hagan ellos!*

   5. *El más informado nos habló.*

   6. *Lo dijeron para que él lo supiera.*

   7. *Es imposible que ellos lo crean.*

   8. *Él dudaba que lo supiéramos.*

   9. *Ellos querían que compráramos el libro.*

   10. *El jefe me dijo que lo hiciera. (El jefe me mandó hacerlo.)*

D. 1. *Me gustaría hablar con la más informada.*
      I would like to talk to the best-informed woman.

   2. *Tenían que ayudar a los heridos.*
      They had to help the wounded.

3. *Que él lo escriba.*
   Let him write it.

4. *Fue imposible que ellos vendieran el coche.*
   It was impossible for them to sell the car.

5. *Sentía que Juan no pudiera venir a la boda.*
   I was sorry that Juan couldn't come to the wedding.

6. *Yo quería que ellos fueran al cine.*
   I wanted them to go to the movies.

7. *Que lo haga Juan.*
   Let Juan do it.

8. *De todos los empleados, Rafael es el preferido.*
   Of all the employees, Rafael is the favorite.

9. *Querían que el jefe lo dijera.*
   They wanted the boss to say it.

10. *Dicen que soy muy inteligente. ¡Ojalá!*
    They say that I am very intelligent. I wish I were!

SUMMARY OF SPANISH GRAMMAR

1.   THE ALPHABET

LETTER	NAME	LETTER	NAME	LETTER	NAME
a	a	*j*	jota	*r*	ere
b	be	*k*	ka	*s*	ese
c	c	*l*	ele	*t*	te
d	de	*m*	eme	*u*	u
e	e	*n*	ene	*v*	ve
f	efe	*ñ*	eñe	*w*	doble ve
g	ge	*o*	o	*x*	equis
h	hache	*p*	pe	*y*	i griega
i	i	*q*	cu	*z*	zeta

The letters *ch, ll,* and *rr* were until recently considered separate letters.

2.   PRONUNCIATION

SIMPLE VOWELS

a   *ah,* like the *a* in f*a*ther
e   like the *ay* in *day,* but cut off sharply
i   like the *i* in mach*i*ne
o   like the *o* in *o*pen
u   like the *u* in r*u*le

VOWEL COMBINATIONS

ai }		*ie*	*ye* in *yes*.
ay }	*ai* in *aisle*.	*io*	*yo* in *yoke*.
au	*ou* in *out*.	*ua*	*wah*.
ei }		*ou*	*wo* in *woe*.
ey }	*áy-ee*.		
eu	*áy-oo*	*iu*	*you*.
oi }		*ui* }	
oy }	*oy* in *boy*.	*uy* }	*óo-ee*.
ia	*ya* in *yard*.		

CONSONANTS

Notice the following points:

b, v   have the same sound. After a pause and after *m*
or *n*, both are like *b* in *boy*. When the sound
occurs between vowels you bring the upper
and lower lips together and blow between
them, the way you do when blowing dust
from something.[1]

c   before *o, a,* and *u*, and before consonants, is like
c in *cut*.

c   before *e* and *i* is pronounced in Spain like *th* in
thin. In Spanish America it is pronounced like
s in *see*.

ch   as in *church*.

d   after a pause or *n* and *l*, like *d*. When it occurs
between vowels, like *th* in *that*.

g   before *a, o,* and *u*, and before consonants, after
a pause, and after *n*, like *g* in *go*.

g   before *e* and *i* is a strong *h* as in *alcohol*.

---

[1] Many Spanish speakers make the same difference between *b* and
v that we do in English. They pronounce *b* whenever a *b* appears in
the spelling and a *v* whenever a *v* appears in the spelling.

h   is not pronounced.
j   is always like *g* before *e* and *i* (see above).
ll   is pronounced like *y* in *yes*.
ñ   is like *ni* in *onion* or *ny* in *canyon*.
qu   is like *k*.
r   is pronounced by tapping the tip of the tongue against the gum ridge back of the upper teeth.
rr   is trilled several times.
s   as in *see*.
x   before a consonant like *s;* between vowels like *x (ks)* in *extra*. Sometimes, however, it is like the *x (gs)* in *examine*.
y   when it begins a word or syllable, like *y* in *yes*.
y   when it serves as a vowel, like *i*.
z   is pronounced the same as the Spanish *c* before *e* and *i* (see above).

3. STRESS

1. Stress the last syllable if the word ends in a consonant other than *n* or *s*.

ciudad   city

2. Stress the next to the last syllable if the word ends in a vowel or *n* or *s*.

amigo   friend
hablan   they speak

3. Otherwise stress the syllable that has the accent (´).

inglés   English
teléfono   telephone

4. PUNCTUATION

There are several differences between Spanish and English.

   1. Exclamation and question marks precede as well as follow the sentence:

¿Adónde va usted?	Where are you going?
¡Hombre! ¿Adónde va Ud.?	Man! Where are you going?
¡Venga!	Come!
¡Qué hermoso día!	What a beautiful day!

   2. The question mark is placed before the question part of the sentence:

Juan, ¿adónde vas?	John, where are you going?
Usted conoce al Sr. Díaz, ¿no es verdad?	You know Mr. Díaz, don't you?

   3. Dashes are often used where we use quotation marks:

Muchas gracias —dijo.	"Thanks a lot," he said.
Esta mañana —dijo— fui al centro.	"This morning," he said, "I went downtown."
—¿Cómo está usted?	"How are you?"
—Muy bien, gracias.	"Very well, thank you."

   4. Capitals are not used as frequently as in English. They are only used at the beginning of sentences

and with proper nouns. *Yo* "I," adjectives of nationality, the days of the week and the months are not capitalized:

Somos americanos.	We're Americans.
Él no es francés sino inglés.	He's not French but English.
Vendré el martes o el miércoles.	I'll come Tuesday or Wednesday.
Hoy es el primero de febrero.	Today is the first of February.

5. Suspension points (. . .) are used more frequently than in English to indicate interruption, hesitation, etc.

5. SOME ORTHOGRAPHIC SIGNS

1. The tilde (~) is used over the letter *n* to indicate the sound of *ni* in *onion* or *ny* in *canyon*.
2. The diéresis (¨) is used over *u* in the combination *gu*. It indicates that the vowel "u" is pronounced (gw).

vergüenza	shame
pingüino	penguin

6. THE DEFINITE ARTICLE

	SINGULAR	PLURAL
MASCULINE	*el*	*los*
FEMININE	*la*	*las*

SINGULAR	
el muchacho	the boy
la muchacha	the girl

PLURAL

los muchachos	the boys
las muchachas	the girls

1. *El* is used before a feminine noun beginning with stressed *a* (or *ha*):

el agua	the water

But—

las aguas	the waters
el hacha	the axe

But—

las hachas	the axes

2. The neuter article *lo* is used before parts of speech other than nouns when they are used as nouns:

lo malo	what is bad, the bad part of it
lo hecho	what is done
lo dicho	what is said
lo útil	the useful
lo difícil	the difficult
lo posible	the possible
lo necesario	the necessary

3. The definite article is used:

a. with abstract nouns:

La verdad vale más que las riquezas.	Truth is worth more than riches.

b. with nouns referring to a class:

los soldados	soldiers
los generales	generals

c. with names of languages (except immediately after common verbs, such as *hablar, saber, aprender, estudiar,* etc. or the prepositions *en* or *de*):

El español no es difícil.	Spanish is not difficult.
Habla bien el portugués.	She speaks Portuguese well.

But—

Dígalo Ud. en inglés.	Say it in English.
Hablo español.	I speak Spanish.

d. in expressions of time:

la una	one o'clock
las dos	two o'clock
las diez	ten o'clock

e. for the days of the week:

Abren los domingos a las dos y media.	They open Sundays at 2:30.
el lunes próximo	next Monday

f. for the year, seasons, etc.

el año 2003	the year 2003
Vino el año pasado.	He came last year.
la primavera	spring
En el invierno hace frío.	It's cold in winter.

g. with certain geographical names:

El Brasil	Brazil
El Canadá	Canada
El Perú	Peru
El Uruguay	Uruguay
El Ecuador	Ecuador
El Japón	Japan

Note: The definite article is used with parts of the body and articles of clothing:

Me duele la cabeza.	My head hurts.
Quítese el abrigo.	Take your coat off.

8. THE INDEFINITE ARTICLE

	SINGULAR	PLURAL
MASCULINE	*un*	*unos*
FEMININE	*una*	*unas*

	SINGULAR
un hombre	a man
una mujer	a woman
unos hombres	men, some (a few) men

	PLURAL
unas mujeres	women, some (a few) women

1. *Unos (unas)* is often used where we use "some" or "a few" in English:

unos días	a few days

2. The indefinite article is omitted:

a. before rank, profession, trade, nationality, etc.:

Soy capitán.	I'm a captain.
Soy médico.	I'm a doctor.
Soy abogado.	I'm a lawyer.
Es profesor.	He's a teacher.
Soy norteamericano	I'm an American.
Ella es española.	She's Spanish.

b. before *ciento* (or *cien*) "hundred," *cierto* "certain," *mil* "thousand":

cien hombres	a hundred men
cierto hombre	a certain man
mil hombres	a thousand men

c. in various idiomatic expressions, such as:

Salió sin sombrero.	He left without a hat.

8. CONTRACTIONS

1. *de + el = del*   of (from) the
   del hermano   from (of) the brother

2. *a + el = al*   to the
   al padre   to the father

9. THE DAYS OF THE WEEK

The days of the week are masculine and are not capitalized. The article is usually necessary, except after *ser:*

el domingo	Sunday
el lunes	Monday

el martes	Tuesday
el miércoles	Wednesday
el jueves	Thursday
el viernes	Friday
el sábado	Saturday
El domingo es el primer día de la semana.	Sunday is the first day of the week.
Van a visitarlos el domingo.	They're going to pay them a visit on Sunday.
Mañana es sábado.	Tomorrow is Saturday.

Notice that "on Sunday," "on Monday," etc., are *el domingo, el lunes;* "on Tuesdays," *los martes,* etc.

10. THE MONTHS OF THE YEAR

The names of the months are masculine and are not capitalized. They are usually used without the definite article:

enero	January
febrero	February
marzo	March
abril	April
mayo	May
junio	June
julio	July
agosto	August
septiembre	September
octubre	October
noviembre	November
diciembre	December

11. THE SEASONS

el invierno	winter
la primavera	spring
el verano	summer
el otoño	fall

The names of seasons are usually not capitalized. They are preceded by the definite article but after *de* and *en* the article may or may not be used:

Hace frío en (el) invierno.	It's cold in (the) winter.
Trabajo durante los meses de verano.	I work during the summer months.

12. MASCULINE AND FEMININE GENDER

Nouns referring to males are masculine; nouns referring to females are feminine:

el padre	the father	*la madre*	the mother
el hijo	the son	*la hija*	the daughter
el hombre	the man	*la mujer*	the woman
el toro	the bull	*la vaca*	the cow
el gato	the tomcat	*la gata*	the she-cat

The masculine plural of certain nouns stands for both genders:

los padres	the parents, the father and mother
los reyes	the king and queen
mis hermanos	my brothers and sisters

Masculine nouns and adjectives usually end in *-o*; feminine nouns and adjectives in *-a*.

1. Nouns ending in -*o* are usually masculine:

el cuerpo	the body
el cielo	the sky .
el dinero	the money

Common Exceptions:

la mano	the hand
la radio/el radio	the radio/the radius

2. Nouns ending in *r, n,* and *l* are generally masculine:

el calor	the heat
el pan	the bread
el sol	the sun

3. Names of trees, days of the week, months, oceans, rivers, mountains, and other parts of speech used as nouns are generally masculine:

el álamo	the poplar
el martes	Tuesday
el Atlántico	The Atlantic Ocean
el Tajo	The Tagus River
los Andes	The Andes
el ser joven	being young, the fact of being young.

1. Nouns ending in -*a* (also -*dad*, -*tad*, -*tud*, -*ción*, -*sión*, -*ez*, -*umbre*, -*ie*) are usually feminine:

la cabeza	the head
la ciudad	the city
la cantidad	quantity
la libertad	liberty
la virtud	virtue
la condición	the condition
la costumbre	the custom
la tensión	tension
la madurez	maturity

Common Exceptions:

el día	the day
el mapa	the map
el drama	the drama
el clima	the climate
el problema	the problem
el poeta	the poet

2. Names of cities, towns, and fruits are generally feminine:

Barcelona es muy bonita.	Barcelona is very nice.
la naranja	the orange
la manzana	the apple

Note: Certain nouns differ in meaning depending on whether they take *el* or *la:*

el orden	order (arrangement)
el capital	capital (money)
el cura	priest

But—

la orden	order (command)
la capital	capital (city)
la cura	cure

13. The Plural

1. Nouns ending in an unstressed vowel add -*s:*

el libro	the book	*los libros*	the books

2. Nouns ending in a consonant add -*es:*

el avión	the airplane
los aviones	the airplanes

3. Nouns ending in -*z* change the *z* to *c* and then add *es:*

la luz	the light	*las luces*	the lights
el lápiz	the pencil	*los lápices*	the pencils

4. Some nouns are unchanged in the plural:

los martes	Tuesdays
los Martínez	the Martínez family

14. The Possessive

English -'s or -s' is translated by *de* "of":

el libro de Juan	John's book ("the book of John")
los libros de los niños	the boys' books ("the books of the boys")

15. Adjectives

1. Singular and Plural

SINGULAR

un muchacho alto	a tall boy
una muchacha alta	a tall girl

PLURAL

dos muchachos altos	two tall boys
dos muchachas altas	two tall girls

Notice that the adjective comes after the noun and is masculine if the noun is masculine, plural if the noun is plural, etc.

2. Feminine Endings

a. If the ending is *-o,* it becomes *-a:*

MASCULINE	FEMININE	
alto	*alta*	tall
rico	*rica*	rich
bajo	*baja*	low

b. In other cases there is no change:

MASCULINE	FEMININE	
grande	*grande*	big, large
azul	*azul*	blue
cortés	*cortés*	polite
útil	*útil*	useful
triste	*triste*	sad

Examples:

una cosa útil	a useful thing
una mujer triste	a sad woman
una muchacha cortés	a polite girl

c. Adjectives of nationality add *-a* or change *o* to *a:*

MASCULINE	FEMININE	
español	*española*	Spanish
francés	*francesa*	French

inglés	*inglesa*	English
americano	*americana*	American

Examples:

una señora inglesa	an English woman
la lengua española	the Spanish language

d. Adjectives ending in *-án* or *-ón*[1] and *-or* add *-a:*

MASCULINE	FEMININE	
holgazán	*holgazana*	lazy
burlón	*burlona*	jesting
preguntón	*preguntona*	inquisitive
encantador	*encantadora*	charming
fascinador	*fascinadora*	fascinating

3. The following adjectives drop the final *-o* when they come before a masculine singular noun:

uno	one
bueno	good
malo	bad
alguno	some one
ninguno	no one
primero	first
tercero	third

Examples:

un buen amigo	a good friend
ningún hombre	no man
el mal tiempo	the bad weather
el primer día	the first day

---

[1] Notice that the accent is dropped in the feminine.

4. *Grande* becomes *gran* when it comes before a singular noun:

un gran amigo	a great friend
un gran poeta	a great poet
un gran hombre	a great (important) man

But—

un hombre grande	a large (tall) man

5. *Santo* becomes *San* when it comes before a noun (except those beginning in *To-* and *Do-*):

San Juan	Saint John
San Luis	Saint Louis

But—

Santo Tomás	Saint Thomas
Santo Domingo	Saint Dominic

6. *Ciento* becomes *cien* before a noun and the number *mil:*

cien dólares	a hundred dollars
cien mil personas	one hundred thousand people

16. POSITION OF ADJECTIVES

1. Descriptive adjectives usually follow the noun:

un libro blanco	a white book
una casa blanca	a white house
mi sombrero nuevo	my new hat

dinero mexicano	Mexican money
un hombre inteligente	an intelligent man
huevos frescos	fresh eggs

2. Exceptions are adjectives which describe an inherent quality:

| *un buen muchacho* | a good boy |

3. Articles, numerals, possessives, and quantitatives usually precede the noun:

muchas personas	many persons
poca gente	few people
cuatro huevos	four eggs
mis libros	my books

4. Some descriptive adjectives can come either before or after the noun:

una niña pequeña or *una pequeña niña*	a little girl
un día hermoso or *un hermoso día*	a nice (beautiful) day
una linda muchacha or *una muchacha linda*	a pretty girl

Other common adjectives used this way are *bueno* "good," *malo* "bad," and *bonito* "pretty."

5. A few adjectives have one meaning when they come before a noun and another when they follow:

| *un hombre pobre* | a poor man |
| *¡Pobre hombre!* | Poor man! |

un hombre grande	a large (tall) man
un gran hombre	a great (important) man
un libro nuevo	a new (recent) book
un nuevo hombre	a different man
cierto hombre	a certain man
una noticia cierta	a true piece of news

17. COMPARISON

1. Regular Comparison

fácil	easy
más fácil	easier
menos fácil	less easy
el más fácil	the easiest
el menos fácil	the least easy

2. Irregular Comparison

bueno	good	*mejor*	better, best
malo	bad	*peor*	worse, worst
mucho	much	*más*	more, most
poco	little	*menos*	less, least
grande	great	{ *mayor* *más grande*	
pequeño	small	{ *menor* *más pequeño*	

Más grande means "larger," "bigger"; *mayor* means "older":

Esta mesa es más grande que aquélla.	This table is larger than that one.
Pedro es mayor que Juan.	Peter is older than John.

Similarly, *más pequeño* means "smaller"; *menor* means "younger."

3. "More (less) . . . than . . ." = *más (menos). . . que . . .*

El español es más fácil que el inglés.	Spanish is easier than English.
Es más inteligente de lo que parece.	He's more intelligent than he looks.

4. "As . . . as . . ." = *tan. . . como. . .* or *tanto. . . como . . .*
   a. before an adjective or adverb:

Tan fácil como. . .	As easy as . . .
El habla español tan bien como yo.	He speaks Spanish as well as I do.

b. before a noun:

Tiene tanto dinero como Ud.	He has as much money as you.

5. "The more (less) . . . the more (less) . . ." = *cuanto más (menos). . . tanto más (menos). . .*

Cuanto más le trate tanto más le agradará.	The more you get to know him (deal with him) the more you like him.

6. "Most" = *-ísimo* (absolute superlative)

Es muy útil.	It's very useful.
Es utilísimo.	It's most useful.

18. PRONOUNS

Pronouns have different forms depending on whether they are:

1. the subject of a verb
2. used after a preposition
3. the direct object of a verb
4. used as indirect objects
5. used with reflexive verbs

1. Pronouns as the subject of a verb:

SINGULAR

yo	I
tú	you
él	he
ella	she
usted	you *(polite)*

PLURAL

nosotros	we *(masc.)*
nosotras	we *(fem.)*
*vosotros**	you *(masc.)*
*vosotras**	you *(fem.)*
ellos	they *(masc.)*
ellas	they *(fem.)*
ustedes	you *(polite)*

SINGULAR

(yo) hablo	I speak
(tú) hablas	you speak *(familiar)*
(él) habla	he speaks
(ella) habla	she speaks
(usted) habla	you speak *(polite)*

* Not used in Latin America, where it is replaced by *ustedes*.

PLURAL

(nosotros) hablamos	we speak *(masc.)*
(nosotras) hablamos	we speak *(fem.)*
(vosotros) habláis	you speak *(masc.)*
(vosotras) habláis	you speak *(fem.)*
(ellos) hablan	they speak *(masc.)*
(ellas) hablan	they speak *(fem.)*
(ustedes) hablan	you speak *(polite)*

The personal pronouns *yo, tú,* etc., are not ordinarily used. "I speak" is just *hablo,* "we speak," *hablamos,* etc. They are used for emphasis or clearness (*usted habla* "you speak" and *él habla* "he speaks").

2. Pronouns used after prepositions:

para mí	for me
para ti	for you *(fam.)*
para él	for him
para ella	for her
para usted	for you *(polite)*
para nosotros	for us *(masc.)*
para nosotras	for us *(fem.)*
para vosotros	for you *(masc./plural)*
para vosotras	for you *(fem./plural)*
para ellos	for them *(masc.)*
para ellas	for them *(fem.)*
para ustedes	for you *(polite/plural)*

Notice that the form of the pronoun used after a preposition is the same as the form of the pronoun used before a verb, except for *mí* "me" and *ti* "you" *(fam.)*.

There is a special form for "with me," "with

you" and "with him": *conmigo* "with me," *contigo* "with you" and *consigo* "with him" or "with her."

3. Pronouns as direct objects:

me	me
te	you *(fam.)*
le	him, you *(polite)* (used only in Spain)
la	her, you, it *(fem.)*
lo	him, you, it *(masc.)*
nos	us
os	you *(fam.)*
los	them, you *(polite)*
las	them, you *(fem.)*

4. Pronouns as indirect objects:

me	to me
te	to you *(fam.)*
le	to him, her, you *(polite)*
nos	to us
os	to you *(fam.)*
les	to them *(masc.* and *fem.)*
	to you *(masc.* and *fem.)* *(polite)*

Le as indirect object means "to him," "to her," "to you" (usted), and *les* means "to them," "to you" (ustedes). The preposition *a* and the prepositional forms *él, ella, usted* and *ellos, ellas, ustedes* are often added for clearness.

SHORT FORM

le doy	=	I give to him I give to her I give to you
les doy	=	I give to them *(masc.)* I give to them *(fem.)* I give to you

FULL FORM

le doy a él	I give (to) him
le doy a ella	I give (to) her
le doy a usted	I give (to) you
les doy a ellos	I give (to) them
les doy a ellas	I give (to) them
les doy a ustedes	I give (to) you

This double construction is used even when the object is a noun:

Le escribí a María ayer.   I wrote to Mary yesterday.

5. Reflexive pronouns:
   Reflexive pronouns are used when a person (or thing) does something to himself, herself (or itself); e.g., "I wash myself."

me	myself
te	yourself *(fam.)*
se	himself, herself, yourself *(polite)*
nos	ourselves
os	yourselves *(fam.)*
se	themselves, yourselves *(polite)*

19. POSITION OF PRONOUNS

1. When there are both direct and indirect object pronouns in a sentence *(he gives it to me)* the Spanish order is the following:

	ENGLISH			SPANISH		
	1		*2*	*2*	*1*	
He gives	it	to	me.	*Me*	*lo*	*da*
	1		*2*	*2*	*1*	
They give	it	to	us.	*Nos*	*lo*	*dan.*

That is, the indirect pronoun precedes the direct. If both begin with *l*, the indirect *(le, les)* becomes *se:*

Se lo diré (instead of *le lo diré*).	I will tell it to him (to her, to you, etc.)

2. When *se* is present it comes before the other object pronouns. It denotes:

a. an impersonal action:

Se dice.	It is said.
Se la trató bien.	She was treated well.

b. a personal object (may or may not be reflexive):

Se lo dice.	He says it to him (her) *or* he says it to himself *or* she says it to herself.

3. If *se* is not present, the first pronoun of the group has the meaning of an indirect object and the second that of a direct object:

Me lo da.	He gives it to me.

4. Object pronouns come before the verb:

Lo veo.	I see him.
Se lo da.	He gives it to him.

They come after an infinitive or present participle:

Tenerlo.	To have it.
Dárselo.	To give it to him.
Quiero verlo.	I want to see him.
Voy a verlo.	I'm going to see him.
Teniéndolo.	Having it.
Diciéndolo.	Saying it.
Estoy mirándolo.	I am looking at him.

Object pronouns follow affirmative commands:

Tómalo.	Take it.
Dígamelo Ud.	Tell it to me.

They come before negative commands (these are always in the subjunctive):

No me lo diga Ud.	Don't tell me.

5. *Te* and *os* precede all pronouns except *se:*

Te lo diré.	I will tell it to you.

But—

Se te dijo.	It was told to you.

20. CONJUNCTIONS

y	and
o	or
pero	but
más	but
que	that
pues	since, as
si	if
sino	but
por qué	why
porque	because
ni. . . ni	neither . . . nor

NOTES

a. *y* "and"

Roberto y Juan son her-manos.	Robert and John are brothers.

e is used instead of *y* before a word beginning with *i-* or *hi-:*

María e Isabel son pri-mas.	Mary and Elizabeth are cousins.
Madre e hija.	Mother and daughter.

b. *o* "or"

Cinco o seis pesos.	Five or six pesos.
Voy con mi hermano o con mi hermana.	I'm going with my brother or with my sister.

u is used instead of *o* before a word beginning with *o-* or *ho-:*

Siete u ocho horas.	Seven or eight hours.
Cinco u ocho meses.	Five or eight months.

c. *pero* "but":

Quiero venir pero no puedo.	I want to come but I can't.

d. *mas* "but" is more formal and literary:

Pensé que vendría mas no pudo.	I thought he would come but he wasn't able to.

e. *sino* "but" is used instead of *pero* after a negative statement:

No es francés sino inglés.	He is not French but English.
No viene hoy sino mañana.	He is not coming today but tomorrow.

21. QUESTION WORDS

1. *¿Qué?*	What?
¿Qué dice usted?	What are you saying?
2. *¿Por qué?*	Why?
¿Por qué dice usted eso?	Why do you say that?
3. *¿Cómo?*	How?
¿Cómo se dice en español esto?	How do you say this in Spanish?

¿Cómo se llama usted?	What's your name? ("How do you call yourself?")
4. *¿Cuánto?*	How much?
¿Cuánto dinero necesita usted?	How much money do you need?
¿Cuántos libros hay?	How many books are there?
¿Cuánto hay de Madrid a Barcelona?	How far is it from Madrid to Barcelona?
5. *¿Cuál?*	What? Which one?
¿Cuál es su nombre?	What's your name?
¿Cuál quiere usted?	Which one do you want?
6. *¿Quién?*	Who?
¿Quién vino con usted?	Who came with you?
¿Quién tiene eso?	Who has that?
7. *¿Dónde?*	Where?
¿Dónde está su amigo?	Where is your friend?
8. *¿Cuándo?*	When?
¿Cuándo se marcha Ud.?	When are you going (leaving)?
¿Cuándo ocurrió eso?	When did that happen?

Notice that the question words are written with an accent.

22. ADVERBS

1. Spanish *-mente* corresponds to "*-ly*" in English. It is added to the feminine form of the adjective:

exclusivamente   exclusively

When there are two adverbs, the ending *-mente* is added only to the last one:

clara y concisamente   clearly and concisely

Adverbs are compared like adjectives.

POSITIVE	*alegremente*	cheerfully
COMPARATIVE	*más alegremente*	more cheerfully
SUPERLATIVE	*lo más alegremente*	most cheerfully

2. Irregular Comparatives:

POSITIVE		COMPARATIVE	
bien	well	*mejor*	better, best
mal	badly	*peor*	worse, worst
mucho	much	*más*	more, most
poco	little	*menos*	less, least

3. Adverbs as prepositions or conjunctions. Many adverbs act as prepositions when *de* is added:

ADVERB:	*después*	afterward
PREPOSITION:	*después de las cinco*	after five o'clock
ADVERB:	*además*	besides
PREPOSITION:	*además de*	besides

When *que* is added they act as conjunctions:

después de que venga   after he comes

Other words which act similarly: *antes* "before"; *cerca* "near"; *delante* "before," "in front of"; *enfrente* "opposite."

4. Adverbs of time:

hoy	today
ayer	yesterday
mañana	tomorrow
temprano	early
tarde	late
a menudo	often
siempre	always
nunca	never
jamás	never
luego	afterward
rápido	quickly
despacio	slowly
antes que	before
después	afterward

5. Adverbs of place:

aquí	here
acá	here*
ahí	there
allí	there (farther away)
adelante	forward, on
atrás	behind
dentro	inside
arriba	up, above
fuera	outside
abajo	down, below
cerca	near
lejos	far

* More common in Latin America.

6. Adverbs of quantity:

muy	very
mucho	much
poco	little
más	more
menos	less
además	besides
cuánto	how much
tan	so much
tanto	so much
demasiado	too much
apenas	scarcely

7. Adverbs expressing affirmation:

sí	yes
verdaderamente	truly
cierto	certainly
ciertamente	certainly
claro	of course
desde luego	of course
por supuesto	of course

8. Adverbs expressing negation:

no	no, not
nunca	never
jamás	never
nunca jamás	never (more emphatic)
ya no	no more, not now
todavía no	not yet
tampoco	neither, either
no tal	no indeed
ni	nor
ni. . . ni	neither . . . not
ni siquiera	not even

9. Here and There:
Aquí "here" refers to something near the speaker:

Tengo aquí los libros.	I have the books here.

Ahí "there" refers to something near the person spoken to:

¿Qué tiene Ud. ahí?	What do you have there?
¿Está Ud. ahí?	Are you there?

Acá "here" expresses motion toward the speaker and is more common in Latin America:

¡Venga Ud. acá! Come here!	

Allá "there" indicates motion away from the speaker and is more common in Latin America:

¡Vaya Ud. allá!	Go there!
Va allá.	He's going there.

Allí "there" refers to something remote from both:

Vienen de allí.	They come from there.
Viví en Sudamérica varios años. ¿Ha estado Ud. allí?	I've lived in South America for several years. Have you ever been there?

23. DIMINUTIVES AND AUGMENTATIVES

The endings *-ito* (*-cito, -ecito*), *-illo* (*-cillo, -ecillo*), *-uelo* (*-zuelo, -ezuelo*) imply smallness. In addition, *-ito* often implies attractiveness or admiration, *-illo* and *-uelo* unattractiveness or depreciation. (They should be used with care.)

chico	boy	*chiquillo*	little boy
señora	lady, Mrs.	*señorita*	young lady, Miss
un poco	a little	*un poquito*	a little bit
pedazo	piece	*pedacito*	a little piece
gato	cat	*gatito*	kitten
papá	papa	*papito*	daddy
cuchara	tablespoon	*cucharita*	teaspoon
Venecia	Venice	*Venezuela*	Venezuela ("little Venice")
cigarro	cigar	*cigarrillo*	cigarette
autor	author	*autorcillo*	unimportant author

The endings *-ón (ona)* and *-ote* indicate largeness (often awkwardness and unattractiveness as well):

tonto	foolish, silly fool	*tontón*	big fool
silla	chair	*sillón*	big chair
cuchara	spoon	*cucharón*	a ladle
hombre	man	*hombrón*	he-man

24. DEMONSTRATIVES

1. Demonstrative Adjectives:

MASCULINE	FEMININE	
este	*esta*	this
ese	*esa*	that
aquel	*aquella*	that (farther removed)

estos	*estas*	these
esos	*esas*	those
aquellos	*aquellas*	those (farther removed)

a. Spanish demonstrative adjectives usually precede the nouns they modify and always agree in gender and number:

este muchacho	this boy
aquellos vecinos	those neighbors

b. *Ese* and *aquel* both mean "that." *Aquel* points out a thing removed in space or time from the speaker or from the person spoken to:

Esa señora es muy amable.	That lady is very kind.
Aquel señor que llegó el mes pasado.	That gentleman who arrived last month.

2. Demonstrative Pronouns:

MASCULINE	FEMININE	
éste	*ésta*	this (one)
ése	*ésa*	that (one)
aquél	*aquélla*	that (one)
éstos	*éstas*	these
ésos	*ésas*	those
aquéllos	*aquéllas*	those

NEUTER	
esto	this (one)
eso	that (one)
aquello	that (one)

The same difference exists between the pronouns *ése* and *aquél* as between the adjectives *ese* and *aquel:*

No quería éste sino aquél.	I didn't want this one but the one over there.

Éste and *aquél* also mean "the latter" and "the former":

Acaban de llegar el embajador y su secretario.	The ambassador and his secretary just arrived.
Éste es joven y aquél es viejo.	The former is old and the latter is young.

Notice that the Spanish order is the opposite of the English: *éste. . . aquél* ("the latter . . . the former").

The neuter demonstrative pronouns *esto, eso,* and *aquello* refer to an idea previously stated and not to a specific thing:

Me dijo que aquello fue horrible.	He told me that that was horrible.

25. Indefinite Adjectives and Pronouns

todos	all
tal	such
ni uno	not one
otro	other
alguien	someone

nadie	nobody
algo	something, anything
ninguno	no one, none
alguno	someone
varios	several
nada	nothing
cualquiera	whatever, whoever
quienquiera	whoever

26. NEGATION

1. *No* "not" comes before the verb:

No veo.	I don't see.
Él no habla.	He isn't speaking.

2. There are two forms for "nothing," "never," "no one," etc.—one with and one without *no:*

No veo nada.	I see nothing.
No voy nunca.	I never go.
No viene nadie.	No one is coming.

Or—

Nada veo.	I see nothing.
Nunca voy.	I never go.
Nadie viene.	No one comes.

27. WORD ORDER

1. The usual order is subject–verb–adverb–object:

Juan vio allí a sus amigos.	John saw his friends there.

2. The tendency in Spanish is to put the longer member of the sentence or the emphasized part last:

Me dio una carta.	He gave me a letter.
¿Compró la casa su padre?	Did your father buy the house?
Han caído veinte soldados.	Twenty soldiers were killed.

3. As in English, questions sometimes have the same order as statements but with the question intonation (that is, with a rise in pitch at the end):

¿Juan va a ir allí?	John is going to go there?

4. However, the more usual way of asking a question is to put the subject after the verb:

¿Va a ir allí Juan?	Is John going to go there?
¿Viene su amigo?	Is your friend coming?
¿Ha comido Ud.?	Have you eaten?
¿Habla usted español?	Do you speak Spanish?
¿Tiene usted dinero?	Do you have any money?
¿Por qué volvió Ud.?	Why did you return?
¿Ha recibido Juan mi carta?	Did John get my letter?

5. Adjectives come right after *ser:*

¿Es tarde?	Is it late?
¿Es bueno?	Is it good?
¿Es difícil la prueba?	Is the test difficult?
¿Es fácil el problema?	Is the problem easy?

28. TENSES OF THE VERB

Spanish verbs are divided into three clauses ("conjugations") according to their infinitives:

Class I—*hablar*
Class II—*comer*
Class III—*vivir*

1. The Present:

I	II	III
-*o*	-*o*	-*o*
-*as*	-*es*	-*es*
-*a*	-*e*	-*e*
-*amos*	-*emos*	-*imos*
-*áis*	-*éis*	-*ís*
-*an*	-*en*	-*en*

hablar to speak	*comer* to eat	*vivir* to live
hablo	*como*	*vivo*
hablas	*comes*	*vives*
habla	*come*	*vive*
hablamos	*comemos*	*vivimos*
habláis	*coméis*	*vivís*
hablan	*comen*	*viven*

The following verbs insert *g* in the first person singular of the present indicative:

tener—tengo	I have
venir—vengo	I come
traer—traigo	I bring
poner—pongo	I put

hacer—hago   I do
decir—digo   I say
salir—salgo   I leave

The present can be translated in several ways:

Hablo español.   I speak Spanish.
                    I am speaking Spanish.
                    I do speak Spanish.

2. The Imperfect:

I	II AND III
-aba	-ía
-abas	-ías
-aba	-ía
-ábamos	-íamos
-abais	-íais
-aban	-ían

a. The imperfect is used:

1. to indicate continued or customary action in the past:

Cuando yo estaba en Madrid, siempre visitaba los teatros.   When I was in Madrid, I always used to visit the theaters.

Lo encontraba todos los días.   I used to meet him every day.

2. to indicate what was happening when something else happened:

Él escribía cuando ella entró.   He was writing when she entered.

b. Irregular Imperfects:
The following are the only Spanish verbs which are irregular in the imperfect:
ser—era, eras, era, éramos, érais, eran
ir—iba, ibas, iba, íbamos, íbais, iban
ver—veía, veías, veía, veíamos, veíais, veían

3. The Future:
The future of regular verbs is formed by adding to the infinitive ending *-é, -ás, -á, -emos, -éis, -án:*

hablar to speak	*comer* to eat	*vivir* to live
hablaré	*comeré*	*viviré*
hablarás	*comerás*	*vivirás*
hablará	*comerá*	*vivirá*
hablaremos	*comeremos*	*viviremos*
hablaréis	*comeréis*	*viviréis*
hablarán	*comerán*	*vivirán*

The future generally expresses a future action:

Lo compraré.	I'll buy it.
Iré mañana.	I'll go tomorrow.

Sometimes it expresses probability or conjecture:

¿Qué hora será?	What time can it be? What time do you think it must be?
Será la una.	It must be almost one.
Estará comiendo ahora.	He's probably eating now.

4. The Preterite:
   There are two sets of preterite endings:

a. One set is used with
   the stem of Conjuga-
   tion I *(-ar)*:

b. The other set is used
   with the stem of Con-
   jugation II *(-er)* and
   Conjugation III *(-ir)*:

-é	*-í*
-aste	*-iste*
-ó	*-ió*
-amos	*-imos*
-asteis	*-isteis*
-aron	*-ieron*

The preterite expresses an action that began in
the past and ended in the past:

Él lo dijo.	He said it.
Habló conmigo.	He spoke with me.
Fui allí.	I went there.
Él nos vio.	He saw us
Escribí una carta.	I wrote a letter.
Llovió todo el día.	It rained all day.
El tren se paró.	The train stopped.
Pasó tres años allí.	He spent three years there.
Lo vi.	I saw him (it).

5. The Present Perfect:
   The present perfect is formed by adding the past
   participle to the present tense of *haber.* It is used
   to indicate a past action which continues into the
   present or which ended only recently:

Ha venido con su amigo.	He has come with his friend.
Nos ha escrito.	He has written to us.

6. The Pluperfect or the Past Perfect:
   The pluperfect is formed by adding the past participle to the imperfect of *haber*. It translates the English pluperfect:

Ya habían llegado.   They had already arrived.

7. The Future Perfect:
   The future perfect is formed by adding the past participle to the future of *haber*. It translates the English future perfect:

Habrán llegado para entonces.   They will have arrived by then.

Sometimes it indicates probability:

Habrán llegado ayer.   They probably arrived yesterday.

8. The Preterite Perfect:
   The preterite perfect, which is rather rare, is formed by adding the past participle to the preterite of *haber*. It is used to indicate that something has occurred immediately before some other action in the past:

Apenas hubo oído eso, se marchó.   No sooner had he heard that than he left.

29. CONDITIONAL

1. The conditional of all verbs is formed by adding to the infinitive the endings: *ía, ías, ía, íamos, íais, ían*. It translates the English "would."

I	II	III
hablar to speak	*comer* to eat	*vivir* to live
hablaría	*comería*	*viviría*
hablarías	*comerías*	*vivirías*
hablaría	*comería*	*viviría*
hablaríamos	*comeríamos*	*viviríamos*
hablaríais	*comeríais*	*viriríais*
hablarían	*comerían*	*vivirían*

Sometimes it expresses probability or conjecture:

Serían las dos cuando él llegó.	It was probably about two o'clock when he arrived.
¿Qué hora sería?	What time could it have been?

2. The perfect conditional is formed by adding the past participle to the conditional of *haber*. It translates the English "would have."

Habría hablado.	I would have spoken.
Habría ido.	I would have gone.

3. If a sentence contains a clause beginning with *si* "if," the tense of the verb is determined by the tense of the verb in the main clause.

If the main clause has a verb in the:	The "if" clause has a verb in the:
Present	Present/Future
Future	Present
Imperfect	Imperfect

Preterite	Preterite
Conditional	Imp. Subjunctive (*-ra* or *-se*)
Si está aquí, trabaja.	If he is here, he is working.
Si estaba aquí, trabajaba.	If he was here, he was working.
Si está aquí mañana, trabajará.	If he's here tomorrow, he'll be working.
Si estuviera aquí, trabajaría.	If he were here, he'd be working.

30. SUBJUNCTIVE

The indicative simply makes a statement; the subjunctive indicates a certain attitude toward the statement —uncertainty, desire, emotion, etc. The subjunctive is used in subordinate clauses when the statement is unreal, doubtful, indefinite, subject to some condition, or is affected by will, emotion, etc.

1. Forms

a. The subjunctive endings of the second and third conjugations are the same.

b. The present subjunctive is formed by adding the subjunctive endings to the stem of the first person singular, present indicative; the imperfect subjunctive, by adding the endings of the stem of the third person plural, preterite.

The subjunctive endings are as follows:

Conjugation I
PRES. SUBJ.   *-e, -es, -e, -emos, -éis, -en*

IMPERF. SUBJ.	-ara, -aras, -ara, -áramos, -arais, -aran
	Or—
	-ase, -ases, -ase, -ásemos, -aseis, -asen

Conjugations II and III

PRES. SUBJ.	-a, -as, -a, -amos, -aís, -an
IMPERF. SUBJ.	-iera, -ieras, -iera, -iéramos, -ierais, -ieran
	Or—
	-iese, -ieses, -iese, -iésemos, -ieseis, -iesen

EXAMPLES

	I	II	III
INFINITIVE	*hablar*	*comer*	*vivir*
PRES. SUBJ.	*hable*	*coma*	*viva*
IMPERF.	*hablara*	*comiera*	*viviera*
SUBJ.	*hablase*	*comiese*	*viviese*

2. Uses

a. The subjunctive is used with verbs of desire, request, suggestion, permission, approval and disapproval, judgment, opinion, uncertainty, emotion, surprise, fear, denial, etc.:

Quisiera verlo.	I'd like to see him.
¡Ojalá que lo haga!	I wish he would do it!
¡Ojalá lo supiera!	I wish I knew it!
Temo que se lo diga a él.	I'm afraid he may tell it to him.
No creo que él lo haya visto.	I don't believe he's seen him.

Niega que lo haya visto.	He denies that he's seen him.
Me sorprende mucho que él no lo haya hecho.	I'm greatly surprised that he hasn't done it.
Espero que no venga.	I hope he doesn't come.
Me alegro de que Ud. esté aquí.	I'm glad you're here!
Temo que esté enfermo.	I'm afraid he's sick.
Temo que no llegue a tiempo.	I'm afraid he won't (may not) come in time.
Duda que lo hagamos.	He doubts that we'll do it.
Dudo que sea verdad.	I doubt that it's true.
Dudo que sea posible.	I doubt whether it's possible.
No creo que lo sepa.	I don't think he knows it.
Se lo digo para que lo sepa.	I'm telling you so you may know it.

b. The subjunctive forms are used in commands: Affirmative or negative commands in the polite form:

¡Abra usted la ventana!	Open the window!
¡No hablen ustedes ahora!	Don't talk now!

1. Negative commands in the familiar form:

No me digas (tú).	Don't tell me!
No habléis ahora.	Don't talk now!

2. Suggestions in which the speaker is included:

Leamos.	Let's read!
Entremos.	Let's go in!

3. Indirect commands (that is, commands in the third person):

Que vaya él.	Let him go.
¡Viva España!	Long live Spain!
¡Que vengan!	Let them come!
¡Que entren!	Let them come in!
¡Que no venga!	Let him not come!

c. The subjunctive is used in conditional sentences which are contrary to fact:

Si estaba allí, yo no le vi.	If he was there, I didn't see him. *(Indicative)*
No iremos si llueve.	If it rains, we won't go. *(Indicative)*

But—

Si fuera él, lo haría.	If I were him (he), I'd do it.
Si fuera mío esto, lo vendería.	If this were mine, I'd sell it.
Si tuviera el dinero, lo compraría.	If I had the money, I'd buy it.
Aunque hubiese tenido dinero no hubiera ido.	Even if I had had the money I wouldn't have gone.
Si lo hubiera sabido, no habría venido.	If I had known it, I wouldn't have come.

Si hubiese estado aquí, habríamos ido.	If he had been here, we would have gone.
Aunque lo hubiese intentado, no hubiera podido hacerlo.	Even if I would have tried, I wouldn't have been able to do it.

d. The subjunctive is used after impersonal verbs which do not express certainty:

Es importante que vengan.	It's important for them to come.
Es preciso que estén aquí.	It's necessary for them to be here.
Es necesario que Ud. venga.	It's necessary that you come.
Es posible que lo tenga.	It's possible that he has it.
Fue una lástima que no vinieran.	It was a pity that they didn't come.

e. The subjunctive is used after various conjunctive adverbs:

1. Certain conjunctive adverbs are always followed by the subjunctive because they never introduce statements of accomplished fact:

antes (de) que	before
a condición de	on condition that
aunque	even if
a (fin de) que	in order that
a menos que	unless
como si	as if
con tal (de) que	provided that, providing
dado que	granted that, given . . .

no obstante que	notwithstanding that
en el supuesto de que	supposing that

2. Other conjunctive adverbs may or may not introduce a statement of accomplished fact. When they do, they take the indicative; otherwise the subjunctive:

a menos que	unless
a pesar de que	in spite of, notwithstanding
antes que	before
así que	as soon as
aunque	although, even though
con tal que	provided (that)
cuando	when
de manera que	so that
de modo que	so that
después (de) que	after
en cuanto	as soon as
hasta que	until
luego que	as soon as
mientras que	as long as, while
para que	in order that, so that
siempre que	provided that, whenever
Aunque él no lo quiera, se lo daré.	I'll give it to him even though he may not want it.
Lo compraré aunque me cueste mucho.	I'll buy it even if it costs me a lot.
Se lo digo para que lo sepa.	I'm telling you so that you may know it.
Aunque llueva mañana.	Although it may rain tomorrow.
Se fue sin que lo supiésemos.	He went away without our knowing it.

Iré con Ud. con tal que tenga tiempo.	I'll go with you provided I have time.
En caso de que llegue.	In case he arrives.

Compare:

Iremos aunque llueve.	We'll go even though it's raining.
Iremos aunque llueva.	We'll go even if it rains (even if it should rain).

f. The subjunctive is used when an indefinite antecedent expresses doubt or denial about a person's existence.:

No hay ningún hombre que entienda esto.	There is no man who understands this.
Busco a alguien que hable español.	I'm looking for someone who speaks Spanish.
No conozco a nadie que pueda hacerlo.	I don't know anyone who can do it (could do it).

g. The subjunctive is used after compounds of *-quiera* "-ever": *quienquiera* "whoever," *dondequiera* "wherever," *cualquier* "whatever," "whichever":

Quienquiera que sea.	Whoever he (it) may be.
Él quiere hacer cualquier cosa que ella haga.	He wants to do whatever she does.
Él quiere ir dondequiera que ella vaya.	He wants to go wherever she goes.

31. COMMANDS AND REQUESTS (THE IMPERATIVE)

There are two types of commands, one with *tú*, *vosotros* and one with *usted, ustedes*.

1. Familiar Commands *(Tú; Vosotros)*
   Familiar commands are used with people to whom you would say *tú*. The singular is the same as the third person singular of the present indicative:

Habla (tú).	Speak!
Come (tú).	Eat!
Sube (tú).	Go up!

The plural *vosotros, -as* is always formed by removing the *-r* of the infinitive and adding *-d*. Remember that this latter form is used only in Spain. (For plural commands, both formal and informal, see 2., below.)

I

hablar   to speak

SINGULAR:	*Habla (tú).*	Speak!
PLURAL:	*Hablad (vosotros, -as).*	Speak!

II

aprender   to learn

SINGULAR:	*Aprende (tú).*	Learn!
PLURAL:	*Aprended (vosotros, -as).*	Learn!

III

escribir   to write

SINGULAR:	*Escribe (tú).*	Write!
PLURAL:	*Escribid (vosotros, -as).*	Write!

Common exceptions in the singular (the plural is always regular):

| | | IMPERATIVE | |
INFINITIVE		SINGULAR	PLURAL
ser	to be	*sé*	*sed*
decir	to say	*di*	*decid*
ir	to go	*ve*	*id*
hacer	to do	*haz*	*haced*
poner	to put	*pon*	*poned*
tener	to hold	*ten*	*tened*
venir	to come	*ven*	*venid*

Familiar commands in the negative are in the present subjunctive:

SINGULAR

No hables.	Don't speak!
No me hables.	Don't talk to me!
No comas.	Don't eat!

PLURAL

No habléis.	Don't speak!
No comáis.	Don't eat!

Other Examples:

Háblame.	Speak to me!
Háblales.	Speak to them!
No les hables.	Don't speak to them!
Hablad.	Speak!
No habléis.	Don't speak!
Dame.	Give me!
No me des.	Don't give me!
Dímelo.	Tell it to me!
No me lo digas (tú).	Don't tell it to me!

No me digas (tú) eso.	Don't tell me that!
Decídnoslo.	Tell it to us!
No nos lo digáis.	Don't tell it to us!
No estudiéis demasiado.	Don't study too much!

Notice that the object pronouns follow the affirmative imperative and precede the negative imperative.

2. Polite Commands *(Usted)*
   Polite commands are used with people to whom you would say *usted* and are formed like the subjunctive. You change the ending of the third person present indicative to *a* if it is *e*, or to *e* if it is *a*.

INDICATIVE		SUBJUNCTIVE	
Habla.	He speaks.	*Hable Ud.*	Speak!
Come.	He eats.	*Coma Ud.*	Eat!

The plural is formed by adding *n* to the singular of the imperative:

Hablen Uds.	Speak!
Coman Uds.	Eat!
Desciendan Uds.	Go down!

Note that this form is used in Latin America to give commands to more than one person.

Other Examples:

Cómalo (Ud.).	Eat it!
Venga (Ud.) a verme.	Come to see me.
Tómelo.	Take it!
Dígamelo.	Tell it to me!

Escríbame (Ud.) una carta.	Write me a letter
Escríbamelo.	Write it to me!
Abra (Ud.) la ventana.	Open the window!

NEGATIVE

No hable Ud.	Don't speak!
No lo coma Ud.	Don't eat it!
No me lo diga Ud.	Don't tell it to me!
No me escriba Ud.	Don't write to me!
No hablen Uds. demasiado.	Don't talk too much!

The pronoun objects follow the affirmative imperative and are attached to it:

Léelo (tú).	Read it!
Habladle.	Speak to him!
Véndamelo.	Sell it to me!
Dígamelo.	Tell it to me!

3. Indirect Commands
   Indirect commands are in the subjunctive and are usually preceded by *que:*

Que entren.	Let them come in!
Que él lo haga.	Let him do it!
Que lo haga Juan.	Let John do it!
Que le hable María.	Let Mary talk to him!
Que venga.	Let him come!
Que vaya él.	Let him go!
¡Que no venga.	Let him not come!
¡Viva España!	Long live Spain!
¡Dios guarde a nuestro país!	God keep our country!

4. "Let's" is expressed by the subjunctive:

Hablemos un rato.	Let's talk a while!
No hablemos.	Let's not talk!
Esperemos.	Let's wait!

Note:

¡Vamos!	Let's go!
No vayamos.	Let's not go!

5. Imperative of Reflexive Verbs
   The final *-d* of the plural is dropped when *-os* is added; that is, *sentados* becomes *sentaos:*

FAMILIAR FORM

SINGULAR

Siéntate.	Sit down!
Despiértate.	Wake up!
No te sientes.	Don't sit down!

PLURAL

Sentaos.	Sit down!
Despertaos.	Wake up!
(despertad + os)	
No os sentéis.	Don't sit down!

POLITE FORM

SINGULAR

Siéntese Ud.	Sit down!
No se siente Ud.	Don't sit down!

PLURAL

Siéntense Uds.	Sit down *(pl.)*!
No se sienten.	Don't sit down!
Sentémonos.	Let's sit down!
(sentemos + nos)	

32. THE PARTICIPLE

1. The present participle (also called the "gerund") of Conjugation I is formed by dropping the *-ar* of the infinitive and adding *-ando;* the present participle of Conjugations II and III is made by dropping the *-er (-ir)* and adding *-iendo:*

I		II	
hablar	to speak	*comer*	to eat
hablando	speaking	*comiendo*	eating

III	
vivir	to live
viviendo	living

Pronoun objects are attached to the present participle (in such cases the verb has a written accent):

comprándolos	buying them
vendiéndomelo	selling it to me
dándoselo	giving it to him

The present participle is often used absolutely, describing some action or state of being of the subject of the sentence:

Durmiendo, no me oyeron.	Since they were sleeping, they didn't hear me. They didn't hear me because they were sleeping.
Estando cansados, dormían.	Being tired, they were sleeping. They were taking a nap because they were tired.

2. The past participle is formed by adding *-ado* to the stem of *-ar* verbs (that is, the infinitive minus *-ar*) and *-ido* to the stem of *-er* and *-ir* verbs:

I			II
hablar	to speak	*comer*	to eat
hablado	spoken	*comido*	eaten

III	
vivir	to live
vivido	lived

3. Irregular Participles
   The following are some of the most common verbs with irregular present and past participles:

	INFINITIVE	IRREGULAR PAST PARTICIPLE	IRREGULAR PRESENT PARTICIPLE
abrir	to open	*abierto*	
caer	to fall	*caído*	*cayendo*
creer	to believe	*creído*	*creyendo*
cubrir	to cover	*cubierto*	
decir	to say	*dicho*	*diciendo*
despedirse	to take leave of		*despidiéndose*
dormir	to sleep	*dormido*	*durmiendo*
escribir	to write	*escrito*	
hacer	to do, make	*hecho*	
ir	to go		*yendo*
leer	to read	*leído*	*leyendo*
morir	to die	*muerto*	*muriendo*
oír	to hear		*oyendo*
pedir	to ask for		*pidiendo*
poder	to be able to		*pudiendo*

poner	to put	*puesto*
seguir	to follow	*siguiendo*
sentir	to feel	*sintiendo*
traer	to bring	*traído* *trayendo*
venir	to come	*viniendo*
ver	to see	*visto*
volver	to return	*vuelto*

33. PROGRESSIVE TENSES

The Spanish progressive tenses are made up of the forms of *estar* plus the present participle. As in English, they denote a continuing action (that is, they describe the action as going on):

Estoy trabajando aquí.	I'm working here.
Estábamos leyendo un periódico.	We were reading a newspaper.
Estoy divirtiéndome.	I'm having a good time.
Está hablando.	He's speaking.
Estaba esperándome.	He was waiting for me.

34. PASSIVE VOICE

The passive voice is made up of the forms of *ser* plus the past participle:

La carta fue escrita por ella.	The letter was written by her.

The passive is used as in English. Very often, however, Spanish uses the reflexive where English uses the passive:

Aquí se habla inglés.	English is spoken here.

35. To Be

There are two verbs in Spanish for "to be": *ser* and *estar*. Here are the present tense forms of *ser* and *estar*. See "The Forms of Irregular Verbs" for other tenses.

SER	ESTAR	
yo soy	yo estoy	I am
tú eres	tú estás	you are
usted es	usted está	you are
él es	él está	he is
ella es	ella está	she is
nosotros somos	nosotros estamos	we are
nosotras somos	nosotras estamos	we are
vosotros sois	vosotros estáis	you are
vosotras sois	vosotras estáis	you are
ustedes son	ustedes están	you are
ellos son	ellos están	they are
ellas son	ellas están	they are

USAGES:

1. *Ser*

a. indicates a characteristic that is unlikely to change:

Mi hermano es alto.	My brother is tall.

b. is used with a predicate noun, in which case it links two equal things:

Él es médico.	He is a doctor
Es escritor.	He's a writer.
Es español.	He's a Spaniard.

c. is used with an adjective to indicate an inherent quality.

El libro es rojo.	The book is red.
Ella es joven.	She is young.
El hielo es frío.	Ice is cold.
Es inteligente.	He's intelligent.
Es encantadora.	She's charming.

d. is used with pronouns:

Soy yo.	It's I.

e. indicates origin, source, or material:

¿De dónde es Ud.?	Where are you from?
Soy de España.	I'm from Spain.
Es de madera.	It's made of wood.
Es de plata.	It's silver.

f. indicates possession:

¿De quién es esto?	Whose is this?
Los libros son del señor Díaz.	The books belong to Mr. Diaz.

g. is used in telling time:

Es la una.	It's one o'clock.
Son las dos.	It's two o'clock.
Son las nueve y diez.	It's ten past nine.

h. is used to indicate cost:

Son a noventa céntimos la docena.	They are 90 cents a dozen.

Son a nueve balboas cada uno.	They are nine balboas each.

i. is used in impersonal constructions:

Es tarde.	It's late.
Es temprano.	It's early.
Es necesario.	It's necessary.
Es una lástima.	It's a pity.
¿No es verdad?	Isn't it?

2. *Estar*

a. expresses position or location:

Está allí.	He's over there.
Está en México.	He's in Mexico.
Nueva York está en los Estados Unidos.	New York is in the United States.
Los Andes están en Sudamérica.	The Andes are in South America.
El Canal está en Panamá.	The Canal is in Panama.
¿Dónde está el libro?	Where's the book?
Está sobre la mesa.	It's on the table.

b. indicates a state or condition which may change:

Ella está contenta.	She's pleased.
Estoy cansado.	I'm tired.
Estoy listo.	I'm ready.
El café está frío.	The coffee's cold.
Está claro.	It's clear.
La ventana está abierta (cerrada).	The window's open (shut).

c. is used to form the present progressive tense:

Están hablando.	They are talking.
Están caminando.	They are walking.

   d. is used to ask about or describe states or conditions of physical or mental health:

¿Cómo está Ud.?	How are you?
¿Cómo están ellos?	How are they?
Estamos tristes.	We're sad.
Están muertos.	They are dead.
Estoy enojada.	I'm angry.

      Some adjectives may be used with either *ser* or *estar* with a difference in meaning.

Él es malo.	He is bad (an evil person).
Él está malo.	He is sick.
Es pálida.	She has a pale complexion.
Está pálida.	She is pale (owing to illness).

	With *ser*	With *estar*
bueno	good	well, in good health
listo	clever	ready, prepared
cansado	tiresome	tired

REGULAR VERBS WITH SPELLING CHANGES

1. VERBS ENDING IN -*CAR*

Example: buscar to look for

Verbs ending in -*car*; *c* changes to *qu* when followed by *e*. This occurs in:

   1. the first person singular of the preterite
   2. all persons of the present subjunctive

PRETERITE INDICATIVE	PRESENT SUBJUNCTIVE
busqué	*busque*
buscaste	*busques*
buscó	*busque*

buscamos	*busquemos*
buscasteis	*busquéis*
buscaron	*busquen*

Verbs conjugated like *buscar:*

acercar	to place near	*sacrificar*	to sacrifice
educar	to educate	*secar*	to dry
explicar	to explain	*significar*	to signify, mean
fabricar	to manu-facture	*tocar*	to touch, play (music)
indicar	to indicate		
pecar	to sin	*verificar*	to verify
sacar	to take out		

2. VERBS ENDING IN -*GAR*

Example: *pagar* to pay

Verbs ending in -*gar:* *g* changes to *gu* when followed by *e*. This occurs in:

1. the first person singular of the preterite indicative
2. all persons of the present subjunctive

PRETERITE INDICATIVE	PRESENT SUBJUNCTIVE
pagué	*pague*
pagaste	*pagues*
pagó	*pague*

pagamos	*paguemos*
pagasteis	*paguéis*
pagaron	*paguen*

Verbs conjugated like *pagar:*

ahogar	to drown	*investigar*	to investi-gate
apagar	to extin-guish	*juzgar*	to judge
arriesgar	to risk	*llegar*	to arrive
cargar	to load, to carry	*obligar*	to compel
castigar	to punish	*otorgar*	to grant
congregar	to congre-gate	*pegar*	to hit
entregar	to deliver	*tragar*	to swallow

3. VERBS ENDING IN *-GUAR*

Example: averiguar to ascertain, investigate

Verbs ending in *-guar: gu* changes to *gü* when followed by *e*. This occurs in:

1. the first person singular of the preterite indicative
2. all persons of the present subjunctive

PRETERITE INDICATIVE	PRESENT SUBJUNCTIVE
averigüé	*averigüe*
averiguaste	*averigües*
averiguó	*averigüe*

averiguamos   *averigüemos*
averiguasteis   *averigüéis*
averiguaron   *averigüen*

Verbs conjugated like *averiguar:*

aguar   to water, dilute
atestiguar   to attest

4. VERBS ENDING IN -*ZAR*

Example: *gozar* to enjoy
Verbs ending in -*zar:* *z* changes to *c* when followed by *e*. This occurs in:

1. the first person singular of the preterite indicative
2. all persons of the present subjunctive

PRETERITE INDICATIVE	PRESENT SUBJUNCTIVE
gocé	*goce*
gozaste	*goces*
gozó	*goce*
gozamos	*gocemos*
gozasteis	*gocéis*
gozaron	*gocen*

Verbs conjugated like *gozar:*

abrazar	to embrace	*organizar*	to organize
alcanzar	to reach	*rechazar*	to reject
cruzar	to cross	*rezar*	to pray
enlazar	to join	*utilizar*	to utilize

5. VERBS ENDING IN -*GER*

Example: *escoger* to choose, select
   Verbs ending in -*ger*: *g* changes to *j* when followed by *o* or *a*. This occurs in:

1. the first person singular of the present indicative
2. all persons of the present subjunctive

PRESENT INDICATIVE	PRESENT SUBJUNCTIVE
escojo	*escoja*
escoges	*escojas*
escoge	*escoja*
escogemos	*escojamos*
escogéis	*escojáis*
escogen	*escojan*

Verbs conjugated like *coger:*

acoger	to welcome	*proteger*	to protect
coger	to catch	*recoger*	to gather

6. VERBS ENDING IN -*GIR*

Example: *dirigir* to direct
   Verbs ending in -*gir*: *g* changes to *j* when followed by *o* or *a*. This occurs in:

1. the first person singular of the present indicative
2. all persons of the present subjunctive

PRESENT INDICATIVE	PRESENT SUBJUNCTIVE
dirijo	*dirija*
diriges	*dirijas*
dirige	*dirija*

dirigimos	*dirijamos*
dirigís	*dirijáis*
dirigen	*dirijan*

Verbs conjugated like *dirigir:*

afligir	to afflict	*rugir*	to roar
erigir	to erect	*surgir*	to come forth
exigir	to demand		

7. VERBS ENDING IN -*GUIR*

Example: *distinguir* to distinguish

Verbs ending in -*guir: gu* changes to *g* when followed by *o* or *a*. This occurs in:

1. the first person singular of the present indicative
2. all persons of the present subjunctive

PRESENT INDICATIVE	PRESENT SUBJUNCTIVE
distingo	*distinga*
distingues	*distingas*
distingue	*distinga*
distinguimos	*distingamos*
distinguís	*distingáis*
distinguen	*distingan*

Verbs conjugated like *distinguir:*

conseguir	to get, obtain	*perseguir*	to persecute
extinguir	to extinguish	*seguir*	to follow

8. VERBS ENDING IN -*CER*, -*CIR*

(Preceded by a vowel)

Examples: *conocer* to know   *lucir* to shine

Verbs ending in -*cer*, -*cir*, preceded by a vowel, change *c* to *zc* before *o* or *a*. This occurs in:

1. the first person singular of the present indicative
2. all persons of the present subjunctive

INDICATIVE	SUBJUNCTIVE	INDICATIVE	SUBJUNCTIVE
conozco	*conozca*	*luzco*	*luzca*
conoces	*conozcas*	*luces*	*luzcas*
conoce	*conozca*	*luce*	*luzca*
conocemos	*conozcamos*	*lucimos*	*luzcamos*
conocéis	*conozcáis*	*lucís*	*luzcáis*
conocen	*conozcan*	*lucen*	*luzcan*

Verbs conjugated like *conocer:*

aborrecer	to hate	*desaparecer*	to disappear
acaecer	to happen	*desobe-decer*	to disobey
acontecer	to happen	*desvanecer*	to vanish
agradecer	to be grate-ful	*embellecer*	to embel-lish
amanecer	to dawn	*envejecer*	to grow old
anochecer	to grow dark	*fallecer*	to die
aparecer	to appear	*favorecer*	to favor
carecer	to lack	*merecer*	to merit
compadecer	to pity	*nacer*	to be born
complacer	to please	*obedecer*	to obey
conducir	to conduct, to drive	*ofrecer*	to offer

crecer	to grow	*oscurecer*	to grow dark
padecer	to suffer	*placer*	to please
parecer	to seem	*reconocer*	to recognize
permanecer	to last	*traducir*	to translate
pertenecer	to belong to		

9. VERBS ENDING IN *-CER*

(Preceded by a Consonant)

Example: *vencer* to conquer

Verbs ending in *-cer,* preceded by a consonant: *c* changes to *z* when followed by *o* or *a*. This occurs in:

1. the first person singular of the present indicative
2. all persons of the present subjunctive

PRESENT INDICATIVE	PRESENT SUBJUNCTIVE
venzo	*venza*
vences	*venzas*
vence	*venza*
vencemos	*venzamos*
vencéis	*venzáis*
vencen	*venzan*

Verbs conjugated like *vencer:*

convencer	to convince	*ejercer*	to exercise

10. VERBS ENDING IN *-UIR*

(But not *-guir* and *-quir*)

Example: *construir* to build

Verbs ending in *-uir,* except those ending in *-guir* or *-quir,* add *y* to the stem of the verb before *a, e, o.* This occurs in:

1. all persons of the present indicative (except the first and second familiar persons plural)
2. all persons of the present and imperfect subjunctive
3. the imperative singular *(tú)*
4. third singular and plural of the preterite

PRESENT INDICATIVE	PRESENT SUBJUNCTIVE
construyo	*construya*
construyes	*construyas*
construye	*construya*
construimos	*construyamos*
construís	*construyáis*
construyen	*construyan*

(*i* between two other vowels changes to *y*)

PRETERITE INDICATIVE	IMPERFECT SUBJUNCTIVE
construí	*construyera (se)*
construiste	*construyeras (ses)*
construyó	*construyera (se)*
construimos	*construyéramos (semos)*
construisteis	*construyerais (seis)*
construyeron	*construyeran (sen)*

IMPERATIVE
construye
construid

Verbs conjugated like *construir:*

atribuir	to attribute	*huir*	to flee
constituir	to constitute	*influir*	to influence
contribuir	to contribute	*instruir*	to instruct
destituir	to deprive	*reconstruir*	to rebuild
destruir	to destroy	*restituir*	to restore
distribuir	to distribute	*substituir*	to substitute
excluir	to exclude		

11. VERBS LIKE *CREER*

Creer to believe

In verbs whose stem ends in *e*, the *i* of the regular endings beginning with *-ie*, *-ió*, becomes *y*. This occurs in:

1. the present participle *creyendo*.
2. the third person singular and plural of the preterite indicative
3. both forms of the imperfect subjunctive

PRETERITE INDICATIVE	IMPERFECT SUBJUNCTIVE
creí	*creyera (se)*
creíste	*creyeras (ses)*
creyó	*creyera (se)*
creímos	*creyéramos (semos)*
creísteis	*creyerais (seis)*
creyeron	*creyeran (sen)*

Verbs conjugated like *creer:*

caer	to fall (irregular)	*leer*	to read
construir	to build	*poseer*	to possess

12. VERBS LIKE *REÍR*

Reír to laugh

In verbs whose stem ends in *i*, the *i* of the regular endings, *-ie*, *-ió*, is dropped to avoid two *i*'s. This occurs in:

1. the present participle *riendo*
2. the third person singular and plural of the preterite indicative
3. all persons of both forms of the imperfect subjunctive

PRETERITE INDICATIVE	IMPERFECT SUBJUNCTIVE
reí	riera (se)
reíste	rieras (ses)
rió	riera (se)
reímos	riéramos (semos)
reísteis	rierais (seis)
rieron	rieran (sen)

Verbs conjugated like *reír; sonreír* to smile.

13. VERBS ENDING IN *-LLER*, *-LLIR*, *-ÑER*, *-ÑIR*

Example: *tañer* to toll (a bell)
PRESENT PARTICIPLE: *tañendo*

PRETERITE INDICATIVE	IMPERFECT SUBJUNCTIVE
tañí	tañera (se)
tañiste	tañeras (ses)
tañó	tañera (se)

tañimos	tañéramos (semos)
tañisteis	tañerais (seis)
tañeron	tañeran (sen)

In verbs whose stem ends in *ll* or *ñ*, the *i* of the regular endings beginning with *-ie*, *-ió* is dropped. This occurs in:

1. the present participle
2. the third person singular and plural of the preterite indicative
3. all persons of both forms of the imperfect subjunctive

Verbs conjugated like *tañer:*

bullir	to boil	*gruñir*	to growl

14. VERBS ENDING IN *-IAR*, *-UAR*

Examples: *enviar* to send   *continuar* to continue

PRES. IND.	PRES. SUBJ.	PRES. IND.	PRES. SUBJ.
envío	*envíe*	*continúo*	*continúe*
envías	*envíes*	*continúas*	*continúes*
envía	*envíe*	*continúa*	*continúe*
enviamos	*enviemos*	*continuamos*	*continuemos*
enviáis	*enviéis*	*continuáis*	*continuéis*
envían	*envíen*	*continúan*	*continúen*

	IMPERATIVE
envía	*continúa*
enviad	*continuad*

Some verbs ending in *-iar* or *-uar* take a written accent over the *i* or the *u* of the stem.

1. in all persons of the present indicative (except the first plural and second plural familiar).
2. in all persons of the present subjunctive (except the first plural and the second plural familiar).
3. in the singular of the imperative *(tú)*.

Verbs conjugated like *enviar:*

confiar	to trust	*desconfiar*	to distrust
criar	to bring up	*fiar*	to give credit
desafiar	to challenge	*guiar*	to guide

Verbs conjugated like *continuar:*

actuar	to act	*evaluar*	to evaluate
efectuar	to carry out	*perpetuar*	to perpetuate

THE FORMS OF THE REGULAR VERBS

CONJUGATIONS I, II, III

INDICATIVE

Infinitive	Pres. & Past Participles	Present Indicative	Imperfect	Preterite	Future	Conditional	Present Perfect	Pluperfect	Preterite Perfect
I. -ar ending *hablar* to speak	hablando hablado	hablo hablas habla hablamos habláis hablan	hablaba hablabas hablaba hablábamos hablabais hablaban	hablé hablaste habló hablamos hablasteis hablaron	hablaré hablarás hablará hablaremos hablaréis hablarán	hablaría hablarías hablaría hablaríamos hablaríais hablarían	he has ha + hablado hemos habéis han	había habías había + hablado habíamos habíais habían	hube hubiste hubo + hablado hubimos hubisteis hubieron
II. -er ending *comer* to eat	comiendo comido	como comes come comemos coméis comen	comía comías comía comíamos comíais comían	comí comiste comió comimos comisteis comieron	comeré comerás comerá comeremos comeréis comerán	comería comerías comería comeríamos comeríais comerían	he has ha + comido hemos habéis han	había habías había + comido habíamos habíais habían	hube hubiste hubo + comido hubimos hubisteis hubieron

Infinitive	Pres. & Past Participles	Present Indicative	Imperfect	Preterite	Future	Conditional	Present Perfect	Pluperfect	Preterite Perfect
III. -ir ending *vivir* to live	viviendo vivido	vivo vives vive vivimos vivís viven	vivía vivías vivía vivíamos vivíais vivían	viví viviste vivió vivimos vivisteis vivieron	viviré virirás vivirá viviremos viviréis vivirán	viviría vivirías viviría viviríamos viviríais vivirían	he has ha + vivido hemos habéis han	había habías había + vivido habíamos habíais habían	hube hubiste hubo + vivido hubimos hubisteis hubieron

INDICATIVE

Future Perfect	Conditional Perfect
habré habrás habrá + hablado habremos habréis habrán	habría habrías habría + hablado habríamos habríais habrían

SUBJUNCTIVE

Present	Imperfect (-r-)	Imperfect (-s-)	Present Perfect	Pluperfect (-r-)	Pluperfect (-s-)	Imperative
hable hables hable hablemos habléis hablen	hablara hablaras hablara habláramos hablarais hablaran	hablase hablases hablase hablásemos hablaseis hablasen	haya hayas haya + hablado hayamos hayáis hayan	hubiera hubieras hubiera + hablado hubiéramos hubierais hubieran	hubiese hubieses hubiese + hablado hubiésemos hubieseis hubiesen	Habla (tú). Hable (Ud.). Hablemos (nosotros). Hablad (vosotros). Hablen (Uds.).

INDICATIVE

SUBJUNCTIVE

	Future Perfect	Conditional Perfect	Present	Imperfect (-r-)	Imperfect (-s-)	Present Perfect	Pluperfect (-r-)	Pluperfect (-s-)	Imperative
	habré	habría	coma	comiera	comiese	haya	hubiera	hubiese	Come (tú).
	habrás	habrías	comas	comieras	comieses	hayas	hubieras	hubieses	Coma (Ud.).
	habrá + comido	habría + comido	coma	comiera	comiese	haya + comido	hubiera + comido	hubiese + comido	Comamos (nosotros).
	habremos	habríamos	comamos	comiéramos	comiésemos	hayamos	hubiéramos	hubiésemos	Comed (vosotros).
	habréis	habríais	comáis	comierais	comieseis	hayáis	hubierais	hubieseis	Coman (Uds.).
	habrán	habrían	coman	comieran	comiesen	hayan	hubieran	hubiesen	
	habré	habría	viva	viviera	viviese	haya	hubiera	hubiese	Vive (tú).
	habrás	habrías	vivas	vivieras	vivieses	hayas	hubieras	hubieses	Viva (Ud.).
	habrá + vivido	habría + vivido	viva	viviera	viviese	haya + vivido	hubiera + vivido	hubiese + vivido	Vivamos (nosotros).
	habremos	habríamos	vivamos	viviéramos	viviésemos	hayamos	hubiéramos	hubiésemos	Vivid (vosotros).
	habréis	habríais	viváis	vivierais	vivieseis	hayáis	hubierais	hubieseis	Vivan (Uds.).
	habrán	habrían	vivan	vivieran	viviesen	hayan	hubieran	hubiesen	

RADICAL CHANGING VERBS

1. GROUP I: -AR AND -ER VERBS ONLY

a) Change the *o* to *ue* when stress falls on root (ex: *contar, volver*).
b) Change the *e* to *ie* when stress falls on root (ex: *pensar, perder*).

Infinitive*	Present Indicative	Present Subjunctive	Imperative	Similarly Conjugated Verbs		
contar(o>ue) to count	cuento	cuente	cuenta	acordar	avergonzar	probar
	cuentas	cuentes	contad	acordarse	avergonzarse	recordar
	cuenta	cuente		acostarse	colgar	recordarse
	contamos	contemos		almorzar	costar	sonar
	contáis	contéis		apostar	encontrar	volar
	cuentan	cuenten		aprobar	jugar (*u to ue*)	volver
volver(o>ue) to return	vuelvo	vuelva	vuelve	devolver	oler	
	vuelves	vuelvas	volved	doler	soler	
	vuelve	vuelva		dolerse		
	volvemos	volvamos		llover		
	volvéis	volváis		morder		
	vuelven	vuelvan		mover		

Infinitive*	Present Indicative	Present Subjunctive	Imperative	Similarly Conjugated Verbs		
pensar(e>ie) to think	pienso piensas piensa pensamos penséis piensan	piense pienses piense pensemos penséis piensen	piensa pensad	acertar apretar calentar cerrar confesar despertar	empezar encerrar gobernar plegar quebrar sentarse	temblar tentar
perder(e>ie) to lose	pierdo pierdes pierde perdemos perdéis pierden	pierda pierdas pierda perdamos perdáis pierdan	pierde perded	ascender atender defender descender encender entender	extender tender	

*In all the other tenses, these verbs are conjugated like all other regular verbs.

347

Radical Changing Verbs

2. GROUP II: -IR VERBS ONLY

a) Change *o* to *ue* when stress falls on root (ex: *dormir*).
b) Change *o* to *u*; a) when stress falls on ending (ex: *dormir*—present subj. only); b) in third persons of preterite.
c) Change *e* to *ie* when stress falls on root (ex: *sentir*).
d) Change *e* to *i*; a) when stress falls on ending (ex: *sentir*—present subj. only); b) in third persons of preterite.

Infinitive*	Present Indicative	Present Subjunctive	Preterite	Imperative	Similarly Conjugated Verbs	
dormir to sleep	duermo duermes duerme dormimos dormís duermen	duerma duermas duerma durmamos durmáis duerman	dormí dormiste durmió dormimos dormisteis durmieron	duerme dormid	morir (past participle: *muerto*)	
sentir to feel	siento sientes siente sentimos sentís sienten	sienta sientas sienta sintamos sintáis sientan	sentí sentiste sintió sentimos sentisteis sintieron	siente sentid	advertir arrepentirse consentir convertir diferir divertir	herir mentir preferir presentir referir sugerir

*In all the other tenses, these verbs are conjugated like all other regular verbs.

3. GROUP III: *-IR* VERBS ONLY

Change *e* to *i*; a) when stress falls on root; b) in third persons of preterite (ex: *pedir*)

Infinitive*	Present Indicative	Present Subjunctive	Preterite Indicative	Imperfect Subjunctive	Imperative	Similarly Conjugated Verbs	
pedir to ask	pido	pida	pedí	pidiera (se)		competir	expedir
	pides	pidas	pediste	pidieras (ses)	pide	conseguir	reír
	pide	pida	pidió	pidiera (se)	pedid	corregir	repetir
	pedimos	pidamos	pedimos	pidiéramos (semos)		despedir	seguir
	pedís	pidáis	pedisteis	pidiérais (seis)		despedirse	servir
	piden	pidan	pidieron	pidieran (sen)		elegir	vestir

*In all the other tenses, these verbs are conjugated like all other regular verbs.

THE FORMS OF THE IRREGULAR VERBS*

Infinitive Present and Past Participles	Present Indicative	Present Subjunctive	Imperfect	Preterite	Future	Conditional	Imperative
andar "to walk"	ando	ande	andaba	anduve	andaré	andaría	anda
andando	andas	andes	andabas	anduviste	andarás	andarías	andad
andado	anda	ande	andaba	anduvo	andará	andaría	
	andamos	andemos	andábamos	anduvimos	andaremos	andaríamos	
	andáis	andéis	andabais	anduvisteis	andaréis	andaríais	
	andan	anden	andaban	anduvieron	andarán	andarían	
caber "to fit," "to be contained in"	quepo	quepa	cabía	cupe	cabré	cabría	cabe
	cabes	quepas	cabías	cupiste	cabrás	cabrías	cabed
	cabe	quepa	cabía	cupo	cabrá	cabría	
cabiendo	cabemos	quepamos	cabíamos	cupimos	cabremos	cabríamos	
cabido	cabéis	quepáis	cabíais	cupisteis	cabréis	cabríais	
	caben	quepan	cabían	cupieron	cabrán	cabrían	

caer "to fall"	caigo	caiga	caía	caí	caeré	caería	cae
cayendo	caes	caigas	caías	caíste	caerás	caerías	caed
caído	cae	caiga	caía	cayó	caerá	caería	
	caemos	caigamos	caíamos	caímos	caeremos	caeríamos	
	caéis	caigáis	caíais	caísteis	caeréis	caeríais	
	caen	caigan	caían	cayeron	caerán	caerían	
conducir "to lead," "to drive"	conduzco	conduzca	conducía	conduje	conduciré	conduciría	conduce
	conduces	conduzcas	conducías	condujiste	conducirás	conducirías	conducid
conduciendo	conduce	conduzca	conducía	condujo	conducirá	conduciría	
conducido	conducimos	conduzcamos	conducíamos	condujimos	conduciremos	conduciríamos	
	conducís	conduzcáis	conducíais	condujisteis	conduciréis	conduciríais	
	conducen	conduzcan	conducían	condujeron	conducirán	conducirían	
dar "to give"	doy	dé	daba	di	daré	daría	da
dando	das	des	dabas	diste	darás	darías	dad
dado	da	dé	daba	dio	dará	daría	
	damos	demos	dábamos	dimos	daremos	daríamos	
	dais	deis	dabais	disteis	daréis	daríais	
	dan	den	daban	dieron	darán	darían	

THE FORMS OF THE IRREGULAR VERBS*

Infinitive Present and Past Participles	Present Indicative	Present Subjunctive	Imperfect	Preterite	Future	Conditional	Imperative
decir "to say," "to tell"	digo	diga	decía	dije	diré	diría	di
diciendo	dices	digas	decías	dijiste	dirás	dirías	decid
dicho	dice	diga	decía	dijo	dirá	diría	
	decimos	digamos	decíamos	dijimos	diremos	diríamos	
	decís	digáis	decíais	dijisteis	diréis	diríais	
	dicen	digan	decían	dijeron	dirán	dirían	
estar "to be"	estoy	esté	estaba	estuve	estaré	estaría	está
estando	estás	estés	estabas	estuviste	estarás	estarías	estad
estado	está	esté	estaba	estuvo	estará	estaría	
	estamos	estemos	estábamos	estuvimos	estaremos	estaríamos	
	estáis	estéis	estábais	estuvisteis	estaréis	estaríais	
	están	estén	estaban	estuvieron	estarán	estarían	

	Present	Subjunctive	Imperfect	Preterite	Future	Conditional	Imperative
haber "to have" (auxiliary)	he	haya	había	hube	habré	habría	
	has	hayas	habías	hubiste	habrás	habrías	
	ha	haya	había	hubo	habrá	habría	
habiendo	hemos	hayamos	habíamos	hubimos	habremos	habríamos	
habido	habéis	hayáis	habíais	hubisteis	habréis	habríais	
	han	hayan	habían	hubieron	habrán	habrían	
hacer "to do," "to make"	hago	haga	hacía	hice	haré	haría	haz
	haces	hagas	hacías	hiciste	harás	harías	haced
	hace	haga	hacía	hizo	hará	haría	
haciendo	hacemos	hagamos	hacíamos	hicimos	haremos	haríamos	
hecho	hacéis	hagáis	hacíais	hicisteis	haréis	haríais	
	hacen	hagan	hacían	hicieron	harán	harían	
ir "to go"	voy	vaya	iba	fui	iré	iría	ve
	vas	vayas	ibas	fuiste	irás	irías	id
	va	vaya	iba	fue	irá	iría	
yendo	vamos	vayamos	íbamos	fuimos	iremos	iríamos	
ido	vais	vayáis	ibais	fuisteis	iréis	iríais	
	van	vayan	iban	fueron	irán	irían	

THE FORMS OF THE IRREGULAR VERBS*

Infinitive Present and Past Participles	Present Indicative	Present Subjunctive	Imperfect	Preterite	Future	Conditional	Imperative
oír "to hear"	oigo	oiga	oía	oí	oiré	oiría	
oyendo	oyes	oigas	oías	oíste	oirás	oirías	oye
oído	oye	oiga	oía	oyó	oirá	oiría	oíd
	oímos	oigamos	oíamos	oímos	oiremos	oiríamos	
	oís	oigáis	oíais	oísteis	oiréis	oiríais	
	oyen	oigan	oían	oyeron	oirán	oirían	
poder "to be able," "can"	puedo	pueda	podía	pude	podré	podría	
pudiendo	puedes	puedas	podías	pudiste	podrás	podrías	puede
podido	puede	pueda	podía	pudo	podrá	podría	poded
	podemos	podamos	podíamos	pudimos	podremos	podríamos	
	podéis	podáis	podíais	pudisteis	podréis	podríais	
	pueden	puedan	podían	pudieron	podrán	podrían	

354

	Present	Pres. Subj.	Imperfect	Preterite	Future	Conditional	Imperative
poner "to put," "to place" *poniendo* *puesto*	pongo	ponga	ponía	puse	pondré	pondría	
	pones	pongas	ponías	pusiste	pondrás	pondrías	pon
	pone	ponga	ponía	puso	pondrá	pondría	
	ponemos	pongamos	poníamos	pusimos	pondremos	pondríamos	
	ponéis	pongáis	poníais	pusisteis	pondréis	pondríais	poned
	ponen	pongan	ponían	pusieron	pondrán	pondrían	
querer "to want," "to love" *queriendo* *querido*	quiero	quiera	quería	quise	querré	querría	
	quieres	quieras	querías	quisiste	querrás	querrías	quiere
	quiere	quiera	quería	quiso	querrá	querría	
	queremos	queramos	queríamos	quisimos	querremos	querríamos	
	queréis	queráis	queríais	quisisteis	querréis	querríais	quered
	quieren	quieran	querían	quisieron	querrán	querrían	
reir "to laugh" *riendo* *reido*	río	ría	reía	reí	reiré	reiría	
	ríes	rías	reías	reíste	reirás	reirías	ríe
	ríe	ría	reía	rió	reirá	reiría	
	reímos	ríamos	reíamos	reímos	reiremos	reiríamos	
	reís	riáis	reíais	reísteis	reiréis	reiríais	reíd
	ríen	rían	reían	rieron	reirán	reirían	

THE FORMS OF THE IRREGULAR VERBS*

Infinitive Present and Past Participles	Present Indicative	Present Subjunctive	Imperfect	Preterite	Future	Conditional	Imperative
saber "to know" *sabiendo* *sabido*	sé sabes sabe sabemos sabéis saben	sepa sepas sepa sepamos sepáis sepan	sabía sabías sabía sabíamos sabíais sabían	supe supiste supo. supimos supisteis supieron	sabré sabrás sabrá sabremos sabréis sabrán	sabría sabrías sabría sabríamos sabríais sabrían	sabe sabed
salir "to go out," "to leave" *saliendo* *salido*	salgo sales sale salimos salís salen	salga salgas salga salgamos salgáis salgan	salía salías salía salíamos salíais salían	salí saliste salió salimos salisteis salieron	saldré saldrás saldrá saldremos saldréis saldrán	saldría saldrías saldría saldríamos saldríais saldrían	sal salid

356

	Present	Present Subj.	Imperfect	Preterite	Future	Conditional	Imperative
ser "to be" *siendo* *sido*	soy	sea	era	same as preterite of *ir.*	seré	sería	sé
	eres	seas	eras		serás	serías	sed
	es	sea	era		será	sería	
	somos	seamos	éramos		seremos	seríamos	
	sois	seáis	erais		seréis	seríais	
	son	sean	eran		serán	serían	
tener "to have" *teniendo* *tenido*	tengo	tenga	tenía	tuve	tendré	tendría	ten
	tienes	tengas	tenías	tuviste	tendrás	tendrías	tened
	tiene	tenga	tenía	tuvo	tendrá	tendría	
	tenemos	tengamos	teníamos	tuvimos	tendremos	tendríamos	
	tenéis	tengáis	teníais	tuvisteis	tendréis	tendríais	
	tienen	tengan	tenían	tuvieron	tendrán	tendrían	
traer "to bring" *trayendo* *traído*	traigo	traiga	traía	traje	traeré	traería	trae
	traes	traigas	traías	trajiste	traerás	traerías	traed
	trae	traiga	traía	trajo	traerá	traería	
	traemos	traigamos	traíamos	trajimos	traeremos	traeríamos	
	traéis	traigáis	traíais	trajisteis	traeréis	traeríais	
	traen	traigan	traían	trajeron	traerán	traerían	

THE FORMS OF THE IRREGULAR VERBS*

Infinitive Present and Past Participles	Present Indicative	Present Subjunctive	Imperfect	Preterite	Future	Conditional	Imperative
valer "to be worth"	valgo	valga	valía	valí	valdré	valdría	vale
valiendo	vales	valgas	valías	valiste	valdrás	valdrías	valed
valido	vale	valga	valía	valió	valdrá	valdría	
	valemos	valgamos	valíamos	valimos	valdremos	valdríamos	
	valéis	valgáis	valíais	valisteis	valdréis	valdríais	
	valen	valgan	valían	valieron	valdrán	valdrían	

	Present	Present Subjunctive	Imperfect	Preterite	Future	Conditional	Commands
venir "to come"	vengo	venga	venía	vine	vendré	vendría	
viniendo	vienes	vengas	venías	viniste	vendrás	vendrías	ven
venido	viene	venga	venía	vino	vendrá	vendría	venid
	venimos	vengamos	veníamos	vinimos	vendremos	vendríamos	
	venís	vengáis	veníais	vinisteis	vendréis	vendríais	
	vienen	vengan	venían	vinieron	vendrán	vendrían	
ver "to see"	veo	vea	veía	vi	veré	vería	
viendo	ves	veas	veías	viste	verás	verías	ve
visto	ve	vea	veía	vio	verá	vería	ved
	vemos	veamos	veíamos	vimos	veremos	veríamos	
	veis	veáis	veíais	visteis	veréis	veríais	
	ven	vean	veían	vieron	verán	verían	

*To form compound tenses, use the appropriate form of *haber* together with the past participle of the irregular verb.

359

LETTER WRITING

Formal Invitations and Responses

INVITATIONS

Marzo de 2006

Jorge Fernández y Sra. tienen el gusto de anunciarles a Ud. y a su familia el próximo enlace matrimonial de su hija Carmen con el Sr. Juan García, y los invitan a la ceremonia que se realizará en la Iglesia de Nuestra Señora de la Merced, el día 6 de este mes, a las 6 de la tarde. A continuación tendrá lugar una recepción en la casa de los padres de la novia en honor de los contrayentes.

March 2006

Mr. and Mrs. George Fernandez take pleasure in announcing the wedding of their daughter Carmen to Mr. Juan Garcia, and invite you to the ceremony that will take place at the Church of Nuestra Señora de la Merced, on the 6th of this month and year at 6 p.m. There will be a reception for the newlyweds afterward at the residence of the bride's parents.

Los señores Suárez ofrecen sus respetos a los señores García y les ruegan que les honren viniendo a comer con ellos el lunes próximo, a las ocho.

Mr. and Mrs. Suárez present their respects to Mr. and Mrs. García and would be honored to have their company at dinner next Monday at 8 o'clock.

Los señores Suárez y Navarro saludan afectuosa-mente a los señores Del Vayo y les ruegan que les hon-ren asistiendo a la recepción que darán en honor de su hija María, el domingo 19 de marzo, a las nueve de la noche.

Mr. and Mrs. Suarez y Navarro ("greet Mr. and Mrs. Del Vayo cordially and") request the honor of their presence at the party given in honor of their daughter Maria, on Sunday evening, March 19, at nine o'clock.

RESPONSES

Los señores Del Vayo les agradecen la invitación y tendrán el honor de asistir a la recepción del domingo 19 de marzo.

Thank you for your kind invitation. We shall be hon-ored to attend the reception on Sunday, March 19th.

Los señores García tendrán el honor de acudir a la cena de los señores Suárez y entretanto les saludan cordialmente.

Mr. and Mrs. García will be honored to have dinner with Mr. and Mrs. Suárez. With kindest regards.

Los señores García ruegan a los señores Suárez se sirvan recibir las gracias por su amable invitación y la expresión de su sentimiento al no poder aceptarla por hallarse comprometidos con anterioridad.

Mr. and Mrs. García thank Mr. and Mrs. Suárez for their kind invitation and regret that they are unable to come owing to a previous engagement.

THANK-YOU NOTES

5 de marzo de 2006

Querida Anita:

La presente es con el fin de saludarte y darte las gracias por el precioso florero que me has enviado de regalo. Lo he colocado encima del piano y no te imaginas el lindo efecto que hace.

Espero verte pasado mañana en la fiesta que da Carmen, la cual parece que va a ser muy animada.

Deseo que estés bien en compañía de los tuyos. Nosotros sin novedad. Te saluda cariñosamente, tu amiga.

Lolita

March 5, 2006

Dear Anita,

This is just to say hello and also to let you know that I received the beautiful vase you sent me as a gift. I've put it on the piano and you can't imagine the beautiful effect.

I hope to see you at Carmen's party tomorrow. I think it's going to be a very lively affair.

I hope your family is all well. Everyone here is fine.

Lolita

BUSINESS LETTERS

C/ Santo Domingo, 104
41019 Sevilla
Tel: 95 435 000 00

16 de enero de 2006

Jorge Rivera
C/ Regalo, 7 - 5ºB
41001 SEVILLA

Estimado Sr. Rivera:

Por la presente quisiera recordarle que el alquiler del mes de enero del apartamento localizado en la C/ Regalo, 7 - 5ºB todavía no ha sido saldado. Recordará que los pagos del alquiler se deben abonar durante la primera semana de cada mes.

Ruego que me envíe un cheque o que ingrese la cantidad pendiente en mi cuenta bancaria a la mayor brevedad posible.

Atentamente,

Ernesto Rincón

104 Santo Domingo Street
41019 SEVILLA
Tel: 95 435 000 00

16th January 2006

Jorge Rivera
Regalo Street, 7 - 5°B
41001 SEVILLA

Dear Mr. Rivera

I write to remind you that the rent for January on the apartment at C/ Regalo, 7 - 5°B is still outstanding. You will remember that rent payment is due during the first week of each month.

I am asking you to please send me a check or deposit the money into my account at your earliest convenience.

Sincerely,

Ernesto Rincón

_____

Envíos Rápidos
Calle Segovia 552
La Paz, Asunción

Sr. Ricardo Hernández
Calle Ensenada 445
La Paz, Asunción

2 de junio de 2006

Estimado Sr. Hernández:

Me dirijo a usted en respuesta a su carta del 17 de mayo en la cual afirma que, debido a la suma pendiente de mi cuenta, se procederá en mi contra a menos que salde por completo la deuda dentro de un plazo de 7 días.

Su carta me ha sorprendido porque llevamos haciendo negocios durante 12 años y en el pasado siempre he pagado a tiempo. Lamento que haya optado por esta vía y le pido una prórroga del plazo para pagar. Le comuniqué en mi última carta que mis propios acreedores se están retrasando últimamente, lo cual explica las dificultades que estoy experimentando en estos momentos.

Le aseguro que tengo la intención de abonar la totalidad de la cuenta dentro de un plazo de 30 días, y como prueba de mi buena fe le adjunto un cheque para cubrir una pequeña parte de la cuenta final.

Con la confianza de poder llegar a un acuerdo amistoso, le saluda cordialmente,

Ricardo García

Envíos Rápidos
552 Segovia Street
La Paz, Asunción

Sr. Ricardo Hernández
445 Ensenada Street
La Paz, Asunción

2nd June 2006

Dear Mr. Hernández

I am writing in reply to your letter of the 17th May in which you state that due to the outstanding amount on my account you will be taking proceedings against me unless full settlement is made within 7 days.

The letter surprised me because I have been doing business with you for twelve years now and in the past I have always paid on time. I regret you should adopt this line of action and ask you to reconsider and allow me an extension. I informed you in my last letter that my own creditors have been holding back payments recently and this explains the difficulties I am experiencing at the moment.

I should like to assure you that I intend to make full payment within 30 days and as evidence of my good faith I have enclosed a check to cover part of the balance.

Yours faithfully,

Ricardo García

David Kamps
23 East 25th Street
New York, NY 10010
Correo electrónico: davidkamps@yupi.com
Tel: 212 345 6666
Fax - 212 345 6666
3 de abril de 2006

Número Uno Guest House
Esperanza, 3
Condado, Puerto Rico

Estimados señores:

Quisiera hacer una reserva de una habitación con cama doble y baño para las noches del viernes 6 hasta el domingo 8 de abril. Nuestra partida será la mañana del lunes 9 de abril.

Si todo es satisfactorio, ruego que me lo confirme por fax o correo electrónico.

Atentamente,

David Kamps

David Kamps
`23 East 25th Street
New York, NY 10010
e-mail - davidkamps@yupi.com
Tel: 212 345 6666
Fax - 212 345 6666
April 3, 2006

Número Uno Guest House
Esperanza, 3
Condado, Puerto Rico

Dear Sirs,

I would like to reserve a room with a double bed and bathroom for the nights of Friday 6th April to Sunday 8th April. We will be departing the morning of Monday, April 9th.

Would you please confirm by fax or E-mail if this is possible.

Yours faithfully,

David Kamps

INFORMAL LETTERS

Mi querido Pepe:

Me ha sido sumamente grato recibir tu última carta. Ante todo déjame darte la gran noticia. Pues he decidido por fin hacer un viaje a Madrid, donde pienso pasar todo el mes de mayo.

Lolita viene conmigo. A ella le encanta la idea de conoceros por fin.

Los negocios marchan bien por ahora y confío en que continuará la buena racha. El otro día estuve con Antonio y me preguntó por ti.

Procura mandar a reservarnos una habitación en el Nacional, que te lo agradeceré mucho.

Escríbeme pronto. Da mis recuerdos a Elena y tú recibe un abrazo de tu amigo,

Juan

Dear Pepe,

I was very happy to get your last letter. First of all, let me give you the big news. I have finally decided to make a trip to Madrid, where I expect to spend all of May.

Lolita is coming with me. She is extremely happy to be able to meet the two of you at last.

Business is good now and I hope will keep up that way ("that the good wind will continue"). I saw Antonio the other day and he asked me about you.

I'd appreciate your trying to reserve a room for us in the "National."

Write soon. Give my regards to Elena.

Yours,
Juan

FORMS OF SALUTATIONS AND COMPLIMENTARY CLOSINGS

A. Salutations:

FORMAL

Señor	Sir
Señora	Madam
Señorita	Miss

Estimado señor Sánchez	Dear Mr. Sanchez
Estimada señora Rodríguez	Dear Ms. Rodriguez
Distinguida señora	Dear Madam
Muy señor mío	Dear Sir
Excelentísimo señor	Your Excellency

INFORMAL

Estimado amigo	Dear friend
Querido amigo	Dear friend
Mi querida Lolita	My dear Lolita
Querida mía	My beloved
Amor mío	My love

B. Complimentary Closings:

FORMAL

Atentamente	Sincerely
Le saluda atentamente	Yours sincerely
Cordialmente	Cordially
Respetuosamente	Respectfully yours
Me despido respetuosamente	I give my respectful farewell
Sinceramente	Sincerely yours
Un cordial saludo	My sincere regard
Le saluda muy cordialmente	My sincere regard

INFORMAL

Cariñosamente	Affectionately yours
Atentamente	Sincerely yours
Sinceramente	Sincerely yours
Afectuosamente	Affectionately

De quien te estima	Affectionately
Un abrazo	A hug
Un fuerte abrazo	A warm hug
Besos y abrazos	Love and kisses
Con todo mi cariño	With all my love
Con todo mi afecto	With all my affection
De todo corazón	With all my heart
Hasta pronto	I hope to hear from you soon

C. Form of the Letter:

FORMAL

Estimado señor:
or *Muy señor mío:*

_____

_____

Atentamente,

INFORMAL

Querido Juan:

_____

_____

Cariñosamente,

D. Common formulas:

Beginning a letter—

1. *Me es grato acusar recibo de su atenta carta del 8 de este mes. Tengo el agrado de. . .* This is to

acknowledge receipt of your letter of the 8th of
this month. I am glad to . . .

2. *Obra en mi poder su apreciable carta de fecha
   10 de marzo.* . . I have received your letter of
   March 10th.

3. *En contestación a su atenta carta de.* . . In
   answer to your letter of . . .

4. *De conformidad con su carta del.* . . In accor-
   dance with your letter of . . .

5. *Con referencia a su anuncio en "La Nación" de
   hoy.* . . In reference to your ad in today's issue of
   "The Nation," . . .

6. *Por la presente me dirijo a Ud. para.* . . This letter is to . . .

7. *Nos es grato anunciarle que.* . . We are pleased
   to announce that . . .

8. *Me es grato recomendarle a Ud. al Sr.* . . . I take
   pleasure in recommending to you Mr. . . . .

9. *La presente tiene por objeto confirmarle nuestra
   conversación telefónica de esta mañana.* . . This
   is to confirm our telephone conversation of this
   morning . . .

Ending a letter—

1. *Anticipándole las gracias, le saludo a Ud. atentamente,*
   Thanking you in advance, I am

                                 Sincerely yours,

2. *Agradecidos por su atención le enviamos un cordial saludo.*
   Thanking you for your attention we send you a warm salute.

3. *En espera de sus noticias, le saludamos.*
   Awaiting your reply, we salute you.

4. *Esperando contar nuevamente con ustedes en futuras transacciones, reciban un cordial saludo.*
   Hoping we can count on you again for future transations, please receive our salute.

5. *Esperamos su grata y pronta contestación.*
                              Atentamente,
   Hoping to hear from you at your earliest convenience, I am

                              Sincerely yours,

6. *Aprovecho esta ocasión para despedirme respetuosamente.*
   I am taking this opportunity to give my respectful farewell.

7. *Quedamos a su disposición para lo que puedan necesitar.*
   We remain at your disposal for anything that you may need.

Form of the Envelope

Félix Valbueña y Cía.
Calle de Zurbarán, 6
Madrid

> Señor Don
> Ricardo Fitó,
> Apartado 5042,
> Barcelona

M. Navarro Suárez
San Martín Vía Aérea 820
Buenos Aires, Argentina

> Señores
> M. Suárez y Coello,
> Paseo de la Castellana, 84
> 28002 Madrid, España

Señorita
Lolita Navarro
Gran Vía de Germanías, 63
Valencia

Antonio de Suárez
Calle del Sol, 2
(Chamartín)
Madrid

OTHER EXAMPLES

Sr. Antonio Aguilar [1]
Provenza, 95
Barcelona
      Señorita
      María Sucre y Navarro
      Paseo de la Castellana, 80
      Madrid

---

[1] To a doctor: *Sr. Dr. Antonio Aguilar.*
To an engineer: *Sr. Ing. Don Antonio Aguilar.*

E-MAIL AND INTERNET

A. Sample E-mail

Fecha: 7 de julio de 2006
Para: enmon@muchocorreo.es
De: cpermar@muchocorreo.es
Asunto: Planes de vacaciones

Querido Enrique:

Ya por fin te podemos escribir con nuestros planes para el fin del verano. Viajaremos a Venecia, vía Barcelona, el 24 de julio. Estaremos allí tres días y el 27 nos vamos a Croacia. Regresaremos a Barcelona el día 7 de agosto y nos quedaremos una semana. La hora prevista de llegada de nuestro vuelo es a las 6 de la tarde. Si todo sale bien, hacia las 8 de la noche estaremos instalados en nuestro hotel que se llama "Hotel Oriente Husa", al lado del Liceo, en Las Ramblas, teléfono: 93-3022558 y la reserva está a nombre de María Jesús. Nuestro teléfono móvil es el 838831007. Quizás tú llegues más tarde o más temprano de tu viaje y estés muy cansado. Ya nos dirás el teléfono y el nombre de tu hotel y, si no podemos cenar juntos, al menos podremos tomar algo después. En cualquier caso, tenemos el día siguiente para vernos. Hacer coincidir el viaje con el tuyo, que esta vez diseñamos entero por Internet, fue bastante complicado, pero, al fin, parece resuelto. Y es que después de saber que estuviste en Londres cuando nosotros también estábamos allí, no queríamos que por unas horas nos quedásemos sin la posibilidad de vernos otra vez. Ya nos dirás si tus fechas siguen como estaban. Si es posible, por favor envíanos tu itinerario. Nos podrías adjuntar tu itinerario con todos tus vuelos cuando respondas a este mensaje. ¡Tenemos muchas ganas de verte!

Cariños,

César y María Jesús

Date: July 7, 2006
To: enmon@muchocorreo.es
From: cpermar@muchocorreo.es
Subject: Vacation Plans

Dear Enrique:

We can finally write to you with our final summer plans. We are flying to Venice, via Barcelona on July 24. We will spend three days there and on the 27 we're off to Croatia. We will be back in Barcelona on August 7, where we'll stay for an extra week. Our flight is expected to arrive at 6 p.m. If everything goes as planned, by 8 p.m. we will have checked into our hotel, which is called "Hotel Oriente Husa," next the the Lyceum on Las Ramblas, telephone: 93-3022558. The reservation is under Maria Jesus's name. Our cell phone number is 838831007. You might arrive earlier or later than that and you might be very tired after your flight. Let us know the name of your hotel and your phone number; if we can't have dinner together, at least we'll have a drink later that night. In any case, we have the next day to see each other. It was very difficult to make our schedule coincide with yours; we planned everything on the Internet and everything seems to be finalized and set. You see, after knowing that we were in London at the same time and we didn't know about it, we didn't want to miss the opportunity to see each other again. Let us know if your dates are still the same. If it's possible, please send us your itinerary. You could attach your itinerary with all your flight information when you reply to this message. We are so much looking forward to seeing you!

Love,

César and María Jesús

B. Vocabulary Related to E-máil and the Internet

Internet related vocabulary:

correo electrónico	E-mail
eliminar	to delete
responder	to reply
correo basura	spam
reenviar	to forward
mover	to move
imprimir	to print
bandeja de entrada	inbox
revisar correo	check E-mail
redactar	to write a draft
dirección de correos	E-mail address
buscar en Internet	to search
impresora	printer
hacer una búsqueda	to do a search
enviar	to send
contraseña	password
perfil	profile
ir al chat	to go to the chat room
sitio web	web site
adjuntar	to attach
archivo	file
asunto	subject

C. Internet Resources

The following is a list of useful websites for those students who want to enhance their language abilities.

1. These three sites are Spanish variations of Yahoo. Their content is adapted for each of the three geographical regions

http://espanol.yahoo.com/   for Spanish speaking
                               users in the USA
http://es.yahoo.com/   for users in Spain
http://mx.yahoo.com/   for users in Mexico

2. CNN en Español. This website contains international news from CNN in Spanish. It is updated regularly throughout the day.

http://www.cnn.com/espanol

3. BBC en Español. This is another news website from the BBC. It provides news in Spanish with a strong emphasis on international coverage.

http://www.bbcmundo.com/

4. Diccionarios. This online dictionary gives synonyms and antonyms as well as translations from Spanish into several other languages, including English, and vice-versa.

http://www.diccionarios.com/

5. Yupimsn.com. This portal is associated with MSN. It is a mainstream portal similar to Yahoo.

http://www.yupimsn.com/

6. Terra.com. This is a major portal in many Spanish and Portuguese speaking countries.

http://www.terra.com/

7. Español.com This website offers links to other websites that relate to Spanish language, Hispanic culture and interests, travel resources, etc.

http://www.espanol.com

8. ESPN Deportes. This is the Spanish version of the ESPN sports website.

http://espndeportes.espn.go.com/

9. Hola en Español. This website is the Spanish equivalent of the British magazine Hello. Its focus is on celebrities and European royalty.

http://www.hola.com/

10. Royal Family. This is the official website of the Royal Family of Spain. It is an official site that gives information about travels and activities of the members of the royal family.

http://www.casareal.es/

INDEX

NOTES

NOTES